Jahrin   6?

WITNESS
TO THE
TRUTH

WITNESS
TO THE
TRUTH

Nathan Shapell

David McKay Company, Inc.

New York

WITNESS TO THE TRUTH

COPYRIGHT © 1974 BY Nathan Shapell

Designed by Remo R. Duchi

LIBRARY OF CONGRESS CATALOG CARD NUMBER: 73-87843

ISBN: 0-679-50456-7

MANUFACTURED IN THE UNITED STATES OF AMERICA

Dedication

TO— My father, Benjamin, *killed in Wolbrom 1942*

My mother, Hela, and my sister, Rochelle, 20, *killed in Auschwitz 1943*

My sister Yadja, 23, *missing and presumed dead somewhere in Russia*

Uncle Joshua Schapelski and his four sons—Baruch, 20, Natan, 16, Samuel, 14, and Abraham, 9—*killed in Ploszow Prison, Cracow 1942*

Aunt Jacheta and her two daughters, Fela, 12, and Luba, 10, *killed in Auschwitz 1942*

Aunt Genya Singer and her daughter, Esther, 23, *killed in Auschwitz 1942;* her son, Natan, 25, *missing and presumed dead in Auschwitz*

Uncle Moshe Schapelski, *killed in Sosnowiec 1942*

Aunt Sara and seven of her children—Cesia, 16, Natan, 12, Chajka, 10, Icek, 9, Zacharias, 8, Srulek, 5, and Smulik, 4—*killed in Auschwitz 1942*

Aunt Chana Friedberg and her daughter, Ruth, 10, *killed in Auschwitz 1942*

Uncle Chaim and his son, Natan, 8, *killed in Auschwitz 1942*

Uncle Natan Schapelski, Aunt Rose, their twin sons, Ben and Simon, 14, and their daughter, Sarah, 11, *killed in Auschwitz 1942*

Uncle Lipma Gelbart and his son, Mordechai, 20, *killed in Ploszow Prison, Cracow 1942*

Aunt Luba and her daughter, Hela, 21, *killed in Auschwitz 1942*

Uncle Simon Gelbart and his sons, Chaim, 14, and Bernard, 13, *killed in Ploszow Prison, Cracow 1942*

Aunt Rachael and her daughter, Miriam, 8, *killed in Wolbrom 1942*

Uncle Abraham Gelbart, 37, *killed in Wolbrom 1942*

Aunt Ethel Chaba and her two daughters, Fela, 17, and Miriam, 14, *killed in Auschwitz 1942*

Uncle Simon and his three sons—Ephraim, Baruch, and Israel—*killed in Ploszow Prison, Cracow 1942*

Cousin David Chaba, *dead of starvation somewhere in Russia*

And to all those who never came back, this book is dedicated with my eternal love.

PREFACE

When I left Europe in 1951 to begin a new life in America, I knew I would never be at peace until these events were recorded so that anyone, of this or future generations, who wanted to know the truth, as I saw it and experienced it, could find it in these pages.

I had no diaries, no notes; only my own vivid memories and those of my wife, Lilly, who shared the turbulent post-war years and my conviction that this book must be written—an almost impossible task without someone unusual who understood me and believed it must be done. I found that person in Rosetta Adler Cohen and to her I offer my deep gratitude.

I owe so much to so many . . . may this book serve in some small way to honor the memory of those who died, to honor the courage of those who survived and the bravery of those who went on to fight for the creation of the State of Israel and are still fighting to keep it alive and free, and to honor those

splendid American officers and soldiers who gave us, the survivors, their hearts and their hands, and who have received so
little of the recognition they richly deserve for their great acts.

Nathan Shapell

Los Angeles, California
November 1973

Part I

Chapter

I

SEPTEMBER 1, 1939—THE FIRST DAY.

Standing with my father on a street in the city of Sosnowiec, Poland, on Friday morning, September 1, 1939, I watched the enemy planes pass overhead. The white swastika markings on the underside of their wings could be seen clearly. There was no longer any doubt that the German monster had lashed out.

We started fighting our way through the panic-ridden stream of people already clogging the streets and sidewalks. All the stores and places of business had closed, and men and women carrying children and large bundles of belongings were trying to navigate the crowded streets.

The apartment building on Schklarnastrasse where we had lived for so many years was in a state of confusion, echoing the panic in the streets. My mother waited anxiously in the doorway for us; behind her, my brother and sisters talked excitedly. Over their voices the crackle of the radio in the neighbor's apartment blared out the news: Hitler had kept his promise; the invasion of Poland had begun.

"Quiet down now, children," Father said, closing the door behind us. "We don't know yet how close they are to Sosnowiec. When we know, we can start to make some plans."

The girls, Rochelle, Yadja, and Sala, calmed by his presence, began to help Mother with the Sabbath evening meal. David and I talked in whispers about the fighting the Polish Army must be faced with now. I was angry and frustrated that at seventeen I was too young to fight the Nazis.

David and I went out into the hall to the superintendent's apartment, where other neighbors gathered around his radio. All news broadcasts had stopped, but the airwaves were sending what were surely code signals to Polish planes; the words "chocolate, chocolate" and "coffee, coffee" were repeated over and over. Because we were only a short distance from the German border, we were frighteningly aware that Poland's surrender to Germany was probably only a matter of days and that Sosnowiec, though not a major city, would be occupied soon.

The same questions came from all sides: "What shall we do?" "What do you think will happen?" "I can't believe it!" "Where is our Army?"

When we returned to our apartment, Mother was lighting the candles. The realization that it was Sabbath night stunned me, the events of the day had so completely erased all normal thoughts.

We ate quickly, after hurried prayers, and then, back to the radio.

Relatives and friends who lived nearby burst into our home all through that night and the Saturday that followed. "Benjamin, what are you going to do?" they asked Father. "Do you think we should leave tonight? We can't just sit here and wait for the Germans, can we?" We had no answers for one another.

The radio had begun to broadcast the same frightening announcement over and over throughout the night and all the following day. "Poland has fallen. German troops have crossed the border at all points. There is little or no resistance." We listened less and less until the radio itself became silent.

The night before, we had seen from our windows streams of people in wagons and trucks and on bicycles, but most of them on foot, holding small children by the hand or carrying them, entire families, all going east toward the railroad station. By Saturday morning a cloud of fear had descended on the city, and the streets were almost empty. Families huddled together, not wanting or daring to venture out into a city that had come so suddenly to a standstill. Almost immediately restrictions were posted, forbidding unauthorized civilians to leave their homes, and patrols of Polish militia quickly cleared the streets of any civilians they found without proper identification.

By the evening of the second day, Saturday, our plans were made. Father decided that we would try for safety to the east, in the small town of Wolbrom about sixty-five kilometers away, where he and Mother and most of us children had been born and spent the early years of our lives. We had many relatives there and could be sure of finding refuge.

We gathered our few valuables and what necessities we felt we would need and could carry. Our small family store had been locked and boarded up on Friday.

Although we had felt the desperate urgency to leave the city as soon as possible, we could not have found a way out other than by foot without breaking faith with the Sabbath. Even in these dark hours no Jew could find it within himself to go against the ancient laws.

On Sunday morning, September 3, 1939, we started out for the railroad station—our family and Uncle Natan, his wife, twin sons, and daughter. Father's other brother, Max, stayed behind with his family.

The streets were crowded with frantic, desperate people. There was no longer any order or control, and most of the communication lines had been bombed out. The crush at the railroad station was unbelievable. No passenger trains had as yet come through, but a line of freight cars stood by the platform, and the mob was fighting, kicking, and pushing to climb aboard. I tried to pull Mother through the crowd, and Yadja and Rochelle held on to shield her. We fought our way to the nearest car and somehow managed to climb on. I looked back for the others, but they were lost in the mob. There was no chance to go back now; we were being crushed and shoved from behind.

We found a place in the freight car and prepared ourselves for the long ride to Wolbrom. But the train did not move. Hours passed, and it seemed we would never leave the station. Finally, with a lurch, the wheels began to turn and the row of freight cars pulled out of the Sosnowiec station, picking up speed. A sigh of relief swept through the jammed car. "Thank God we're finally moving." It seemed only a few minutes had passed when the train stopped suddenly and then, after what seemed an interminable length of time, started again.

Time after time the train slowed to a stop and then eventually started again. We speculated on the delays while we waited impatiently for the jolt that would restart us on our way.

Finally, at one stop, the waiting became so unbearable in the packed car that the women began to cry out in fright. I fought my way to the open doorway and called out, "What happened? How long will we be here?" Voices yelled back, "The rails are gone—bombed out. The train can't go any farther. This is the end of the line."

As the news spread, the train was evacuated. We joined the stream of people on the road, bundles slung over our shoulders. I watched along the way for the faces of Father, Sala, and David, hoping they had been able to board the train even for this short a journey.

We walked on through the night, stopping only long enough to take a few bites of the food we carried and to give Mother a chance to rest. The girls and I could have gone on, but she was frail and the strain of the past few days had already taken its toll. The sound of artillery fire could be heard in the distance,

6

and when daylight came, we saw in the fields alongside the road spent shells and the craters they had dug.

We walked on and on until, late Tuesday afternoon, we reached the heavy forest on the outskirts of Wolbrom. The shelling from the heavy guns to the east continued over our heads.

At the edge of town we left the shelter of the forest and made our way to Uncle Gelbart's house on the Schulestrasse. Mother's brother and his wife took us in; their own fear and anxiety were put aside at the sight of our exhaustion. But the relief we felt at knowing we were with our family did not last long. The Germans had already attacked the town, and the token resistance of the Poles had ended only a few hours before.

Some good news awaited us. Father, David and the others had made the journey to Wolbrom ahead of us by truck and were waiting for us at Uncle Joshua's house. "But where is Sala?" the Gelbarts asked. "Isn't she with you?" We realized then that Sala must have become separated from all of us and was probably alone in Sosnowiec.

I waited until late afternoon and then walked out into the deserted streets of the small town. When I reached the corner of Pilzerstrasse, where Uncle Joshua lived, I stopped short. The body of a man lay in the street before me, riddled with bullets and surrounded by empty kerosene cans he had apparently been carrying—the first victim of the Germans that I had seen.

Forcing myself to circle around him, I hurried into Uncle Joshua's house. There was little time for conversation. David and Father slipped out with me and we made our way back to the Gelbarts', through the fields in back of the houses.

There was no joy in the reunion. We had escaped from Sosnowiec, hoping to find ourselves behind the Polish Army lines, only to discover our refuge already the scene of disaster.

I told them of the dead man I had seen, but they knew of the body already. A German motorcycle patrol had come through Wolbrom from Piltz earlier, and they had all heard the shoot-

7

ing in the streets. The Germans had reached Wolbrom before us.

We sat and talked far into the night. My mind raced in a million directions while I listened to the hushed and hopeless voices. We tried to reassure one another that with the end of hostilities the Germans would merely occupy the country. It would be terrible, but, after all, what more could happen? All of Hitler's threats and promises to destroy the Jews would surely end now that he held Poland. All of his words had been only propaganda to frighten and cow the people.

We talked endlessly about what we could or would do if and when the future brought every conceivable problem. The conversation went around and around, aimlessly and hopelessly. I was terrified at the thought that harm might come to my family and that I would be helpless to prevent it.

Finally, we went upstairs, into the living quarters over the store, and found room to lie down and wait for the morning.

It came quickly and brutally. There was shouting in the streets: "All male Jews, *heraus*—out." We dressed quickly, and Uncle Natan, Father, my brother David and I started down the stairs. Halfway, German soldiers blocked our way.

"Get your hands up and keep them up," they barked and prodded us with the butts of their rifles. At gunpoint they herded us into an area behind the houses where others already stood, hands raised above their heads.

When the soldiers had cleared the entire block of Jewish men and boys, they marched us off, surrounded by special squads still in battle gear who had come into town with specific orders—"Get the Jews." They pushed us toward the marketplace, already crowded with Jewish men of all ages, and encircled us with troops holding machine guns.

We stood for hours, bunched together like cattle. As the day passed, some of our women tried to approach the square with food and water, only to be beaten back by the soldiers. Many of the older and weaker men fainted from shock and lack of water and lay on the cobblestone street. From their dazed faces we

8

could see that they would be unable to stand much more.

The afternoon had begun to fade into dusk when a German officer, a special commander, strode up to the edge of the crowd and shouted for silence through a loudspeaker. "All male Jews under the age of sixteen years will line up over there," he yelled, pointing to one side of the marketplace. "If your papers are in order, we will permit you to return home. The rest of you will remain here."

"Natan, you go, go right now," my father whispered to me. "You can pass for sixteen. Get back to Mother and the girls. They need you."

I slipped away and joined the small group of young boys forming to one side. But when my turn came in line at a release point, the guard looked at my papers and barked, "Get back in there. You're too old." I tried the other release points, only to be rejected each time.

Finally, at the last point in the circle, I approached the line, concealing my clenched hands in the pockets of my breeches. The German officer became enraged at what he thought to be an air of defiance on my part. "You goddamned dog! Get your goddamned hands out of your pockets, or else!" he ordered and struck me across the face. Then he motioned me toward the Polish interpreter. In another moment I was out of the encirclement.

I walked past the soldiers quickly, not daring to circle back to where my family stood, under guard. When I was past the view of the Germans I broke into a run and got back to Uncle's house as fast as my legs could carry me.

Several hours later Yadja arrived. She had followed us to the marketplace and stayed until the soldiers had marched the remaining men, six abreast, through the dusk to the town of Zawiercha, a few miles away. Yadja and the other women whose men were in the column had followed the march for a while and then had turned back.

It wasn't until the next morning that the news of their destination became known to us. The Germans had used the daylight hours, while they held the men in the square, to empty a large factory of all its workers and turn it into a detention camp for these two to three thousand men.

Yadja made the journey to Zawiercha, again with many other women, and returned white-faced and in tears. She told us how the officers had posted armed guards around the factory and on the rooftops. The women who had had the courage to approach and question the soldiers about their men inside had been pushed back and mistreated.

My mother and aunt exhausted themselves weeping. They were frantic, and my helplessness infuriated me. When their tears and the tears of my sisters had subsided, they decided to try to get food to the men.

In the morning the girls hitched a horse to a rented buggy, our last remaining means of transportation, since, in the past hours, the Germans had confiscated all motorized vehicles and fuel. They drove to the factory in Zawiercha.

Other women had had the same idea, and when they approached the guards with their food parcels, they were permitted to write the name of the recipient on the package and hand it over to the guards for delivery. We had no way of knowing whether or not they actually would pass the food through, but it gave us hope, at least, that the Germans had some interest in keeping the internees alive.

Days passed, two, three, four. We learned later that one morning all of the men had been marched into the courtyard of the factory, encircled by soldiers with drawn guns and held in suspense for more than two hours. But the order to fire on them, or the man to give the order to execute them, never came. They were marched back into the factory and held for two more days.

On the sixth day the women came again, bearing food and parcels of clothing, to find empty buildings—the guards gone—the prisoners gone. Their immediate fears were erased when people living across from the factory told them that all the men had been released. The doors had been opened in the morning and the men permitted to leave. A few older, weaker men had succumbed, but most of the men had the strength to walk out and back to their homes. Father and the men of our family came back to us; David had gone directly back to Sosnowiec. Somehow they had passed the women on the roads.

The men regained their strength and with it the need returned to resolve the question that had become an obsession with us: "What shall we do? Shall we stay here or go back to Sosnowiec?"

In the past days other refugees had streamed into and through Wolbrom, bringing news, horrible news, of the terror the Germans were spreading through the occupied city we had left. The synagogues had all been burned to the ground and other atrocities committed.

We were caught between two hells—the known one in Wolbrom and the unknown one in Sosnowiec. If they were equally horrible, it would be better to go home and rejoin Sala and David, my parents concluded. But a fateful decision had to be made. My father's deep religious beliefs would have no place of expression in Sosnowiec; the temples were smoldering ashes now. He would remain behind in Wolbrom for the time being, and when some semblance of order had been restored he would either send for us or he would return home.

My mother was grief-stricken; they had never been parted before for any length of time. "Who will take care of you?" she said. "I can't leave you here alone. You'll get sick and there'll be no one to take care of you. Please come back with us."

But he had made his decision and tried to soothe her. "Listen, it will only be a little while before we are all together again. Let's use our heads. We have to be practical at a time like this. I can stay with our family and friends here. I have many friends in the temple. I'll be all right, I promise you."

As always, we did as he asked; his decision was to be respected.

It was a grueling trip back, both physically and emotionally. The wagon could barely support the weight of our belongings, and so the girls and I took turns walking alongside. We had known fear, seen death, felt the hand of naked brutality on us already. The days ahead loomed dark and hopeless. We had had no time to think or plan. The responsibility Father had placed upon David and me came first; we had to see that Mother and the girls were protected and cared for, and until their safety was secured we could not plan for ourselves.

Chapter

2

WE RETURNED to a city so changed in a few weeks' time that it was almost unrecognizable at first. The buildings were the same, except for the burned-out synagogues and a few factories on the outskirts that had been badly bombed. Few residents walked the streets, but the Germans were everywhere, strutting arrogantly, pushing their way past now silent, sullen men and women.

Sala and David told us that all the rumors we had heard were true. Not only had the temples been burned, but when the Germans first occupied the town they had forcibly taken every young Jewish man they could find and marched them, several hundred young boys and men, to the outskirts of the city, forced them to dig their own mass graves, and then shot them in cold blood. Our neighbor's son, young Kohan, had been among them.

We saw terrible and horrible things going on around us each moment and were powerless to do anything. The Gestapo had already taken steps to set up a Jewish Council, the Kultusgemeinde. Mr. Merin was installed by them as chairman. Their plans were efficient, thorough, and well laid in advance. In order to get food, every Jew had to have a ration card, which could be obtained only from the Kultusgemeinde where we had to register.

The first order came: All Jews had to wear a yellow Star of David over their hearts. Later another order proclaimed that every Jew must wear an identifying armband on the left sleeve of his outer garment, and it must be displayed at all times. Failure to comply meant instant imprisonment. As the Gestapo's control of our lives tightened, a Jewish police force, the militia, was established and quartered across the street from the Kultusgemeinde headquarters.

Within a few days an order came to our house, hand-carried by a militiaman. It was addressed to David. He was ordered to appear at a certain time and place for transport to an unstated destination for labor. David had already been the victim of one of the ever-increasing street raids. German soldiers had swooped down on one street, picked up David and every other Jew they could find, young and old, man and woman, and put them to work sweeping the streets. Poles, encouraged by the Germans, gathered around, jeering and insulting them. The degradation and frustration were more than David could bear, and so, faced with forced labor, he decided to make a break for it to the east. We encouraged him to go; he had nothing to lose, since he faced an unknown fate if he went to the labor camp. At least he might have a chance if he made it into the Russian-occupied eastern zone. And David left with our blessings and part of Mother's heart.

The next to go was 23-year-old. Yadja. She came home a few days after David's departure and told us that some of her girlfriends had plans to leave for the east, too. We could see the first faint handwriting on the wall. The Germans were taking only one member of a family at a time, and if splitting up meant survival for more of us, we could only encourage her to leave with her friends. As David had done, she and the other girls headed east and disappeared. We heard that the German border guards were not stopping women, and therefore she stood a better chance than David to make it to safety. For David, our hopes were not high. The Germans had transported young Jewish men to the Russian zone, turned them loose, ordered them to run, and shot them down when they obeyed. Had David been among them? No word came back from the east of either David or Yadja.

Slowly, most of the Jewish families that had fled the city had returned to their homes and what remained of their lives. Some had already lost sons to raids and transports. So many shocks had hit us in such a short period of time that a feeling of numbness and unreality had set in. It was almost impossible to imagine being affected or hurt by any new terror. Father was in Wolbrom, and now that the Germans had annexed the territory to their Third Reich, we were cut off from him as if from another world. Our closely knit family had dwindled in a few shattering weeks to Mother, Sala, Rochelle, and me.

The next move against us by the German occupation forces was the takeover of Jewish-held businesses. The big enterprises and factories owned by Jews were either confiscated, closed and stripped of their inventories and machinery, which were then shipped into Germany, or put into the hands of German custodians. The former owners were forced to work under the Germans with little or no compensation and no authority or voice in the affairs of the company. This lasted only until the Germans had replaced the Jews with their own trained personnel. Then the Jews were evicted permanently.

Most of our people were of moderate circumstances, tradesmen and shopkeepers; others, like our dear friends the Koplowich and Gold families, were people of great wealth and power in the city. The Gold family had vast wineries that had been in their family for generations, and these were taken from them. The Koplowich family had one of the largest wholesale textile businesses in our area, with huge warehouses of merchandise, and these were seized and placed under German custodians. Our own small, family-run wholesale poultry business that we had reopened was bypassed in the Nazi confiscation, but our sources of supply and our contacts were cut off and the business dwindled rapidly. Sala and I did our best to run it in our father's absence.

My sisters and I made a few dangerous trips by night in a wagon past the border guards and into Wolbrom to see Father and our family there. On the return trips we smuggled food and supplies back for ourselves and friends and to sell on the black market that had sprung up.

Even these trips became too dangerous, and we had to give them up. Our last contact with Father and our family in Wolbrom was broken, and Mother began to realize she might never see him again.

If we had had any doubts about the willingness of the Germans to inflict the promised punishment on anyone trying to conceal merchandise or materials, our doubts were soon laid to rest. The Kultusgemeinde issued an announcement that the father and son of one of our most prominent Jewish families had been accused by the Gestapo of concealing and removing materials from their store on Mungeyofska and that their punishment was to be carried out publicly as a lesson to all of us. As if in some ghastly nightmare, we watched a gallows erected in the city square and saw the two men led roughly up the steps. Nooses were placed over their heads, and after a few seconds their lifeless bodies swayed in the cold winter air. Their bodies were left there, for how long I don't remember. It was the Germans' way to instill fear in us, and in that they were partly successful.

But they were even more successful in bringing home to us the ultimate realization that a Jew's life was meaningless to them. We determined to resist in the only ways left open to us, one of which was to conceal whatever possessions we could without being caught. We had also learned that the Kultusgemeinde was merely a tool of the Gestapo and could do nothing to protect us.

Our family and friends drew even closer together in suffering and mutual need. We shared whatever we had and tried to comfort one another and maintain some order and sanity in our lives.

The rationing of food, severe in the beginning, became even less endurable. The Poles and Jews had been issued different ration cards. The Poles were allowed a subsistence diet. But the Nazis had limited the number of calories a Jew could have a day and even specified where food could be obtained, if available. Two Jewish bakeries were permitted to operate, and only there could the thousands of Jews in the city come to look for bread. We stood in queues for hours, many times all through the icy nights, often to find when our turn came in line that there was nothing left for us and the hundreds behind us, not even crumbs.

As hungry as our bodies became, our souls were even hungrier. Our synagogues were gone, but our religion was too strong a part of our lives for us not to find a way to carry on. In many Jewish homes a room was set aside where the Torahs and Holy Arks saved from the Germans were hidden. On Friday nights small groups of men and boys made their way silently and cautiously to these rooms and, with or without a rabbi, delivered the age-old prayers to God.

We were hungry, frightened, and filled with an anger we dared not display. A curtain of ice and hatred came down between us and the Poles. Their faces turned from us in the streets, half guilty and half relieved that the Germans had found in us a scapegoat, leaving them to go on with their lives, captive but, by comparison, free. We waited for the next blow.

Chapter 3

ONE DAY IN NOVEMBER a militiaman delivered another notice to our home. I, Natan Schapelski, was ordered by the German Government of Occupation, through the Kultusgemeinde, to prepare myself to appear at the time and place stated. I was instructed to report to the Kultusgemeinde for a supply of food, and I would be permitted to carry the two or three days' supply in a knapsack only; no hand luggage would be permitted. The order went on to state very simply that if I did not appear as ordered, my entire family would be seized and sent to a concentration camp. I learned that the same order had been sent to some four hundred Jewish men between the ages of seventeen and twenty-five years, and it appeared that only one male member of a family had been called.

I had no choice. If my going meant time gained for the rest of my family, I would go willingly.

The Germans obviously understood only too well the family

structure of the European Jew. They knew that it was part of our heritage and training to feel a deep and abiding responsibility for one another—a brother for a sister, a daughter for a mother, a father for his children. Hitler, his Gestapo and SS had made the cruelly accurate analysis of our extraordinarily close family ties. The European Jew, although technically a citizen of the country of his birth, was traditionally and effectively isolated by religion and heritage from his fellow citizens. We might be natives of Poland and feel love for the country, but the years of discrimination and isolation had turned us inward to our own people. We relied on one another, so there was no question of self-sacrifice in the actions of one family member for another; it had always been so and would always be so. We Jews took it for granted, and now so did the Germans. Our family devotion became a deadly weapon in their sadistic hands.

We dared to believe from day to day that this nightmare would be short-lived and that the outside world would awaken to what was taking place and put a stop to it. So, if I and thousands of others went unresistingly in the beginning, buying time for our families with our captivity, it was because we felt there was reason to hope that Hitler would find himself under attack from the west and we would be freed at last. On the other hand, the Germans knew that as long as they took only one at a time from each family, holding the lives and safety of the others as hostage for the behavior of the chosen victim, they could control us.

We could not fight them openly. We were without arms, and the few Jews taken into the Polish resistance and partisan groups were eventually betrayed or murdered by them. It would be a very long time before we finally realized that our hopes were false.

Mr. Koplowich heard the news and came to offer his help. "Don't worry, Natan, I'll do everything I can to get you out of this," he assured me. "I'll go to Merin at the Kultusgemeinde and talk to him."

We were reassured; Mr. Koplowich was still a powerful

influence in the community and respected by everyone. If anyone could help me, he could. The Golds came to comfort us also. They repeated what Mr. Koplowich had said and, as he had done, offered their help without limit. I knew that if money could buy my name off the list, these friends would pay out their last zloty for me. But when they returned the following day I could tell from their faces that their efforts had been useless.

"Natan," Mr. Koplowich told me, "the Gestapo has a copy of the list in their hands, and we can't get to it. We talked to Merin's assistant at the Kultusgemeinde, and he says he can't do anything about it. I'm going to try again tonight, so don't give up hope."

I was not the only boy they tried so desperately to save. Other friends of theirs had sons due to leave with me, and these wonderful people put their resources to work for them at the risk of their own safety. When they returned that night we had to face the truth. If any more attempts were made to remove names from the list, it would inevitably cost the lives of our families and friends. I resigned myself to leaving in the morning for the designated gathering place on the Third of May Street.

Before the last evening at home had ended, all our friends and relatives came to wish me well and to offer their protection to Mother and the girls. Mr. and Mrs. Gold presented me with a bottle of wine that represented a gift of love and compassion beyond its considerable worth. This wine had been many years in the wine cellars of their family, and in offering it to me they gave also their hearts and prayers.

Uncle Max and Uncle Natan came with their wives and my young cousins to help us through the last minutes in the morning of the final day.

I fought back tears and kissed Sala and Rochelle. "Take care of Mother," I whispered to them. "No matter what happens, see that she is safe." They didn't have to promise me; I knew they would lay down their lives for her, as I would.

When I put my arms around my mother's tiny body, words failed me. I held her for a moment, not even hearing her words. She touched my face and murmured something to me, and then it was time to go.

With my knapsack on my back, I walked out alone into the street. I turned into Descartes toward the *punkt* (the assembly point) and as I neared the big textile factory on Persnayer where we had been ordered to gather, cries and shouts came from all sides. As I got closer I heard what sounded like hysterical laughter. I began to run toward the noise.

"It's true, it's true," the voices yelled. "The transport's been called off!"

"We don't have to go, Natan! They've changed their minds."

I stopped short, dazed, unbelieving. A wild surge of hope ran through me. My God, it's finally happened, the miracle we had been praying for. Somewhere in the world outside, forces had come together and put a stop to the nightmare.

I began to laugh and yell with the others, then turned and ran crazily back through the streets. Only a moment before I had left behind all that was dear to me, and now my life had been handed back and, with it, new hope for my loved ones.

I ran into the house, calling the good news ahead of me. "I'm back, Mother! I don't have to go!"

The joy in our house was echoed throughout the other Jewish homes where young men returned, even though the reason for the counterorder remained a mystery. We tried through every channel to find out who had been responsible for the order to cancel the transport, but no answer was ever found.

So we accepted this gift of hope and life, and for a few weeks we waited for the other horrors to stop. But they did not, and each passing day brought the realization that this one miracle was just that—a solitary miracle—beyond explanation and without any possibility of happening again. In the endless, tragic time that followed, we spoke of this one day less and less. The brief hope that had flamed up in our hearts and then died had left us even less prepared for what came after. After that no other transport was ever called off in our city or, as far as I could tell, in any other city.

Chapter

4

LATER THAT SAME MONTH, in November, we heard a rumor that more than a thousand, perhaps as many as fifteen hundred, Jewish men had been brought into Sosnowiec from Theresienstadt in Czechoslovakia.

The rumors said that these men were intellectuals, doctors, teachers, professors, white-collar workers, and professional men of the highest level. We soon learned that it was true. They were interned in a textile factory the Germans had previously emptied and were being kept there without being put to forced labor. No one knew, least of all the prisoners, the purpose of their imprisonment. It appeared that they were being treated fairly decently by the Germans.

Their welfare began to concern us as the mystery of their confinement and destination deepened. In discussing their situation one day with a family friend, Mrs. Silverstein, we agreed that it was our responsibility to help these men in any way we could. She and I went to see the German official in charge of the guards stationed around the building and on the rooftops with machine guns cradled in their arms.

He said, "What do you want? What business do you have here?"

We explained to him that we merely wanted permission to offer some food and supplies to the people in the factory, not daring to hope that he would agree.

"All right, you two can come here once a week, say, a week from tonight—Friday," he said, pointing at Mrs. Silverstein and me. "And you can bring in food and clothing, but only you two and only what you can carry yourselves. No one else is to come without my permission."

It seemed to us that he was acting under orders to proceed very cautiously in the treatment of his prisoners, and this, again, gave us some hope. I felt that the Germans did not know as yet precisely what to do with these men and wanted to see how the outside world would react to reports of the imprisonment of a large group of Jewish men representing the cream of the cultural, intellectual, and professional society of their communities.

We returned to our homes and immediately spread the story to our families and friends.

On the next Friday night Mrs. Silverstein and I collected from our friends what they could spare of their own meager supplies—packages of bread, dried fruit, extra blankets—and when we had as much as we could carry we made our way to the factory.

The guards let us pass, and at last we came face to face with the prisoners. We were stunned! These were men from another society and country. Physically, they were striking in their height and manly proportions. To me, accustomed as I was to the moderate stature of the Poles, my own family included, these well-dressed, tall and handsome men seemed almost of another race.

Several men approached us, and in our common languages of Yiddish and German introduced themselves courteously, and

24

presented a spokesman to whom we could direct our questions. He thanked us for bringing food and supplies and for showing them that someone cared. More men gathered around us while others lay on crude bunks or sat on the factory floor.

We asked when and how they had come to Sosnowiec. Until we came, they had not known where they were. We heard the story of how they had been taken without warning from their homes at night—a sudden, unexplained round-up of leaders of their Jewish communities—and carried off in secrecy across the border.

When the guards indicated that we had to leave, after almost an hour, we promised the prisoners we would be back the following Friday night and left with their thanks and warm words following us through the gates.

My mind was reeling. I had been prepared to find prisoners like those confined in Zawiercha, men and boys like my father and brother, but these men were different.

Every Friday night in the weeks that followed, Mrs. Silverstein and I entered the factory, loaded with supplies. Our people never let us down, and often we had more than we could carry. I looked forward to this short trip each week even though we could offer them no explanation of their imprisonment nor any hope for their future.

Almost two months passed, and my esteem and respect for these men grew, as did my admiration for their courage in the face of their uncertain future. They were always courteous and warmly grateful for our limited offerings of food and spoke of their concern for the safety and well-being of the wives and children from whom they had been torn so brutally.

One Friday night we went as usual to the factory and found the guards missing. We entered the building quickly, unchallenged. It was empty! Every one of the prisoners was gone without a trace, and not one of them was ever heard from again.

The world's obvious indifference to their disappearance must have encouraged the Germans to move. There was little or no reaction or protest, and what there was certainly was not loud enough to reach Sosnowiec that black day.

We grieved for them and cursed the darkness that had swallowed them. I felt bereft, as if I had lost my father, brother, and uncles again. And indeed I had, for had we Jews not become even more one family?

Chapter
5

WE WERE FRIGHTENED uncontrollably by the swift disappearance of the Czechs, and our fear was heightened by the apparent isolation from the world beyond our borders.

"If no one cared enough to question their fate, what will happen to us?" we asked one another in growing terror. The answer was not long in coming.

It started again suddenly one day with the Arbeitseinsatz, the labor command. The Germans used the same successful formula in enlisting their slave labor. Either one or two young members from each family were called up (never the entire family at one time), or the SS, Gestapo, and Kriminalpolizei raided the streets, and the young men and women they caught were sent away to work camps. Some of my dearest friends were among the first taken in these raids, never to be heard from or seen again.

Then local shops and factories were converted to manufacture supplies for the German military. Uniforms and other equipment, such as shoes and boots for their troops, were to be made in Sosnowiec.

The Germans were short of trained labor and technicians, and if a young Jewish man or woman was fortunate enough to have the required training, an official paper was provided, exempting them from the street raids. They were put to work in the factories in town instead of disappearing on the transports to the German labor camps.

Refugees straggled through the city every day and brought with them rumors of the evacuation of the city of Oswiecim —Auschwitz in German—and the nearby town of Birkenau.

At first we heard and believed that they were preparing the site of a huge labor camp; later, new rumors began to circulate about the strange structures being erected on that once desolate plain, unlike any imaginable work camp. At the same time, several hundred miles away, Maidanek was being built in the same pattern as Auschwitz.

No news came from Yadja or David. Father, while only a few miles away, was as cut off from us as they were.

While the raids in the streets and in the houses continued, the local German officials apparently began to feel the need to retain at least a semblance of what remained of Jewish business life. Bulletins were posted at the Jewish centers notifying us that the legal heads and license holders of business firms would be immune for the time being from the local Arbeitseinsatz and the camps.

In Father's absence, we determined to get our business, diminished as it was, transferred to my name to provide me with some immunity from the orders to join work transports that came from the Kultusgemeinde.

After days of persuasion, Sala was finally able to exact the help we needed from the landlord of our apartment building, an influential Pole who had large property holdings in the community. He smoothed the way for the license to be issued in my name, but even though I now had official recognition as head of our business, we knew this immunity was only temporary. If I was caught in a street raid, the license had no value.

I realized that the ceaseless raiding of our people would inevitably and eventually expand to include not only the young men and women but entire families. I had only to look around me. The German soldiers were grabbing people off the streets under any pretext and forcing them to clean out barracks, or taking them to the private homes of German officials and officers to do menial work. They loaded them down with sacks of coal or put them to work at any humiliating task. Others, caught in the planned raids, went out in transports.

Sosnowiec, Bedzin, Dabrowa, and all the other surrounding towns and cities had been emptied of more than 20 percent of their Jewish population in just these few short months of occupation. And most of the first victims were the young men and women. I knew I had to find some exemption more permanent than the business license, for if I was taken, Mother and the girls would be unprotected.

Uncle Chaim told me that he had just been given a job with the city sanitation department and that they were taking on hundreds of people to do street cleaning, rubbish removal, and recovery of scrap material. The Germans found they needed many workers to keep the city functioning and to fill the gap between the few mechanized vehicles and the still horse-drawn snowplows and fire engines.

Before the war most of the work force had, of course, been Poles. Now the department was drafting its labor from the many Jews who were without work and forbidden to practice their trade or operate a business. Uncle Chaim had heard that this work entitled the employees to a *sonder* pass that carried some weight with the authorities.

"They say if you're caught in a raid and you have this *sonder*, they let you go," he told me.

"How did you get into this department, Uncle?" I asked.

"I got an introduction to this man Rainer who's in charge. He's a Volksdeutsche from Katowitz. He does the hiring for the street-cleaning crews. I talked to him about you yesterday, Natan, so you meet me tomorrow after work and we'll see if we can get you in.

I left the house the next afternoon and hurried through the chill gray light.

At the gathering place, Uncle Chaim left the group of men waiting to be counted and released after their day of work in the city streets and came over to me. "That's Rainer over there," he said, pointing to a man near the door of the office.

As we walked over to him, I could see he was a typical Volksdeutsche, one of the many Polish-born German civilians the Nazis had brought in to take over the city government and its departments under their military occupation.

Rainer looked at me curiously as Uncle Chaim introduced us. Uncle mentioned casually that I had some connections in the textile industry, but since the occupation it was impossible for me to carry on the business.

"It's very difficult to get fabrics now, *nein?*" Rainer asked, speaking directly to me for the first time.

I understood immediately what his question implied. We were not allowed any fabric at all, but it was also rationed to the Germans very strictly.

"Well, of course, Herr Rainer," I answered. "The textile business is out of our hands, but we might have some left over. Possibly I could find some in the house."

"I see. That's very interesting, because I could use some material," he said evenly. "I think I can use you in the department on one of the crews. Report in the morning with the rest of the men and I'll put you to work."

I held my breath for a moment, and then he said what we had been waiting to hear.

"You'll be issued a *sonder* to show you are now working for the city. Pick it up in the morning at the office before you start work." He turned abruptly and walked away.

Uncle Chaim and I congratulated each other with our eyes. I felt a temporary sense of relief. If I understood this Rainer, and I knew I had, then the *sonder*, the special pass, was to be mine for a price. I knew I could get all the material I needed from Mr. Koplowich, so that was no problem. But I had to be concerned about how I dealt with Rainer so that our unspoken agreement would not endanger the safety of Uncle Chaim, the others, or myself, now that I had found safety for the moment under his patronage.

The pass was ready for me when I came for it the next morning. I folded the unimpressive-looking piece of paper and placed it securely in my pocket, hoping I would not need to test its value. Uncle Chaim took me with him on his crew, and we set off with push brooms and carts, clearing the debris of the city from its streets and gutters.

The anger and humiliation that welled up in my throat when I saw my uncle and the other once respected men, no longer young, reduced to this menial labor took days to subside. "At least we're still alive" became the phrase that checked my desire to strike out. I clenched my teeth against the angry words I wanted to yell and gripped the handle of the broom until my knuckles turned white. I wanted to fight back, show these beasts that we were human and men, not passive slaves. But the lives of my mother and sisters were my first responsibility, and I could not afford to lose my self-control.

My first day on the crew ended, and we returned to the department headquarters for roll call and to check in our equipment.

Rainer nodded to me and motioned me over to one side. "Well, Schapelski, you have your job now, *ja?*"

I thanked him for putting me to work and for the paper I found myself clutching in my pocket.

"Did you bring me any goods, Schapelski?" he asked. "The clothes I brought from Katowice are just about worn out, and I really could use some new trousers."

"I think I have some fabric you can use, Herr Rainer, but I don't want to bring it here. With your permission, I would rather bring it to your house, you understand?"

He agreed that it would be wiser and gave me his address.

I went to see Koplowich that evening, and he assured me I could take whatever material I needed from the personal stock he had kept for his own family's use. I explained to him that in this situation I saw a way to get other Jews into the city department with *sonders* for their protection.

"Certainly, Mr. Koplowich, there will be other Germans

who will want material, and Herr Rainer will not be satisfied with just one piece. If this turns out to be the case, then we can take advantage of it and ask them to open the department to more people."

He understood at once the opportunity we had and was only concerned that I might be walking into a trap laid by Rainer.

"Be careful. He could turn you in for trying to bribe him and for concealing confiscated material."

I assured him I would not put myself in a position where Rainer could say that I was demanding any payment or give him any chance to trace back the source of the fabric.

When I went to Rainer's house and was admitted, I unwound material from my mid-section and handed it to him folded. He was very pleased.

"How do you happen to have such a fine piece of cloth?" he asked. "I would think you would have used it for yourself by now."

"Well, you see, Herr Rainer, my father had this put away to make a suit for himself, but somehow he never got around to taking it to the tailor, and then, of course, the war . . ."

He seemed to accept my explanation, and I left with no mention of payment between us then or in the days that followed when he found opportunity time after time to let me know that his wife could use a new coat, a warm dress, and that he had "friends" also in need of material.

Our bargain had been struck. I delivered material always in small pieces so that he would not get too greedy and always from the "family" supply. Each time I would mention to him that I had a friend or friends who could use a job. In the days that passed he took into the department Mr. Gold, his twin sons, and two of the Chaba men and gave them *sonders*, too.

One evening after roll call Rainer called me into his office. "I want to talk to you for a minute," he said. "I am leaving Sosnowiec for another assignment, and a friend of mine is taking over as chairman of the Arbeitseinsatz." He described the friend briefly to me as a casualty of the war who was being transferred to non-combatant service because he was no longer able to serve at the front.

I began to wonder what this story would lead to.

"You see, Schapelski," Rainer continued, "Chairman Smoloz has been in uniform, and now that he is taking over this important civilian post he will need suitable clothes. It would be unfortunate if he had to wait for his year's ration."

So that was it! I explained to Rainer that our modest inventory consisted only of prewar fabrics, and even those were limited, as he well knew. He repeated that his friend would need a certain amount of material, and, further, since Herr Smoloz would be assuming a post of some importance in the department, perhaps I could arrange for a reliable tailor to make up a suit.

I understood that Rainer was using me in order to ingratiate himself with his friend, but I had no choice. Over a period of days I brought the fabric in small pieces to let him know how difficult it was to obtain, and I also gave him the name of a tailor to whom I had already spoken and who understood his payment would be coming from me, not from any German he outfitted.

I was curious about the success of Rainer's obvious courtship of the new chairman, whom I had not seen. And when Rainer offered to introduce me to him, I was relieved to find out that the plot had gone smoothly. If Rainer was successful, it also meant renewed opportunity to bring more people into the department under the new chairman.

Smoloz looked down at his feet when Rainer brought me to him. He was a dark, slender man of medium height. Only when he glanced up briefly to acknowledge my presence and I saw the brutal, unsmiling face could I picture him in uniform. He thanked me curtly for the material I had provided and indicated, by looking down again, that the introduction was over. I could see from Rainer's manner that he was afraid of him and wanted to gain his confidence and friendship. A glance at the man's hands during our brief exchange of words showed that several of his fingers were missing. At the time it occurred to me that this man's bitter countenance might be due to his wounds, but as I came to know Smoloz and later his wife, and as their demands on me for fabrics and other scarce

33

goods grew, I came to the conclusion it was more likely that he had deliberately shot off his own fingers to escape combat.

As the demands grew, I made frequent trips to their living quarters in the row of new apartment houses that had been made *Judenrein*—Jew-free—for the number of Volksdeutsche now living in and running the city departments. Frau Smoloz would meet me at the door and take the parcels from me with a few words of thanks in German.

They made an odd pair when they walked together—he, thin, always in somber, dark clothing, striding forcefully; she, slender and blond, with a delicate face and almost unnoticeable limp, trying to keep up with him.

Our strange relationship grew, and I called on every source I had to keep up with their demands. Each time I delivered a length of cloth or a parcel of scarce food, I asked that a few more people be taken into the department, sometimes two or three at a time.

So it went, each delivery gaining safety for another friend, each piece of fabric or parcel of food meaning another *sonder* in the pocket of a Jewish man or boy.

Where at first my youth had been a handicap in bargaining with them, they came to understand that I knew this was no child's game and that I cared only about the safety they extended to my people.

Chapter
6

SOON ANOTHER PLAYER ENTERED THE GAME.

At roll call one day the Polish clerk who worked in the office came out to the assembly and said, "Schapelski, Herr Smoloz wants to see you inside. You, too, Friedman."

Uncle Chaim and I left the others waiting to be dismissed for the evening and went through the door. I glanced back and noticed that the clerk was not following us inside.

Smoloz broke off his conversation with the tall, handsome young blond man we had seen around the office for several days and called to us, "Friedman, Schapelski, come in, come in. Herr Schmidt, these are the two men I was telling you about."

Smoloz introduced us briefly, stressing for our benefit what we had already heard—that Herr Schmidt was the superintendent of the Public Works Department in the City Hall and was related to the German Burgermeister who had replaced the Polish mayor. He was an attractive man and impressed me with his warmth and outgoing manner. He made no attempt to convey his authority and power but asked only a few simple questions about our work.

35

"I hear from Herr Smoloz that you are both good workers. I am pleased to know this," he said. "I like to hear good reports when I make inspections."

My instinctive distrust of any German put me on my guard against the unexpectedly decent way he spoke to us. In a moment, when I looked around, we were alone. Smoloz had left the office, taking Uncle Chaim with him. I took the initiative finally and asked, "Is there anything I can do for you, Herr Schmidt?"

"Well, that's very nice of you, Schapelski. Not now, but if I think of anything I'll let you know."

Nothing more was said along personal lines. We had a quiet discussion about the work in general, and then he excused me and I left.

Smoloz found an early opportunity to tell me that it might be well for me to stop by Schmidt's apartment and talk to his housekeeper. He gave me her name and suggested I ask her if there was anything she needed for the house.

I knew the neighborhood well. It was an exclusive area of new upper-class homes where many professional people—doctors, professors, attorneys—and wealthy Poles and Jews had lived before the occupation.

The housekeeper seemed to have been expecting me, and when I identified myself she was ready with a list of her needs to run Schmidt's bachelor household. She wanted fresh meat, a really scarce commodity, and other hard-to-get groceries.

I did my best to get what she asked for, and everyone I approached for help cooperated, because they understood how vital it was that more and more men be brought under the protection of the sanitation department.

I made the requested deliveries to Schmidt's house, and I could tell that his housekeeper was satisfied.

From then on I called on her frequently, and, as the weeks passed, I saw Schmidt at the house often. He was increasingly cordial to me, and my initial favorable reaction to him strengthened and grew. He was a German—unquestionably an oppressor, one of them—but apparently a decent human being.

All his actions and words bore this out, and try as I might I could detect no falseness or hidden brutality in him. He carried the responsibility for the entire Public Works Department of the city on his shoulders.

Since Sosnowiec had just started to mechanize before the war, our equipment was, by German standards, fairly primitive, and we depended for the most part on manual labor and horse-drawn equipment, even though we did have some trucks for rubbish collection and heavy-duty hauling.

I had become increasingly conscious during this period of a German obsession for which I later had many reasons to be grateful. The Germans had an almost abnormal fear of disease and epidemic, and the strictest orders had come down from the High Command that streets and public places were to be kept clean and free of debris at all times. ·

The street and house raids continued. Trying desperately to buy room in the department for more people, I became so occupied with maintaining the supply line connecting me with Schmidt and Smoloz that my actual work had to be slighted.

I met with Schmidt and Smoloz separately several times and told them how difficult it was becoming for me to have to report to work, spend the day with the crew, and then, in the short time before curfew, try to round up all the materials and food they required. I asked for a permit to allow me to be out after hours so that I would have time to take care of my many errands.

Smoloz went to Chief Knoeller at the SS headquarters and obtained a special SS exemption for me on the ground that I was needed to notify workers if any emergency arose at night. The SS chief agreed that it was an urgent matter.

I was taken off the work crew and given a job at the warehouse, distributing equipment to the men in the morning and checking it back in at night. Also I was ostensibly to make inspection tours during the day and was issued what had become an almost priceless object, a means of transportation, a bicycle. Jews had been forbidden access to any public transportation from the first days of the occupation.

I received advance warning of night raids, and with the curfew exemption and the bicycle I was able to warn friends that they could expect a night visit from the soldiers so that they could hide.

I had proven to these men that I could deliver what they needed, and they were willing to gamble with their power to gain these few luxuries and privileges. Smoloz wanted to stay on good terms with Schmidt because of Schmidt's relationship with the Burgermeister, so he played his game for personal advantage. For the most part they were fair with me. But Schmidt was the only one for whom I had any respect. I could not despise him as I did the others.

I traveled the city streets day and night now in comparative safety, with my special paper stamped and signed by the SS and with the official armband of the city seal riding on my upper arm, level with the yellow star over my heart.

Chapter
7

OUR DAILY LIFE, already a chaotic nightmare of large and small horrors, became a waiting game—the intended victims waiting to see the next move the hunters would make.

Food and other essentials became scarcer, and when money ceased to have value, our possessions went.

The Polish farmers, although forbidden to trade with us under threat of death, made deals for food, taking in exchange whatever we had to offer. We traded hoarded goods from our dwindling stocks and then personal belongings for an occasional bit of fresh meat, a chicken or a few vegetables.

I watched my mother's tiny face become more pinched with each passing day, even though I brought her and my sisters every bit of food I could pry away from whatever sources I had. The strain and tension that never stopped, day or night, exacted a toll from us for which the inadequate nourishment could not hope to compensate.

The sound of heavy boots in the street below at night or, even worse, in the hallways of the building would strike terror into all of us. Few mornings dawned that were not emptier by one or two or three or more young friends, gone from us, taken on a raid.

When these kidnappings no longer produced enough young laborers to fill the growing needs, the Kultusgemeinde received orders to conscript workers and see that they reported for assignment to camps or, for the few fortunate ones, to local shops and factories.

And every few weeks the Germans came up with new confiscatory demands on the Jews. At first it was that we must turn in all gold watches to the Kultusgemeinde, then all gold of every type, then any and all jewelry, and finally, time after time, cash assessments, until we were drained.

While making my usual rounds one Monday morning, without warning, I found myself in the midst of a raid. Soldiers grabbed me, and, with all the others, I was forced onto a truck and taken downtown to a special *punkt*, round-up point, where we were to be held until transportation was available to the ultimate destination.

As soon as they had us locked in the courtyard they began weeding out the elderly men and women and those whose obvious disabilities made them unfit for the work camps. These few were released and permitted to return home. But even for them the shock and brutality to which they had been exposed left wounds and mental anguish their freedom could not erase.

I was frantic. It had finally happened; my turn had come. Now what would happen to my mother and the girls? I wracked my mind. Had I been careless? So many nights, forewarned by a few words from Schmidt or Smoloz, I had made my way to the homes of others to warn of upcoming night raids. But the street raids were not preplanned, so for me there had been no warning.

When I had almost given up hope of any help, the gate was opened by the guards and Smoloz walked in.

"All right, Schapelski, you are free. Come with me," he said and walked me past the guards.

I was dazed and stumbled after him.

"How did you know where I was?" I asked him as soon as we were clear of the *punkt*.

"You're a lucky boy. Your sister Sala came straight to me when some friends of yours told her they had seen you taken in the street. I went to the Burgermeister's office and convinced them you were needed in the department and should be released to me. They gave me official orders for the officer in charge of the *punkt* that he could not disregard, so you're a free boy."

That narrow escape only sharpened my awareness of the desperate need among our people for protection. I had been able to get many friends and relatives jobs and *sonders*, but it was not enough. I had to try to get immunity extended as widely and as fast as possible.

I had to see Schmidt immediately.

Entrance to the City Hall was *verboten* to Jews. Schmidt was surprised to see me but displayed no anger. As a result of that meeting, acting on my recommendation that we increase our labor force and pulling strings and using every connection he had, we took over two hundred more Jews into the department. They were relatives and friends and others in desperate need of help who were facing impending transport to the camps because they lacked the technical skills and knowledge to make them useful in the local shops and factories.

Some of our new recruits were later caught in raids and released as I had been, because they had the magical *sonder*.

Encouraged by success, I approached Schmidt and Smoloz again, and once more we increased the labor force, using as our reason this time the need for "reserves."

I was able to convince them that women should be employed by the city to do cleaning in the offices of the City Hall, to maintain the stock and equipment in the warehouse, and, of course, that additional numbers were needed in "reserve." Now, at last, Sala and Rochelle held *sonders*, too. Naturally, most of our new "laborers," men and women, never appeared for work; but they carried in their pockets the little piece of paper that gave some security and protection. These favors and *sonders* cost more and more. I was hard pressed to keep up with the need for supplies and funds to satisfy the men whose protection had been extended to so many. But I knew I did not dare let them down or their favor could be quickly withdrawn. And in my eagerness to keep them pleased, I came within a breath of losing everything, including my own life and that of Uncle Chaim.

Smoloz, in the course of a casual conversation one evening at his house, indicated that he could use a loan of some money but that he was hesitant to take it from me. I, in turn, made it clear, as subtly as I could, that I would be glad to see that some money found its way into his pocket. I said I could see nothing wrong in loaning him as little as fifty marks. When he did not respond to my suggestion, I thought my intent had not been made sufficiently clear and I wanted to reassure him that there would be no problem in his accepting money from me.

"After all, Herr Smoloz," I told him, "even Herr Schmidt might borrow fifty marks from me—as a loan, you understand—so you needn't be concerned if you find yourself in need of funds."

He seemed pleased with my clarification, and we let the subject drop.

When I wheeled up to the office on my bicycle at the end of work the next day, the men were turning in their equipment. This was always a very lengthy process, made even longer by the German insistence on counting all the men then, as they did every morning. With several hundred men and women reporting in and checking out every day, a considerable amount of time was consumed by this ritual. I called out a greeting to Uncle Chaim and looked over to see what Schmidt was doing. He was watching us with a peculiar look on his face, and when he saw he had our attention, he motioned us to him.

"Both of you get into the office at once," he said coldly.

We walked inside. The room was empty and quiet for two or three minutes, then Schmidt and Smoloz walked in and closed the door behind them. Schmidt said evenly and without expression, "Both of you walk to the wall and face me."

42

I couldn't believe I had really heard what he said, but when I saw Uncle Chaim's face go white, I started for the wall with him. We stood facing them, the two Germans. Schmidt reached into his coat and drew a gun from his shoulder holster. I could hear a loud click as he cocked it and pointed it at us.

"Did you ever give me any money?"

My mind raced, and before I could actually think I blurted out, "There's been a terrible mistake. I may have mentioned to Herr Smoloz that *if* Herr Schmidt should need a loan, I would be more than happy to secure it for him."

Schmidt did not change expression. "Did you ever give me any money?"

I could feel my uncle trembling beside me. "No, Herr Schmidt. It looks as if Herr Smoloz misunderstood me," I answered.

Smoloz had not lifted his gaze from the floor during this exchange. Schmidt stared at us for a moment, and I felt that the end had come. He needed no excuse to shoot us down if he so decided. No one would have questioned the execution of two Jews at this stage of the war, particularly not by him. Then, as suddenly as he had drawn it, he replaced the gun in his holster and said to Smoloz, "From tomorrow morning on, these two men are to be assigned to street work and are to be checked at least three times a day to see that they are performing their duties."

With that, he wheeled and left the office.

Smoloz said nothing as we walked slowly by him and out of the office.

I reported for work with Uncle every day thereafter, and, as Schmidt had ordered, we were watched closely and checked three times a day to see that we were not shirking our work. All privileges were taken away from me, and I was despondent at what damage had been done. For days I did not dare to get in touch with either Smoloz or Schmidt for fear they would take more drastic action.

I could not let the situation deteriorate, so the following week I contacted Schmidt's housekeeper several times. Each time she asked me not to come back. She had instructions from Herr Schmidt. But I persisted in asking for an interview until one day she said he had agreed to talk to me.

We met that evening in his house, and he allowed me to state my side of the misunderstanding. I was relieved when he accepted my explanation and agreed to try to forget what had happened. He made it clear there would be no second chance if a like situation should occur again, and I understood precisely what he meant.

The tension and crisis had passed, but for how long? For every Jew holding a *sonder,* ten, twenty, thirty of those without one disappeared every day and every night.

We counted the time of the occupation no longer in days or weeks but now in months. And then a year had passed.

Fear was our constant companion. We gradually gave up hope that help would ever come, and the future lost all meaning. We could not be certain of awakening next morning in our own beds, much less plan for tomorrow or next week.

Chapter
8

THE GRAY SADNESS had spread even to the little children. I could not bear to look at my young cousins, old before their time, silent, with every childish instinct for laughter and play stamped out by the heavy German boots that walked our streets.

We lived on rumors. Anyone who had any contact with the SS, Gestapo, or Kultusgemeinde, or knew anyone who did, tried to read into every remark or happening some indication of how the war was going or what the next move against us might be. From the world outside the perimeter of Sosnowiec, beyond which we dared not venture, came the first hideous, whispered explanations of the camps at Auschwitz and Birkenau.

"They are burning Jews. Those funny buildings—they're crematories!" We instinctively protested against these wild stories, denied their plausibility, but in our hearts was the unspoken acceptance of the truth. Hitler had promised his German people he would exterminate us. He had found the way to fulfill his promise.

The summer of 1941 had long passed, and the darkness of the early winter closed in around us.

It seemed I had only closed my eyes after saying good night to Mother and the girls when I heard the dreaded pounding on our door.

"Open up, *Juden*. Open up immediately!"

I motioned the women into the other room and went to the door. The soldiers pushed past me and held me to one side, while others went into the next room and dragged Rochelle and Sala out, my mother trying to hold on to them, weeping, "No, no, not my girls!"

We were helpless. The building had been completely surrounded before the raid began, so there could be no escape, and they swept through so swiftly that there was no time to conceal anyone even if a hiding place had existed. We tried to explain to the soldiers that the girls had papers and were special workers. "Wait, listen, they have *sonders*. Look, here they are, please look," we begged. But it was to no avail. They were on a special raid for young Jewish women, and no *sonders* had any meaning to them.

Two or three minutes later my sisters were gone into the night with dozens of other young girls and women. My mother was in a state of hysteria, and I could hear the wailing and crying from the other apartments down the hall.

"Mother, please stay here. I'm going to get help. I'll get them back, I promise you. Or go next door and stay with Mrs. Kohan. I'll be back as soon as I can."

I ran to the building's entrance door, and when the last soldier had swung aboard the trucks loaded with terrified, half-clad women, dressed only in whatever they had been able to grab when dragged out into the icy night, I slipped out into the snow-covered streets.

Once clear of our street and out of sight of the Germans, I broke into a run. The ten minutes it took to cover the distance to Smoloz's house seemed like an eternity. I tapped on his door, trying not to rouse his neighbors, until finally I heard his heavy, sleepy voice ask, "Who is it? What do you want?"

"Herr Smoloz, please open up. It's me, Natan Schapelski," I whispered.

"Schapelski? Just a minute," he answered and opened the door, motioning me inside.

I didn't give him an opportunity to ask what had happened. The words tumbled out.

"They've taken my sisters. Sala and Rochelle—they're gone. Please, Herr Smoloz, help me! They wouldn't look at the *sonders*. If we don't do something, I know they will be gone by tomorrow."

I fought back tears; he was my only hope.

Smoloz whistled under his breath. "Uh-huh, I see, I see," he said.

Frau Smoloz called from the bedroom, "Who is it?"

He went to the door and said something quietly to her and returned to me, closing the door behind him.

"There is nothing that can be done right now. Schapelski. I have to find out exactly where they have taken them. I will take steps first thing in the morning when it's light. Go home and wait. Don't do or say anything to anyone until you hear from me. All right?"

I leaned against the wall, breathless and frantic, still gasping. I had to trust him; these was no one else I could turn to.

"All right, I'll do whatever you say, but please get them released whatever it costs. You know there is nothing I won't do to get them back. You are the only man who can help them now."

He opened the door and looked around to see if anyone had been awakened by the noise.

"It's clear. Go now and do as I said," he whispered, and I slipped out quietly.

I ran back home, more slowly and cautiously than I had come. He would help me if he could. I knew that. He could have thrown me out for having endangered him by coming to his home at night. Instead he had promised his assistance. If I had been seen entering his apartment and one of his Volksdeutsche neighbors had reported him to the Gestapo, he would have been in trouble for associating with a Jew and would have had

47

to explain my presence in his home at that hour. Fortunately, no one saw me.

I spent the night consoling and reassuring my mother that the girls were all right and would be home by morning, only half daring to believe what I swore to her was the truth.

Morning came and with it a sleigh gliding up to our apartment with Smoloz, Sala, and Rochelle. They were free!

Our joy at their release was overwhelming, and I could not find the words to thank Smoloz for this gift of their lives and for the humanity and decency he had shown me.

But the tragedy that had befallen the other families that same night did not end as fortunately as did ours. Their girls and young women did not come back; they were gone that same day into the silent world that lay beyond Sosnowiec.

Chapter

9

NOT LONG AFTER THE INCIDENT with my sisters came shocking news: The city of Wolbrom had been made *Judenrein*—Jew-free—and all the Jews still surviving in that town had been taken to Maidanek, except my father and a group of fellow worshippers, who had been dragged out of the synagogue and machine-gunned to death in the street. Father was gone and all my uncles, aunts, and cousins, too.

The shock of my father's death was more than my mother could bear. She had believed until that moment that someday they would be together again or she would never have consented to leave him behind in Wolbrom. And the almost two years that had passed had never weakened her faith. Now even that was gone and with it almost all her will to live. She wept constantly, reciting Father's name and David's and Yadja's. I stood by helplessly, filled with hatred and fury at the insanity and barbarity that had done this to her. What had she or any of us ever done to bring such disaster and desolation down upon ourselves? I raged inwardly. Could it be that God and the world were completely blind and indifferent to our suffering?

I felt old and tired inside, but I renewed my promise to my father. I would take care of Mother and my sisters with my last breath, and when the Sabbath came I sat in our secret little place of worship and said Kaddish for him in the age-old prayers I had learned in another life, in a lost world.

Our circle of family and friends grew smaller and more intimate. We became one family in our fear and in our suffering. And the strength we drew from one another gave us what little will to survive we could muster from day to day.

Every human weakness seemed to diminish in our common tragedy. There was no quarreling among our group of closely knit families, no arguments or jealousies. We shared our material possessions, our food and our lives, drew what little beauty and warmth we could from the sense of kinship that grew between us.

We went on struggling month after month, fighting in every way still left to us to sustain and prolong our lives. There were times when reason threatened to leave us altogether and the will to survive seemed to disappear. It was far from easy to keep our heads and sanity in the midst of the growing madness around us. Whatever contacts we had with most of the Poles, our lifelong neighbors and fellow citizens, were brief and strange. People we had known all our lives became sullen strangers and enemies who turned away from us in hatred and fear, as if we were contaminated with some dread disease (as indeed we were, for we were Jews; nothing could be more deadly).

Life was far from easy for them; they too suffered from lack of food, and they too were oppressed by the Germans. And they too were forced to work for their conquerors. But they had their freedom, and there were no camps being built to imprison them.

So they withdrew from us, and some made a special point of insulting and betraying us, conspiring to achieve our ultimate removal from the world. Yet each Sunday found them at their places of worship, and I wondered what they said to their God when they lifted their voices in prayer.

To our everlasting shame, even among our own people were those inevitable few who in their own private hells fought other Jews. As I continued using my German contacts to extract jobs and papers for more people, I began to experience increasing opposition from the Arbeitsgemeinde in the Jewish Council because they resented anyone exercising so much influence. But they had no jurisdiction or control over my activities.

One of the heads of the Jewish Council, Mr. Wulkan, met with me and made his opposition to my actions very clear. He told me to leave the labor force alone, not to interfere with or usurp the authority of the council.

My evaluation of their authority and effectiveness was quite different from his. Every day people were being sent away to the camps. So his warnings to me fell on deaf ears.

By this time I was committed to my course, and at every opportunity I used any means at my command to get help however I could.

The Germans began to take entire families without regard to age or sex, and we refused to accept the rumors of their fate. Now that little children were being taken, surely this meant that Birkenau, Auschwitz, and Maidanek must be labor camps and that they were putting the children under special care while the adults were doing forced labor.

I, like all the others, was unable to grasp the complete horror of the time within which we were all trapped.

The Kohans had lost one son in the first week of the occupation. Another son, Mendel, had been in a labor camp from the earliest days.

Ruschka, their daughter, worked as a secretary in the Jewish Council, and even with the contacts available to her, she had been unable to prevent her brothers from being taken. The Kohans shared with us the one letter a month they received from Mendel, recounting the torture and hunger he was experiencing. They had spent every penny they could afford to try to buy his freedom, when it was still possible to return from a labor camp.

But as the war began to go badly for the Germans, casting the first doubts on their pathological belief that they would win, the lot of the prisoners in the camps worsened, and the monthly letter, carefully worded in the code we had adopted, only intensified the Kohans' anguish. Although they wrote to their son constantly, promising he would be released, we all knew it was hopeless.

I dreaded seeing their faces each time his letters were brought next door to our apartment, their misery was so abject.

Time and again they would discuss wild schemes to get him back, and when they asked me if there was anything I could do I had to tell them it was impossible; no man had come back from any camp for more than a year now. But after reading his letters and seeing their sorrow and heartbreak, I decided I must at least make an attempt.

Smoloz and Kurt Schmidt had influence and power in Sosnowiec, and Schmidt had proven himself to be a decent man as well. I could believe his often repeated statement that he had never belonged to the Nazi party. Relying on his many acts of kindness to me and his proven willingness to help, I decided to approach him and Smoloz on the Kohans' behalf.

I went first to Schmidt and told him Mendel's background and how desperately his family wanted him back.

"You are very close to Knoeller and Ludwig in the SS. Perhaps you could talk to them, convince them that we need this man in the department, that he has special training or some such story."

I had known for some time that Schmidt was friendly with the heads of the SS department responsible for sending young Jews to the work camps, but we had never spoken of it openly before.

Schmidt laughed at me. "Natan, you know as well as I do that it's impossible. Who ever heard of anyone coming back from the camps lately? Show me just one."

I had no answer. It was true; no one had come back since the first few months.

But when I faced the Kohans with this discouraging news, they begged me to try again.

I began nagging Schmidt and Smoloz, asking each to use his personal power and prestige—to talk to the SS, talk to the headquarters in Katowice, convince them Mendel Kohan was a vitally needed specialist. I even resorted to telling Schmidt that my special interest stemmed from my love for Ruschka Kohan and that I intended to marry her. To help convince him, she accompanied me on a visit to Schmidt and Smoloz.

The pressure I put on Schmidt almost nightly finally wore down his resistance, and he agreed to confront Knoeller with the story I had fabricated.

The weeks of incessant talk had not been wasted. Knoeller listened to his friend and set the wheels in motion.

When Schmidt broke the news to me that an order had been issued to the SS Headquarters for Mendel's release, I could not believe it. The possibility of succeeding against such insurmountable odds had been only a very faint hope.

And now I had the joy of seeing the faces of Mr. and Mrs. Kohan when they heard their son would be returning to them.

The news spread through the city like wildfire. Mendel Kohan had come home!

Half dead of starvation and illness, a pitiful apparition, he had gotten off the train in the custody of an SS guard and had been hurried through the streets to SS Headquarters.

Already confused by the miracle of his release, Mendel was further confused when Ludwig queried, "You have been brought back because you are a specialist in the care of the city horses; isn't that right? And you are to report for work immediately at the sanitation department, right?"

Mendel, of course, agreed immediately, anxious to be out of the building and to get home. He was detained only a few moments, and then, without papers or molestation from the SS guards posted outside, he left and hurried home with his coat collar turned up to hide his emaciated face from the townspeople he passed.

Word came to me immediately, and my first thought was to

tell Ruschka. I went to her office in the Kultusgemeinde building with the news. Through tears of joy she said, "I knew if he came back you would be the first to let me know."

The Kohan apartment became the scene of a procession. As the news spread, each hour brought a stream of people eager to see a man who had practically returned from the dead. They came in disbelief, stared at Mendel, congratulated the family, and left, shaking their heads, not daring to dream of their lost loved ones returning to them. It was cruel to know that hope of rescue stopped there. We could not do it again.

The family nursed Mendel back to health with love and care, and when his strength returned he went to work. He brought back with him endless stories of the suffering and senseless brutality being inflicted on the Jews in the camps. He told us of the deaths he had witnessed—deliberate murders, death from starvation, the hunger typhus that swept through the camps, and deaths from the Nazis' sheer indifference to the slave laborers they drove unmercifully.

There was no room for further doubt. It was only a question of time for all of us.

Chapter

10

IT WAS THE SUMMER OF 1942.

The terror spread without any relief. Most of the young people were gone, and there was scarcely a family still untouched by the loss of at least one of its members. Our food supply was cut from very little to almost nothing. Life became even less endurable for those of us still alive.

By the end of the year the records of the Kultusgemeinde would show that over 60 percent of the Jewish people of our community, thousands of refugees who had come to Sosnowiec, almost forty thousand human beings, had disappeared, into Auschwitz, Birkenau, or the forced-labor camps which eventually became as deadly.

The momentum of the three years of terror accelerated. Entire families began to disappear and with them any hope we still had of an end to our nightmare.

Each day was filled with horrors, old and new. At night the raids terrorized and separated family after family, and by day the streets echoed with the shrieks and groans of the victims of vicious beatings.

We faced each morning never knowing what acts of brutality we would witness during the day, certain only that dusk would find more of us gone to some terrible fate.

After curfew we sat, trapped in our rooms, unable to move, waiting for the sound of the boots outside, or lay sleepless in the dark, our eyes open and our ears straining for the telltale sounds we hoped we wouldn't hear, knowing that the morning light would only bring another tragic day.

An order came from the Gestapo—"No Jews will be permitted to live anywhere in a city except in ghettos!"

And they set the stage for a vicious trick.

Official notification was sent to every Jewish community, separately addressed to each adult and child. In Sosnowiec and the surrounding towns we received ours hand-delivered by militiamen. The orders stated that it would be necessary for all of us to assemble on a certain day at a specific hour in one predetermined place, two weeks hence, in order that our identification papers could be stamped with the designation of the ghetto for which we were destined. The orders were clear: We were to appear as commanded or be shot.

The propaganda went on for days; loudspeakers in the streets blared it.

Without the new stamp on our papers we would be unable to get a ration card and consequently would have no food—if we were not immediately shot.

No one knew where the ghettos would be. There was much speculation, but this time the rumors stopped there.

Over and over the propaganda machines stressed that each and every remaining Jew had to report on the appointed day. If one member of a family did not appear, the entire family would be executed in reprisal. The Gestapo claimed to have the records of every family member left in Sosnowiec and stated that the processing would be merely routine. The Jewish Council reassured us they had the Gestapo's promise that everybody would be sent home after the census was completed and our papers had been stamped for the ghettos. They were convinced that all the Gestapo wanted was to count us and determine to which ghetto each of us would be assigned. Toward the end of the two-week period we heard that two ghettos were to be used.

When the day came to assemble at the huge sports arena on the outskirts of the city, virtually all of the Jews reported. They came in the early morning to the grass-covered field, of all ages, sick, bedridden, weak, strong, all came. What was left of our family, all my remaining friends from childhood, the Koplowiches, the Golds, the Kohans, the Chabas—everybody came. All of us empty-handed, prepared to be counted, handed our stamped papers and returned to our homes until the time came to move into the new ghettos, wherever they might be.

Mr. Koplowich had questioned Merin thoroughly and had been assured there was no need to bring any food or supplies.

"Don't worry. All we have to do is line up, get our cards stamped and go home. Nothing else will happen. I have the Gestapo's promise," Merin had told him.

There was nothing to arouse our suspicions. Only a few soldiers stood around, seemingly unconcerned. I saw Merin's assistant from the council near us with his family, repeating to those around him that there was nothing to fear.

"Listen, if this were a trick, wouldn't I know about it? Would I bring my own family?" he repeated.

An officer yelled through a loudspeaker, "All of you sit down on the ground immediately."

And no sooner had we lowered ourselves to the earth than the trap was sprung. Hundreds of helmeted and armed SS and Gestapo troops swarmed completely around us, forming a tight cordon. On the rooftops of nearby buildings the figures of more soldiers stood out against the morning sun, whipping the camouflage from machine guns.

Frightened cries went up from the crowd, and I felt my pulse quicken. Tricked, tricked again!

Merin's aide, staggered by the treachery, fell over, stricken with a heart attack. He had led his own wife and children into the trap.

They held us like this, pinned to the ground, far into the night, without food, without water. The children whimpered and cried. We huddled together in the dark, miserably cold and hungry and filled with fear at what the day would bring.

Moving spears of light pierced the darkness from a ring of spotlights that encircled us, and the faces, drawn and frightened, of those around me appeared and disappeared in their beams.

In the morning, openings appeared around the perimeter of the crowd, and the loudspeaker blared out instructions.

"Now, line up, all of you, according to your last names."

At each opening stood two soldiers, Gestapo or SS, and one representative of the Jewish Council.

The huge throng got slowly to its feet and formed long lines. Mothers cradled children in their arms, trying to quiet them, and old people leaned on the arms of those nearest them for support.

As the lines approached each opening, some people were allowed to pass through, but others were marched under guard to an adjoining field and again encircled.

As Rochelle, Sala, Mother and I approached the head of the line, I saw Wulkan, my opponent at the Jewish Council, at the opening. It was too late to change. If I had seen him sooner, I would have gone to the other line. Sala and I held out our *sonders*, and our papers were stamped for release—we could return to the city—but Rochelle and Mother were marched away to the new cordon of prisoners being assembled nearby. It appeared that if one had a *sonder* of some importance and looked physically strong, one would be freed.

The families of our friends suffered similar separation. Some were marched away and some were released with stamped papers. We saw Mrs. Gold taken to join those gathered in the field nearby.

Again, the cleverly devised blackmail was being practiced against us, the policy of using some family members as hostages

58

to keep the others in line. The Germans had demonstrated to us once more, if we had any lingering doubts, that they were devoid of conscience and willing to exploit the most basic emotions of human beings.

The sorting process went on through the entire day and far into the night. Sala and I stayed with others outside the encirclement for as long as we could without attracting attention, to see if we could help. But there was nothing to be done. When we realized how futile it was, we went wearily home. Two of us were left, five gone.

That night, ironically enough, the curfew for Jews had been lifted, and we passed through the streets virtually unchallenged. Those who were stopped showed their papers and, on seeing the stamp, the guards withdrew.

We used the hours of darkness to race back and forth between the field and the city, seeking help without success. No influence, no price, could buy freedom for anyone trapped out there.

In the late hours of the night I went to Mr. Koplowich, who had just returned.

"Please," I begged him, "try to find out what they are going to do with those people."

He went to the council and found them shattered by their betrayal and just as helpless as we.

In desperation I went to the City Hall to see Schmidt. He, too, though genuinely sorry, told me sadly there was nothing he could do.

The thought of Mother and Rochelle and what could be happening to them made Sala and me frantic. We wanted to act; do something—but what? We faced each other hopelessly.

The following day two city blocks of apartments were completely evacuated, one just a short distance from our house, the other in the downtown section. The people from the field, who had been kept under heavy guard, without food or water, were now marched into the city and crowded into both ghettos. Hundreds and thousands of them were jammed into the obviously inadequate apartment buildings.

59

Daylight was almost gone when the march took place, and Sala and I were stunned when, at that late hour, our door suddenly opened and Rochelle slipped in, almost faint from exhaustion.

"How did you get away? Where's Mother?" we gasped.

She regained her control and told us of the last few hours at the *punkt*. The Germans had separated the crowd into two groups and taken one toward Targowa Street and the other in the direction of the downtown ghetto.

"There were a lot of Jewish militiamen helping the SS and Gestapo who were willing to let us escape," she said. "They motioned to us to slip out of the line, so when we passed a dark alley I took Mother's hand and tried to pull her with me, but she couldn't make it. I had to leave her." She began to cry. "Mrs. Gold and quite a few others got away. I think they took Mother and the rest to Targowa."

Once I knew where Mother had been interned, my only thought was to find her and get her out, no matter what the cost. I went immediately to Koplowich and Gold. My anxiety had left me almost speechless, but it wasn't necessary for me to say much. They understood there was no limit to what I would do to bring Mother back and tried their best to calm me. "Natan, we will do everything humanly possible for your mother. You can count on us. In the morning we'll go to see Merin."

They spoke hopefully of contacting a man who had connections in the German Kriminalpolizei. I was encouraged. Something would be done.

At their urging I went home and tried to get some rest until the morning light would let me move more freely through the streets.

But sleep was impossible for all of us, even in our state of exhaustion and depression. No blow, physical or emotional, no loss or meaningless cruelty to which we had been subjected had taken such a toll as the absence from our sight and protection of this one frail, no-longer-young woman who was the center and most important part of our world. I had fought in every way I knew to protect her, to stay alive and by her side as long as I could. If anything happened to her now, it would be the end for me, too.

I could count on our friends to exert pressure and influence through the council and the other contacts and sources available to them, but was that enough? I wondered. What would be happening to her and the others in the morning? How long would they be held? If the Jewish Council and the others could not help, could I afford to waste time waiting for their answer? I decided I could not remain immobilized until morning.

I got up and left the house, determined to try, once again, to get help from Smoloz. I arrived at his house in the off-limits area, and he let me in. "I know where she is," I said to him. "And I don't have to tell you, Herr Smoloz, that there is no limit to what I will do to bring her back, and no cost is too high for her safety. Please help her and help me."

"I know, Schapelski. I know what she means to you. I'll contact Schmidt first thing in the morning, and we'll see what we can do through the Burgermeister's office."

Schmidt represented German influence in the city, real influence. This, coupled with the power and resources of Koplowich and Gold, gave me some hope. After I left Smoloz I went back to see them again, and then I went home to wait out the long night.

Chapter

I I

As soon as it was faintly light I walked to Targowa.

The street was blocked off from Mungeyofska to Malachawskaya. A guard made up of Gestapo, SS, and an occasional militiaman encircled the entire area. I moved closer and immediately a challenge rang out: "No civilians are allowed in this area. Move on!"

Several soldiers half raised their guns. I walked away silently.

I had to get inside, but how? By this hour the sanitation department warehouse was open. I went in unchallenged.

Since I had the authority to requisition whatever supplies I needed, I loaded a push broom on one of the big covered collection carts and dragged it out of the warehouse into the street. I put a city armband around my upper arm and then, pushing the cart ahead of me, went directly back to Targowa.

It seemed that all the guards followed me with their eyes as I trundled the cart across the deserted street toward their station. Before I got within close range they yelled at me to stop.

"No civilians are allowed in this area. You are to leave immediately."

Keeping the cart before me, I moved closer to them.

"I have my orders to clean the street inside. See, here is my *sonder* from the City Hall." A guard examined my papers while I went on rapidly. "The Superintendent of Public Works is concerned about the sanitation problem in there. If we don't keep the area clean, there could be an epidemic and many soldiers and officers could become ill and die. You understand?"

"All right, let him through," the guard said.

And I walked through. I was inside the ghetto, past the guards blocking the entrance to the inner street. But I had yet to get past the guards posted at the main entrance to the hollow square of buildings that imprisoned my mother and hundreds of others.

I used the same approach with the soldiers inside, explaining that I had to clean the street. They watched me curiously for a few minutes as I passed them, pretending to sweep, and then ignored me. I walked back and forth, guiding the push broom mechanically across the pavement. The silence in the street chilled me. What had once been one of the busiest thoroughfares in our section was deserted except for the few uniformed Gestapo and SS men. Not another living thing moved except me.

I racked my mind for an idea, a plan, thinking all the while, desperately, "Dear God, there has to be something I can do!"

I stayed in the street long enough to satisfy the guards that my work was legitimate and then left Targowa.

Immediately I sought out Smoloz. He was far less encouraging than he had been the night before.

"I don't know how much help we can be, if any. We can't get her out on any official pretext, since she has no *sonder* for work and this is a Gestapo operation from outside the city. But we'll keep working on it, I promise you."

The slight relief I had felt a few hours before disappeared. I went back to Koplowich, hoping for better news, but the Kultusgemeinde had also given him a "No." There was nothing they could do for my mother or any of the others.

But he had a new hope to hold out to me. Rumors had been circulating that morning that some of the people had been smuggled out of the ghetto during the night by the militiamen, after bribing the German guards. It was too early to know if the rumors were true, but at this stage any hope was better than none. There was a militiaman living in the same building as Koplowich, and he was on duty at Targowa. Koplowich went to see him and sounded him out in confidence about the situation. The man admitted that the rumors were true; a few had been helped to escape. Koplowich made a deal with him. For fifteen thousand marks the militiaman would bring my mother out at night. Koplowich paid him part of the money at once—ten thousand marks.

I went to the militiaman with a photograph of my mother and to give him a physical description of her.

"Are you sure you can get her out?" I asked insistently. I knew that any slip-up would place her in even greater danger.

"I can get into the ghetto any time I want," he answered, "and I'll get her away at night, don't you worry."

"What if you are caught? Aren't you afraid they will shoot you, too?"

"I don't have to worry. There are certain guards who can be persuaded to look the other way for a price."

"Then give them whatever they ask, do you hear? I don't care what it costs. The money is available, so don't let that stand in your way. Offer them anything but get her out, and *soon.*"

This was the only way now, I thought. No one else had been able to offer a plan, and he had to know what he was talking about or he would not dare to suggest it.

Again, I felt a sense of relief. It was even possible she would be home this very night. But I had to get through to her, to tell her we were planning for her escape. And in the back of my mind I had to know that she was still alive.

If I could get into the buildings on Targowa on the strength of my papers and the Germans' fear of disease, then perhaps, with Smoloz's backing, I could get all the way inside.

The morning was still young, although it seemed days rather than hours since I had been in Targowa.

Smoloz agreed to come with me to persuade the guards that it was the desire of the superintendent of sanitation, the Burgermeister, and the German city government that the premises be kept orderly and sanitary.

"But what will you do inside alone?" Smoloz asked me.

"I only want to find my mother and see that she is all right."

At the guard station he snapped "Heil Hitler," and thrust his arm out in salute.

The guards responded crisply, "Heil Hitler."

"Where is the officer in charge?" he asked. "Please tell him I would like to talk with him."

An officer came out and they began to converse after Smoloz had identified himself and they had exchanged greetings. I could hear him repeating almost word for word what I had suggested.

"You can understand our concern for the welfare of our soldiers. The slightest infection in there could start an epidemic among our own men," Smoloz stressed.

The officer agreed, nodding his head and muttering, *"Ja, ja,* they are so right. We must take precautions, Herr Smoloz. What do you propose to do?"

"I'm sending this man in to find out how big the job is and how many men we will need. He'll report back to me." Smoloz beckoned me with a motion of his hand.

The officer spoke curtly to the guards, and they stepped aside so that we could pass.

The gateway we entered was as wide as the opening to a city street. It passed through the first floor of the building on Targowa and opened into a central courtyard that was surrounded on all four sides by the apartment houses.

Smoloz stopped and I went on alone.

The passageway had been dark for the short distance we had walked together, and when I was finally inside the light temporarily blinded me. I stood for a moment, waiting for my eyes to focus. Whatever misery I could have foreseen, whatever suffering I might have conceived beforehand, was nothing

65

compared to the sight that now lay before me. As far as the eye could see, human beings were packed like cattle, standing upright in the open area between the buildings. There was not enough space between them to lie down, except for some lifeless bodies on the ground. As my ears became accustomed to the noise, I could make out individual cries of women and children weeping and screaming and men calling desperately to their families and to one another.

I looked up, dreading what I might see and yet afraid not to find out. The windows of the enormous buildings were filled with the faces of distraught men, women, and children.

In a few seconds I was surrounded.

"What's going to happen?"

"What are they going to do with us?"

"Does anyone know where they will take us?"

"Can we get food?"

"The children are starving."

"There isn't enough water."

Voices called out, begging me to take messages to loved ones on the outside. I stood there suddenly drained, powerless. I had nothing, absolutely nothing, to hold out to them that could pass for help or hope.

"I'll try to find out as much as I can. Nobody knows yet what they are planning. We won't forget you. I'll do whatever I can."

I began to press through the crowd, looking for familiar faces. Each time I heard my name called I called back, "Have you seen my mother? Do you know where she is, which building?"

At last a neighbor of ours answered, "She's over there in that house, on one of the top floors. I think she's all right."

The misery and suffering of their confinement without water or sanitation fed the hate and fury welling up inside me as I struggled to reach the entrance to the apartment building. But if I thought the conditions of the people in the courtyard were bad, exposed as they were to the weather, conditions inside the building were no better. Every inch of space, literally every corner of the entrance, every room of each apartment, the staircases, all were jammed solid. Where a family of five had lived in two or three rooms, a hundred or more people were compressed. And there were thousands imprisoned in this way.

As I struggled through, hundreds of faces turned toward me in hope. Hands reached out just to touch me, as if to confirm that someone had really come from the outside.

On one of the upper floors, huddled in a corner crowded with starved and frightened people, I found my mother. She didn't see me until I was almost at her side. The others, with kindness and compassion still alive in their pain-racked bodies, drew as far away as they could to give us room. I knelt to put my arms about her, afraid to hold her tiny frame too closely, yet wanting with every bone in my body to pick her up and carry her away. There was only time to say a few words of reassurance and love. It was difficult to know which of us was comforting the other. With my mouth held close to her ear I whispered, "Mother, I am going to get you out of here. A Jewish militiaman will come for you." I described him to her. "All you have to do is stay where you are at all times so that when he comes he'll know where to find you."

Not once did she ask what I planned or how I had managed to get inside.

"Is Sala all right, Natan? Did Rochelle get home safely? Are you all together?" she asked. "Natan, isn't it dangerous for you to be in here?"

I slipped into her hand a small packet of food I had concealed in my jacket.

"Eat this. I'll be back with more as soon as I can. Try to hold on and remember to stay right where you are, please, Mother," I begged her.

"Yes, my son," she promised. "I'll do whatever you say. Natan, take care of your sisters and be careful."

I tore myself away. The few minutes I could safely spend inside were rapidly slipping away, and Smoloz still waited at the gate.

On my way back to the entrance the faces of the children and the elderly seemed to spring out at me—white, drained of color and expression, most in a state of shock. The least able to protect themselves, they were the soonest broken. Women held infants above their heads, struggling for a breath of air.

The success of the subterfuge I had used to get inside went through my mind as I fought my way back down the stairs and across the courtyard to where I had left my cart hidden in the crush of people. The militiaman would get my mother out that very night, I hoped. I had to believe that he would keep his word. But if I could get into the *punkt* again, perhaps some of the other people could be rescued too.

The militiaman was waiting for me in the courtyard. I took him back to point out my mother's location.

"When the time is right, maybe tonight, I'll bring her home," he told me. I had to believe him.

I loaded the cart with debris as rapidly as I could, and as I wheeled it toward the entrance an idea came to me.

Smoloz stood outside, chatting with SS officers and guards. He excused himself and brusquely called me over, using his official tone of voice for their benefit.

"Well, what do you have to report?" he asked.

"It's a big job, Herr Smoloz. We'll need a crew of men and carts. There are a lot of people in there. That means a lot of work," I said.

"How many men do you think you will need to handle this, Schapelski?"

I did not want to commit myself to a number, so I answered merely that it would take at least three carts each trip.

He turned to the officer and asked him to permit me to return the following morning with three carts and sufficient men to handle the job and to permit me to leave whenever the carts needed to be emptied. He informed the officer that we could be identified by our armbands with the city seal. He asked that the information be passed along to the officers in command of later shifts so that they, too, would expect us. Understanding was quickly reached, and they exchanged a parting "Heil Hitler" as we walked away.

"Did you find your mother? Is she well?" was all he asked.

I told him of her condition and no more. He asked no other questions, although it had to be obvious to him that I had some motive for what I had led him to say in front of the officers and guards. I left the cart to be emptied at the warehouse dump and hurried back to Koplowich.

"I found her. It's terrible. I can't even tell you how horrible it is inside."

I sat with my head held tightly between my hands, trying to translate the hideous memory into words.

"Those people are in agony. They're almost crazy with fear. They're starving. Some are dead. I saw bodies. We've got to do something. Do you believe the militiaman? Will he be able to get Mother out?"

They listened in stunned disbelief, knowing I spoke the truth. The women moaned softly when I told of the infants and little children crying for food and water. We sat in helpless silence for a few minutes.

Koplowich put his arm across my shoulders and comforted me. "Natan, I believe your mother will be out tonight. I have every hope our neighbor will be able to carry out his bargain."

I was encouraged by his words but still terribly anxious. She had been so near the end of her strength when I left her. It would have to happen that night or I was sure she would not survive.

At home I had to tell the same terrible story to my sisters. While they sat weeping, I tried to convince them I was confident we would have Mother back that very night.

I tried to pass the hours, thinking of the next time I would enter the *punkt*, taking other men in with me. It would be dangerous—execution or internment if we were caught. But it had to be done. I would go in with several of the city volunteers, one of us to each cart. We would try to get through just before the shift changed at noon. If they didn't ask for our identification cards on the way in or out and relied only on our armbands, we would have a chance of rescuing a few men. I had already talked to Max and Schejack Gold about my idea before leaving the Koplowich house, and they had both insisted on going in with me. I could not take the responsibility of endangering two sons from one family, and so, over their protests, I agreed that one of them would come along each time, alternately. We needed a third man, and they suggested that their young uncle be approached. Again I refused; too many from one family.

I don't remember sleeping that night, nor can I recall how many times my sisters and I thought we heard the sound of someone coming down the hallway. And as the hours dragged by with no word from the militiaman our anxiety grew.

The sky became light, and with the disappearing night our hope dwindled. Mother was still inside.

I went to roll call, the morning count of the workers, and asked Smoloz if he would mind relieving two of my friends from their regular work and leaving them behind so we could go to the *punkt* to clean. He looked at me curiously for a moment, then ordered them to stay behind. I hoped that of the two young men, one might join us.

Inside the warehouse I approached the first, and he promptly volunteered. I went to the second and explained the plan and the dangers involved and he, too, insisted on being included. His sweetheart's parents were inside.

So we were five. We decided that one of the Gold twins and one of the two young men should stay behind to wait for our return. The other three of us each requisitioned a cart and broom. I grabbed a handful of armbands and stuffed them in my pocket.

Smoloz stopped me outside his office and handed me an official letter over his signature stating that Kurt Schmidt as head of the department had authorized me to enter Targowa to clean and remove all health hazards, under orders from the Burgermeister of the city of Sosnowiec. The seal of the city, overprinted with the swastika, made the letter impressive.

We wheeled the carts across the empty streets to where the guards were posted. I showed the letter to the officer in charge, silently praying he would not take it away. He read it, examined our red and white armbands, handed the letter back to me, and signaled the guards to let us pass. The German mania for numerical order prevailed. They counted the armbands—one, two, three.

"All right, go through."

We went to the danger spot—the checkpoint at the gateway into the *punkt*. They were expecting us and stepped aside to let us pass. Again they counted armbands—one, two, three. The two boys and I passed through, and even with the memory of the previous day still fresh in my mind I was unprepared for this second experience. The two others reacted in stunned disbelief as we were surrounded by the mob.

We wheeled our carts as far away from the view of the German guards as we could. Then, safely engulfed by the crowd, I was able to struggle through to my mother. She was, if possible, even paler and weaker than before. I pressed another parcel of food into her hands and tried to comfort her with the promise that we were definitely going to be able to get her out that night. She asked no questions of me.

I had to watch the time. We had entered at almost eleven o'clock. The guards changed their shift at noon. Time was running out. I had to leave her again.

Some order had been established since my first visit. The strongest men and women were trying to get as many children and old people as possible into the apartments so that they could get water from the faucets. In addition, the Kultusgemeinde had somehow gotten permission to bring big kettles of soup once a day. They were left at the checkpoint and from there the militiamen carried them inside. Containers from the empty apartments were passed around to serve the starving people. I counted fifteen to twenty empty kettles waiting to be carried back to the checkpoint to be reclaimed by the Kultusgemeinde for the next day's delivery. I didn't realize it then, but they would later give me an idea.

The two boys and I stood uncertainly for a moment. We were going to attempt to take three men out with us, and they were waiting for me to choose. In this split second I realized what it was like to play God. Who should it be? A young man?

A friend? A man whose family was on the outside? There was no time to stall. I decided I could not single anyone out. Whoever was nearest and wanted to go I would take. There were no male members of our family inside.

As quietly as possible I signaled three men to follow us into a nearby hallway. One face was vaguely familiar, but I could not identify any of them.

"We are going out as soon as the new shift of guards comes on duty. Will you come with us?" I said to them. "I have an armband for each of you. They won't look at your faces, just check your armbands."

They agreed hurriedly, and I slipped each one an armband from my pocket. "When we go out, there will be two of us to each car. That is the normal crew. Say nothing," I cautioned them.

The militiaman who was to have brought Mother out watched knowingly but said nothing as we walked past, looking straight ahead, pushing the carts, which we had carefully filled with sweepings. The new shift of German guards checked our armbands and watched us walk by. We continued down the street to the entrance. Again, the guards, all new faces, checked the armbands and stepped aside to let us pass. The new officer on duty checked the armbands again, this time more closely, and waved us through.

Across one street, still under the watchful eyes of the soldiers, then the next, and then around the corner to Descartes, and we had done it. The impossible, crazy scheme had worked. They were free. Within seconds the armbands were back in my pocket and the three men gone, already on their way home.

Three men safe, right under the noses of the SS and Gestapo! But only three men; there were countless more inside. And women and children. The two boys and I went our separate ways, each taking a cart.

Our luck continued to hold. We went back again that afternoon, before the shift changed, and left with three more men when the late shift came on. The choice was made in the same way as the first time. Wherever we stood, the first three men I saw I called aside. But only lone prisoners volunteered. Not one man who had a wife or children or family inside the *punkt* would come out with us, even if asked. I was tortured by the blindness of the selection, but there was no rational or equitable way it could be done.

Night came again with no sign of my mother. The militiaman made more excuses and more promises. He insisted he would be able to bribe the guards for certain the following night. I was desperate, but he was still our only hope, and I believed he was trying.

The next day we went in and out of the *punkt* three times—nine more men freed. The news of what we were doing spread, and each time we entered the crowd fought to get near us. Women begged us to take their sons, and the children of the old and weak pleaded with us to take their fathers. I could not risk the other lives involved by taking any man obviously too old to be a worker. It would have drawn suspicion to us.

Each time I went into the room to see my mother, my heart sank. The food I brought couldn't compensate for the overall conditions of congestion and filth. Her spirit was almost broken. Others had told her what I was doing for the men. She never questioned me or complained.

As the freed men reached home, word of the small rescue operation spread swiftly and silently through the Jewish homes still remaining. Relatives and friends of the prisoners came to our home and begged me to bring their loved ones out, but I couldn't. I tried to make them understand that it would be impossible to locate anyone in such a crowd and an injustice to single anyone out. They were all entitled to a chance for life.

On the afternoon of the fourth day I raced home for a few minutes to eat. As I sat in the kitchen, gulping down the food Sala and Rochelle had prepared, a delegation visited me. They were leaders of the Jewish community, men known for their charity and community service. These fine, respected men came to ask if I would try to bring out a very old man I knew by reputation, a prominent and charitable gentleman whom they revered, for years head of the Jewish Free Loan Society and other benevolent causes.

They assured me they understood how dangerous it was, but

73

they felt that he deserved some special consideration because he had given so much of his life to our people. I could not refuse them, especially not Gold and Koplowich. I would have gone through fire for them. So I agreed to try. This time I was really frightened. The chance that I could get the old man out seemed very slim, and if I was caught the possibility of getting Mother out could be endangered or lost.

I entered the *punkt* alone, not wanting the other boys to take the risk. Word was sent through the crowd that I was looking for the old man and would be back. On my return he was there, shaking with weakness. I slipped an armband on his thin, trembling arm and asked him simply to walk alongside the cart and try to appear strong. He followed my instructions, and by some miracle we passed safely through and out of the *punkt* area.

Friends took him in and cared for him until his health returned. Subsequently, the community sent representatives to thank me for saving his life.

Every evening after work my four friends and I met to make our plans for the next day. We were not permitted to enter the *punkt* at night or we would have gone in then, too.

Each time I entered and left I tried to think of some plan for saving women and children. We had discarded the idea of hiding children in the rubbish carts for fear they would suffocate. And no other ideas came to us.

On the evening of the fourth or fifth day my four friends and I sat talking. As we decided on the crew for our next trips, I suddenly had a mental picture of the soup kettles I had seen left empty.

"Listen," I said, "I think I know how to bring out some children along with the men."

"How?" they chorused.

I reminded them of the size of the soup pots. "We can put three children in three pots and each of us can carry out a pot while the other three men wheel out the carts. We'll have to alert the militiamen. If they let slip to the Germans what we're doing, we're dead."

Thus began our rescue of the children. However, instead of

taking only three carts into the *punkt*, I decided to increase our crew to five. Time was running out.

No one, not Smoloz, Schmidt or the Kultusgemeinde, knew when the Germans would make their next move, but we knew it had to be soon. And so the very next trip all five of us entered, each with a cart.

I had only to mention that we would try to take out children, and their mothers thrust them at me.

"Take my son," one said. Then more voices joined in.

"Take mine, take mine." They knew the danger, but in their mothers' hearts they also knew it was preferable to whatever horror lay ahead for them.

When we left that trip Gold and I carried out our first two soup kettles with a little child in each one. Four men from the *punkt* brought out our two carts, and three more from the *punkt*, together with our three colleagues, brought out the other three carts. Neither Gold nor I knew the children we carried, nor did they know us. As in the case of the men, we rescued whoever was at hand. On that first trip and the ones that followed, we took whom we could as fast as we could.

The children we brought out in those few days left an indelible mark on my life. Although they were strangers to me, their faces live forever in my memory. I have never forgotten, nor can I ever forget, their suffering.

Especially one child, a little girl of five or six years who had suffered unknown tragedy. Like the rest, she dumbly accepted being placed in the greasy pot and made no sound as I carried her past the guards and into the street. When I set her down at the nearest safe corner, the child turned her face up to me and asked, "Where shall I go?"

I had to tell her, "Child, I don't know. Run, run."

I no longer knew one Jewish household still intact that could possibly take her in. We had no way of planning for the safety of the children once they were outside the *punkt*. I could only hope that they would find a place, not with a Jewish family but with a Christian family still courageous enough to shelter them and pass them off as one of their own.

In the moment I looked down at her tiny, pinched face and

heard my voice telling her, an infant still, that she was on her own, the insanity and depravity of the monsters who had made this moment happen engraved her small face indelibly on my heart, and to me hers will always be the face of all the children who suffered.

I had managed to save men and children—only a few, but still they were safe. But my own mother and the other women I had not been able to help. I still relied on the militiaman. But with each hour that passed I feared she would die. Each night we waited for her, and every day, between trips in and out of the *punkt*, Sala and I ran to Koplowich.

The five men of our escape team had been relieved from reporting to work, with the unspoken understanding that this would end when my mother was rescued. Not once did either Schmidt or Smoloz indicate in the slightest way that they knew what I was doing. To all appearances they were merely aware that I was attempting to rescue my mother. I had long given up hope of their direct assistance. They had tried futilely. Control of the ghettos rested in Gestapo and SS offices outside their field of influence.

One day at Smoloz's house, while I sat with him and his wife in their kitchen and spoke of my mother, tears formed against my will, and I began to weep out of sorrow and exhaustion. Frau Smoloz also began to weep and begged her husband to do everything he could to help me get my mother out.

"Why are they making the Jews suffer so?" she sobbed. "Why are they doing this?" She ran out of the room.

Chapter
12

THE FOURTH, FIFTH, AND SIXTH DAYS of the imprisonment in the *punkt* passed, and I became increasingly nervous and impatient. I began to leave the house earlier and earlier, sometimes at five o'clock. At first light, I was in the streets with my cart, waiting for the others. When we were all together we would enter the *punkt*. The Germans had long since stopped counting and checked only the armbands.

On the morning of the seventh or eighth day I stood as usual at the corner of Targowa and Mungeyofska, waiting for the other boys to arrive. My mother was still inside, and her condition and the condition of the others were at the lowest ebb.

As I stood in the morning chill, very nervous, hope fading, I recognized a stream of black cars outside as those used by the Gestapo and SS in other raids. I froze. I knew this could only mean that the waiting was over.

I went closer with my cart. This time the sentries stopped me at the checkpoint, but I insisted I was there on express orders of the Burgermeister, and in the confusion they permitted me to pass. I entered the *punkt* alone.

What I saw is impossible to describe. The courtyard, now overflowing inconceivably with people, was the scene of a planned, animalistic round-up. No other word can serve. SS men stationed at intervals held a thick rope encircling the hysterical mob. People poured out of the buildings at gunpoint and were pushed behind the rope as those holding the rope drew the noose, the enormous noose, tighter and tighter.

Other SS men went through the buildings, room by room, with pistols and dogs. Some came down and took men from inside the noose to bring out the bodies of the dead and dump them inside the rope. Guards in leather coats strutted around the rim, kicking the bodies where they lay. Others with snarling shepherd dogs on leashes charged the edges of the crowd, forcing everyone inside the rope. Loudspeakers screamed, "*Heraus, heraus*—out, out," and the shrieks and cries of their victims split the air.

Still they came, the sick, the dead, the old, women, men, boys, girls, babies, pushed, beaten, kicked, shoved, abused. Soldiers, SS and Gestapo milled around with militiamen helping them at gunpoint.

"Get them down and get them out."

Every room was checked to see that no one dead or alive had been left behind. I was helpless, choked with fury and dread. I knew that the other boys must be outside, watching the street filled with the black cars. I stood to one side, pushing my broom back and forth to appear occupied, and watched dazedly what was happening, trying not to draw attention to myself. At last I saw my mother and circled around to be near her.

The militiaman who had promised to take her out of the *punkt* came by, and I watched as he went up to her and said quickly in Polish, "Lie down with the dead ones over there." She and others obediently dropped to the ground among the bodies piled nearby.

Then the transport started. The cordon was drawn tight and the prisoners forced to march in the direction of the gates. SS men ran into the courtyard and began to kick the bodies for any sign of life.

I stood horrified when one walked over to my mother and pushed his boot into her body. Oh, God, she moved!

"Get up!" he screamed at her.

She was beaten and forced to join the others. When I could, I worked my way closer and begged her in Yiddish to lie down again.

"Please, Mother, lie down in the center of the bodies and for God's sake, whatever happens, don't move, don't move!"

Amid the screaming and confusion, she did as I pleaded. Other women did the same thing and lay down among the corpses wherever they could.

The militiaman stood by, watching over them. The panic and confusion mounted.

The prisoners were marched out to Mungeyofska and then left on Czerchegemaya in a precisely-planned operation that took almost four hours.

From the beginning I stood at the doorway and watched, deathly afraid my mother would get up again and pass through with the rest. If she did, I was determined to remove my armband and go with her.

Suddenly I saw my aunt and her little girl, my cousin, passing through. My uncle had refused to let me try to smuggle the child out. He too had been relying on a militiaman for their rescue, and now it was too late, too late.

Dear God, more familiar faces almost unrecognizably contorted with fear and pain. A neighbor, another, and still another, until at last the end of the column disappeared. I walked back into the *punkt*.

My mother lay quietly with the others. Near her lay a neighbor. Here and there a body moved, twitched. A chest rose and fell, demanding air.

I went back to the guards and told them I would have to bring in my cart to clean up the area. "What's going to happen to the bodies in there?" I asked them.

"Don't worry," they said, "the trucks will be back to pick up the ones who were too sick to walk. The bodies will be thrown in with them."

They would not be leaving anyone, dead or alive, in the *punkt*. No evidence of their crime. I made it clear that my only concern was to clean the area as fast as possible to prevent the spread of disease. With their permission I suggested that I could help in the removal of the bodies.

"How would you get them out of here?" they asked.

"Just a few blocks away there's a cab stand," I said, gambling that there would be the usual line-up of big horse-drawn cabs. "I'll get a few of them to come here, load them with bodies, and take them to the station."

"Just get them out of here," one of the guards replied.

"Yes," said another, "get the filth out of here."

I ran, pushing my cart ahead of me. Thank God the cabs were there, standing in line as I had expected. The transport had passed right by them, and the cabbies' faces were a study in horror.

"I'll pay you any amount of money. Follow me and do as I say," I yelled at them. Four of the cabs, all that were available, followed me into the *punkt*.

I guided one driver over to the area where my mother lay. I picked her up and put her in the cab. Other heads moved. Mrs. Grinzeiger opened her eyes, and I leaned over and picked her up, placing her beside my mother. I turned and picked up a cold and lifeless woman's body and placed it gently beside them. The other drivers had loaded up as many as they could, all dead.

"All right, let's go," I yelled. And we wheeled out of the *punkt*, headed for the station.

I dared not trust the driver, so I waited until we were only four blocks from our house before ordering him to turn. Thank God, he obeyed without question, and we pulled up in front of the house. Heads popped from every window. By now the whole city knew what was happening at the *punkt*.

"Take the bodies to the station and go back to the *punkt*. I'll meet you there," I told the driver. Then I helped my mother and Mrs. Grinzeiger out of the cab and into the house.

Sala and Rochelle grabbed Mother from me as we entered the apartment, and when I saw she was all right I raced back to the *punkt*.

While I still could, I tried to get everyone still alive out with my cab, but there were few. Eventually I came back to find the trucks had returned and were already loading bodies. If there were still some alive that I had missed, I'd never know.

I went home to reassure myself my mother was really there, and later in the evening I went back to the *punkt*. Only a few guards were still posted. Everyone else was gone.

Home again to my mother, now sitting up in bed having a hot meal. My happiness at her survival would be forever marred by what I had witnessed. Although her safety had been my prime concern, I could not stop thinking of the others.

A few hours later Max Gold come in. "Natan, a miracle has happened. One of the militiamen, a friend of my girlfriend's family, says her mother and sister are hiding in the attic of one of the buildings at the *punkt*. We have to get them out."

Max and I went back to the *punkt* for the last time. He circled around to the back of the building on a street safe to stand guard, and I went in alone, into a silence of empty rooms, deathly silence, screaming silence, where thousands had passed through into oblivion only a few hours before.

I crossed the courtyard and climbed the stairs of the building where they were reported to be hiding. When I reached the attic I walked through to the adjoining attic and then from one building to another until I saw them. There was a group of almost twenty-five people huddled in the dark, airless space between the floors. The last ones alive, they who had run back into the building after the transport had left. I asked for the woman and her child, and they stepped forward.

"Max is waiting for us. Come on," I said. The woman and child came with me, and the others followed.

I led them through the maze of attics up to the roof and then from one roof to another to avoid being seen from the street. We had planned to exit through a non-Jewish area, so, to escape notice, the woman and child took off their Stars of David and walked ahead of us into the street. The others disappeared into the dark.

Max and I walked behind, pretending not to know them, still wearing our city armbands.

I never went back to Targowa again. The downtown ghetto, which I never had a chance to enter, had been emptied, too. Babies and old people along with the young had been taken, their destination predetermined. We knew about the crematory at Auschwitz. All the thousands were gone. Their screams were stilled, except in my head, where, sometimes, they still go on and on.

Chapter 13

It was now early winter of 1943. The city was in a state of mourning. Families had been split or were gone altogether. The desperation increased from hour to hour. We were four, my mother, Rochelle, Sala, and I.

The people who were still officially free carried little pieces of paper with a green or yellow stamp to show that they had been released from the *punkt*. Those like Mother and Rochelle who had escaped had none.

Now came rumors of the creation of new ghettos. We heard that the Germans would set up two, one downtown and one in Schrodula, a suburb of Sosnowiec. The rumors were that the downtown ghetto would be liquidated shortly after it was occupied but that the ghetto at Schrodula would be kept a ghetto and the people interned there would work in factories and other industries the Germans regarded as vital to their war effort. Those were the rumors.

Sala and I had our stamped papers, but we were slated for the downtown ghetto. Rochelle and my mother did not have papers. We would have to get papers for them and change ours. The Kultusgemeinde told us there was nothing they could do.

As the days went by, our people went through the motions of living. We went to our jobs and waited.

I talked to Schmidt and Smoloz about our new problem. I had heard that some people had been successful, through some means, in getting stamped papers. Schmidt called Wulkan at the Kultusgemeinde and asked him to see that papers were issued to Mother and Rochelle, but either Wulkan was not in a position to do so or he did not want to cooperate in any effort on my behalf. He did nothing.

However, pressure was brought to bear on the Kultusgemeinde through the Burgermeister's office, and papers were eventually issued so that the four of us would go to Schrodula together.

In the meantime we had received a long-awaited letter from Yadja, who had crossed the border into the Russian-occupied zone of Poland. There was joy in our home, knowing that she was alive and well. We tried to correspond with her, but somehow she never received our letters, although we continued to get hers.

One day a letter came saying that she had met a young man from our town and they planned to marry. Somewhere life was going on in our family. We contacted the boy's parents, who were still alive in Sosnowiec, and they were overjoyed to know their son was safe and planned to marry my sister.

A few weeks later we received another letter. Yadja and the boy had married. They were both working, he as a muralist and she at the fine embroidery she did so well.

Unable to share with them what in another time and in another life would have been an occasion for great joy and festivity, we decided to give a little party in their honor for our relatives and close friends and the family of the young bridegroom. I remember so well the few hours we spent together on that Saturday afternoon, about thirty of us, united in the midst of our tragedy in a prayer for the happiness and future life of these two young people. Letters came a few times after that and then silence.

The raids continued. There was seldom a quiet night when the boots did not echo through the streets and through the halls of the houses.

Late one night—I don't recall the month—the Gestapo knocked on our door. They were looking for girls and young women for a special labor camp. Sala was home and she was taken; no *sonder* or paper could help her. That night they did not look at any papers.

We knew that after the raids the Germans usually took the prisoners downtown to the Punkt Ludwig, where they kept them until there was transportation available to sent them off to the camps. For this particular group transportation had been prepared in advance, and they were sent off immediately. Before I was able to contact anybody it was already too late.

This was a terrible shock after what the family had already gone through. Once more, another part of our family had been torn away. My father dead, Yadja and David only God knew where, and now Sala.

Sala's group was sent to a forced-labor camp, an Arbeitzeinsatz, little better than a concentration camp.

We received a letter from her after a few weeks. At least she was alive! Eventually we were permitted to send her a package once a month.

Meanwhile, Rochelle, Mother and I faced our uncertain future. Was it going to be the new ghetto at Schrodula or another fate the Germans had planned for us?

The rumors proved to be true. One day Schrodula and the downtown area were evacuated, and the Poles who lived there were transferred to living quarters elsewhere. At the same time, more streets were made off limits to Jews, and the empty houses and apartments from which they had been evicted were quickly filled.

The Germans took the best for themselves and what was left

the Polish people occupied. And the now deserted Schrodula and downtown areas were turned over to the Kultusgemeinde to assign living quarters to those Jews still left in Sosnowiec.

Schrodula was a small village on the outskirts of the city that had housed civil servants, policemen, firemen, postmen, people of that class. It was a community of modest one-family homes and apartments.

The Kultusgemeinde prepared housing lists. Individual families were assigned to a single house or a single apartment, depending on how many were left in the family. Relatives and friends tried to stay together or close. Numbers ranging from as few as three families to as many as thirty people were assigned to each house.

Mother, Rochelle and I were to share common quarters with our former neighbors, Mrs. Halpern and her daughter, and young Cuker, a close friend of mine who worked as a furniture-maker in the City Hall, doing work for highly placed German officials. Because he and I had connections, we had been given one large room.

And so we moved at last from our home, taking with us whatever we were able to use, leaving behind almost all our possessions, books and pictures for the looters who followed on our heels.

We walked to Schrodula, carrying what we could across the four or five miles that separated our old life from the new emptiness that lay ahead.

On my last trip, I stood for a moment at the door and stared back into the rooms filled with the memories of our life. I wondered if I would ever see our house again or any of the beloved faces that had surrounded my days with love and affection. I closed the door for the last time and walked back to Schrodula.

To maintain some illusion of privacy while occupying the same room, we hung a curtain down the center, but the women shared the kitchen, and we all took our meals together. It was difficult, especially for Mother, but we were as well off as

86

anyone in the same circumstances and in some ways perhaps better off. We had no choice but to adjust to our new surroundings and life.

Our friends, the Golds and Chabas, were assigned a small house for their group of nine people. The Koplowich family had one room, and the Kohans were assigned two rooms. They had been lucky. There was just one young man missing from their group. Frederick Gold, a younger brother of the twins, had left to cross the border into the Russian-occupied zone and had not been heard from since. Others who had tried it and been spotted had been shot on sight. The Golds, their friends and I tried every possible source to find out what had happened to him, without success. He had disappeared, leaving no trace.

The people who worked in town on specially assigned jobs labored mostly in one factory. There were other factories and shops which came under the classification of being essential to the Nazi war effort, such as manufacturing plants for uniforms for their troops. Such work entitled the worker to a *sonder*. The only transportation from Schrodula to the city was by foot, since no Jew was permitted to ride on the streetcars or trains, and even to own or ride a bicycle required special permission.

Every morning at five or five-thirty the early light saw columns of men and women leaving for work. A few of us in the sanitation department had been assigned bicycles on the ground that if an emergency arose in public sanitation, we needed speedy transportation into town.

We went to work every morning, drained by the anxiety of the night, and came home again in the evening to face more hopeless hours.

A strict curfew was imposed, and if we were not at home when the hour came, we remained wherever we were for the night. The lights went off early, however, and stayed off under the tight blackout, so at times we risked moving about under the cover of darkness, out of necessity.

About this time I had a recurring nightmare that persisted into my waking hours. Somehow I would be forced to go away and leave my mother and sister in the hands of the Germans and abandon my family, relatives, and friends, with no one to help them. I was haunted by this possibility and frustrated at my helplessness.

We kept telling one another that if we were allowed to remain like this in Schrodula, we could survive. Food was scarce, but there was food. We had shelter no matter how crowded we were. We counted the days.

They were not so fortunate in the ghetto in the downtown area. The rumors of liquidation had turned out to be true. One night it was encircled, and every person, man, woman, and child, was taken away. Their destination: Auschwitz.

I had never gone near the downtown ghetto in the short time it had been occupied, and now, in one night, every soul had disappeared so fast that it was as if they had never really existed at all.

I could only guess the number—some six to ten thousand Jews from Sosnowiec, many more from other towns within a radius of some twenty miles, evacuees from Bedzin, and all the places that had been made *Judenrein* like Sosnowiec.

When the order had come to report to the ghettos, those who carried the stamp for the downtown area had been mostly older people and young women with children, people the Germans considered unsuitable for labor and, therefore, slated for liquidation first.

The Kultusgemeinde tried to assure us at Schrodula that since we were resettled and working no one would touch us; we were necessary to the German war machine. And Schmidt and Smoloz, more often Smoloz, came to see us and helped to keep hope alive.

Whenever I would go to town during the day I would ride my bicycle through streets off limits to Jews and visit with the Polish family who lived across the street from our old home.

The wife bought food for me from the Polish farmers and merchants, either for money or in exchange for valuables. Once or twice a week I would take home small packages on my bicycle or by truck.

The older people clung together in the ghetto, talking constantly and seeking reassurance from one another. The women held onto their children, frantic when they were out of sight.

We younger men and women talked, too, discussing bits and pieces of news that came to us through many routes. The war had started to turn against the Germans, and we dared to speculate that maybe now they would stop these unspeakable outrages and murders for fear of the reckoning to come.

But, try as we might, no stretch of our desperate imaginations could convince us that this insanity would end soon enough to find us still alive. Despite the reassurances of the Kultusgemeinde, despite the words we used to buoy one another's hopes, we knew the Germans had long since gone beyond the point of no return. Each day, each death, each missing loved one only led us to expect more of the same until our own turn would come. We had learned by bitter experience that rumors of impending tragedy more often than not eventually became tragic realities.

Chapter
14

THE WORST REALITY that came to pass had no forewarning rumor; it just happened.

I stopped my bicycle in the streets of the city one morning, unable to believe what I heard.

"Schrodula is encircled," people were saying. "The whole place is cut off!"

In a moment I turned and pedaled blindly toward the village, praying it wasn't true or, if it was, that I would still have time to get my mother and sister out.

As I approached the settlement I could see a solid blockade already cutting off the entrances to the streets. A special Gestapo group from Katowice stood guard at each point.

I tried to get past them, showing my *sonder*, but they shoved me back. "No one will be let in or out. There are no exceptions or special papers. Get back or else."

When I saw that the situation was desperate I cycled back into town and found Schmidt and Smoloz.

"You know what's happening out there. Help me to get my family out, please," I begged them.

"What can we do?" they protested. "This is Gestapo and not even from our area. They won't listen to us."

I convinced them that if they went with me in an official truck, the guards would let us through. At least we would be able to get into the ghetto and find out what was taking place inside. I had to know if this was a selective raid, if everyone was involved or if possibly my family and friends were safe. I had to show my mother and sister I was there to protect them if I could.

After much time had been lost arguing and persuading, they finally ordered out an official city truck with the emblem on the door. I pulled my bicycle up beside me in the back, and Schmidt and Smoloz got into the cab with the driver. They ordered the driver to Schrodula, and the truck lumbered off slowly, too slowly.

Again, the entrance to the village. The truck was halted by troops and we were told in no uncertain terms that nobody could enter or leave.

Schmidt got out. It was apparent to the guards that he was someone of authority and position. He identified himself and Smoloz. I could hear the exchange of conversation from the back of the truck. The two Germans tried to explain that they were on official business: a serious sanitation problem existed inside the ghetto, and it was their responsibility to clean it up immediately.

"You go on about your business and let us do our job," Schmidt told them. "We won't interfere in your work."

The answer was: "We have special orders not to let anybody in except officers and men from our own Gestapo unit and no one else will get in. Now, get back."

Schmidt repeated, "I am under special orders, too. The Burgermeister wants this truck inside the ghetto to clean up the area before an epidemic breaks out. I have to obey my orders, just like you, or answer to the Burgermeister."

It was in vain; the Burgermeister's power and authority had no importance to them.

After a few more minutes of futile conversation, Schmidt got back into the truck, followed by Smoloz, and we drove to another corner. I could see that they had now become angry. For the first time their prestige had been dimmed by other Germans, and they were determined not to give in. At the next blockade they dismounted, but the exchange was even briefer.

"You cannot enter, and if you persist we have orders to shoot anyone who does not obey. There are no exceptions. Now, get out, and *schnell!*"

We drove away, past others who had run from town and who milled about the guards, trying to get to their families. I saw the uniforms of the local Kriminalpolizei among the civilians, and they, too, were pushed back. Something terrible had to be happening in there. A chill of fear ran through me.

For hours we drove from checkpoint to checkpoint and argued frantically with the guards, using every lie, story and alibi we could manufacture. It was hopeless.

The driver turned the truck back to Sosnowiec, and I jumped off.

Schmidt and Smoloz were grim with anger, yet they had tried to help me in every way they could. I had to try alone. I walked back and forth at the gates amid an ever-increasing number of people.

From eleven o'clock in the morning throughout the afternoon, no sight of a familiar face appeared to us from behind the wall of Gestapo. Early in the evening it was over as suddenly as it had begun. At a word the guards left the area, and we poured through the streets.

I ran to the apartment house and burst through the door. Mrs. Halpern and her daughter sat there looking at me, and I knew that something terrible had happened.

"Tell me, tell me!" I screamed at them. They cried but said nothing. I wanted to shake them and force an answer out of them, but I could not move.

Again I yelled, "For God's sake, tell me, where are they?"

Mrs. Halpern raised her head finally and choked out, "They're gone, Natan. The Germans took them." And they cried even more loudly. I could get nothing else out of them.

I ran back into the street. Where had they gone? There must still be time to get them back.

Someone said the transport had left for Bedzin. Dear God, maybe it was not too late. I began to run toward Bedzin in a state of deep shock. In my personal torment and confusion I was barely aware of the agonizing uproar I was leaving behind.

My legs moved automatically beneath me and my lungs gasped for air. At last I reached the railroad station, where someone said they were being kept.

Empty—not a trace. Nobody was left. All of them had been shipped by trucks that same night to Auschwitz. The tracks were empty, and no waiting trucks stood at the siding. It had been perfectly executed.

I don't remember my journey back to Schrodula. Of all the blows, the shocks, the unbearably tortuous experiences I had lived through, this final loss was the hardest to endure. It shattered my will to survive. I had had only one reason for going on with life until this day. As long as my mother and sister lived, my life had value and purpose. Now there was nothing left.

Of my family, my father was long since gone; David's and Yadja's fates were a mystery; Sala, the last we had heard, was still alive but beyond my power to help her. And now, in this moment, my mother taken and Rochelle with her. It was the end. My life had no further meaning. I had no function as a human being any more.

I lay tortured in the home of the Kohan family, wild questions racing through my head. What had happened that day in the house where I had left the Halperns and my mother and sister? Why was one family left and the other taken? How did the Halperns manage to survive?

I have never gotten the answers to those questions. The people who were left alive in that house in Schrodula that day, all of them, may they rest in eternal peace, are dead. While they still lived, I could not bring myself to go back into the tragic events of that day. I never went back to that room in Schrodula again.

I lay for days on that bed, my face buried in a pillow soaked

93

with tears, all desire to go on living gone. Why couldn't I at least have been with them? Where was I when they needed me? Had I neglected them and their safety? Maybe if I had done this or thought of that . . .

I reached the lowest point in my existence.

The family group closed around me with love and grief. But their words of comfort sounded futile even to them, I knew.

My young cousin, Chaba, came to stand by the side of the bed. "Natan, please come home with me. You belong with your family. All we have is each other now. We want you with us, please."

He stood there trying to display courage and hope. We looked at each other and the wall broke. He had gotten through to me, and we wept unashamedly together.

Although the Kohans wanted very much for me to stay, I left with my cousin to join his family group, which included the Golds and the Koplowiches. They were now my only remaining relatives.

Time after time I made up my mind to give up the struggle and go with the others in the next raid. Let them take me. What use was there in trying to stay here? Why stay alive? But my friends and relatives surrounded me with warmth and love. They drew me into their hearts and lives and homes. They wanted me to live. And this alone was responsible for my surviving those dreadful days.

Chapter
15

MORE THAN TWO WEEKS went by before I could bring myself to go back to the old job and feel concern again as to what was going to happen to the rest of us. I told myself coldly and firmly that, though I had lost everything, I had to try to save, for the others, as much as I could.

With each passing day a semblance of order returned to Schrodula. Those who had jobs went back to work in order to keep their papers, still shattered and numb from the losses and shock they had suffered.

Slowly at first and then faster and faster came new rumors. Someone heard from someone else who knew someone that there was going to be another entrapment. Fear showed in every face old enough to understand, and the children sensed our terror and grew unnaturally quiet. Since the majority of the young people were already gone, those left were mostly very young or very old.

We stopped speculating about the probable end of the war. We stopped trying to hold out empty hope to one another. Only two possible avenues were open to us: to find either a delaying factor or a place of concealment.

Surreptitious construction started all through Schrodula. Bunkers and hiding places were constructed, under cover. Our experience from the last raid had demonstrated that those who were able to hide themselves had secured their own safety. The Germans had filled their quotas from those they were able to find easily without having to search for others.

One day Mr. Koplowich came home and told me he had heard from a reliable source that we were approaching final *Judenrein.*

"You know what this means, Natan. It's a matter of time now. Any hour they will come for us. It's the writing on the wall."

"Not if the bunkers and other hiding places are ready in time," I protested.

"It won't do," he concluded sadly. "When they come this time they won't be so easy to satisfy. There aren't that many of us left. Sooner or later they'll find the bunkers or they'll blow up the entire ghetto. Let's face it—there's no way out."

He was right; I had known it before he had begun to speak.

If there was no safe place of concealment inside Schrodula, perhaps we could find a place outside the ghetto to hide. We could try to escape to Switzerland, a place of safety. We could survive once we got there. But to get there was the problem, without being caught or dying on the way.

The Golds suggested we make a try for Zawiercha, their original home town. Zawiercha was already *Judenrein,* and the Germans would not be looking for Jews there.

If we could get to Zawiercha unharmed, we would have to find an Aryan family to hide and feed us. We would pay them well from the few valuables we had managed to conceal, but how would we go about finding a family we could trust?

Impossible dreams, all of them.

Where, then?

After roll call one morning in the city, when the others had left for work, I walked slowly across the street, lost in thought over this last, desperate problem. I found myself looking at the hollow, city-owned fire tower which was lined with scaling ladders once used by the firemen for practicing their climbing skill.

Across the courtyard from the fire tower there were barns and a stable for the horses and wagons. The area was completely exposed to passersby because it was so much a part of the street, but as far as I knew no one ever went up into the tower. Its very openness made it an ideal place to hide.

I turned the thought over in my head all through the day, and that night when we were huddled together in Schrodula, dismissing one impossible plan after another, I mentioned it to my friends. They were excited—at last a ray of hope, however small. They asked me to try to arrange it as soon as possible. The nights had become unbearable in Schrodula.

Schmidt had jurisdiction over the fire tower. I went to him once more. We had come to know each other extremely well by now. I understood his every weakness and strength, and he knew I sought his help only when I could find no solution on my own.

Almost casually I asked him, "Would you mind if I brought a few families into Sosnowiec and hid them in the fire tower and stable hayloft?"

"What are you suggesting, Schapelski?" he replied, startled. "You know people go by there all the time, and they would certainly notice it if people suddenly started coming and going from the area. No, it's too dangerous. I can't permit it. I'm sorry."

I could not blame him for his concern. There was a very real danger to him if his part in it were exposed.

I told him, "I understand your concern, but, please, we are desperate and the gamble will be all on our part, not yours. I promise. You will know nothing of this arrangement."

He understood I was guaranteeing that if we were caught his name would never be divulged by anyone as having permitted us to use the tower. But he still looked troubled.

"I will be with the group myself," I added.

He looked up, surprised. Now he knew just how desperate we were.

"Let me think it over and discuss it with Smoloz. I'll have to talk to the man in charge of the fire tower, too. If he doesn't go along with us, it's no use even thinking about it."

"Herr Schmidt, there isn't time. You know and Herr Smoloz knows what happened just a few weeks ago. It could happen again at any minute—maybe tonight and it'll be too late. Please help us." I put every ounce of pleading and persuasion I could into my voice.

He made no promise, but I had some hope. I spent the day anxiously awaiting word, and when he called me aside later in the evening the suspense was unbearable.

"Schapelski, I talked to Smoloz and the man at the stable. We have your word that none of us knows anything about this, no matter what happens?"

"Yes, you have my promise," I swore. "If we're caught, they'll never find out from us that you or Smoloz or the stableman knew we were there."

He gave me permission to make the move. They would go along with our plans and keep our secret.

That night I took a city truck into Schrodula and we loaded a few personal possessions, the bare necessities, and climbed aboard. There were eighteen people: Mr. and Mrs. Koplowich, Mr. and Mrs. Gold, Mr. and Mrs. Kohan, Mr. and Mrs. Chaba, Franya Gold and her sister, Ruschka and Mendel Kohan and their sister and brother, the Gold twin boys, the little Chaba boy, and myself.

In dead silence we rode through the streets of Schrodula and a few minutes later entered the equally empty streets of the city and slowly pulled up at the fire tower.

The women were sent up to the top of the tower, even though it was difficult for them to scale the inside ladders. If anyone searched the area, the tower would be the last place they would look, and we wanted the women to have that extra measure of safety.

The men and young boys went into the hayloft in the barn. Ruschka stayed down in the hayloft, too, because she had to report for work every day to the Kultusgemeinde. The Chabas' little boy stayed in the tower with the women.

We had blankets and warm clothing and whatever food we had been able to carry.

The first night passed tensely. Every little noise outside made us freeze, and I worried for the women alone in the tower with no one to reassure them.

Morning came, and those of us who had to go to work reported to our jobs as usual, including the girls. I waited at the entrance to the fire tower and motioned to them one by one when to come out, and when it was safe we slipped into the streets as unobtrusively as possible, mingling with other people on their way to work.

During the day I cycled back time after time to check on those left in the tower. At night we all returned to the tower and hayloft.

I watched the tower during the day, never leaving the area for very long except to find food. It came from the black market and especially from Yablonska, the Polish woman who had been our neighbor. She risked her own safety by selling me black-market food for our own use and for bribing the Germans, and she even cooked some of it for me. She must have known that the amount of already cooked food I required could only mean that there were some of us hiding in the city, but she never asked a question. She even let me store food and supplies in her house, and sometimes at night I would slip into the streets to get to them. There were so many of us that food was a problem second only to concealment. Neither her husband nor her two grown children knew exactly how involved she was in her dealings with farmers and with me.

Usually I brought bread and cooked meat back with me to the tower and sometimes, if I was lucky, a little piece of butter for the bread.

My special permit still allowed me to ignore the curfew which forbade Jews to be in the streets after seven-thirty. With it I could pass freely through any street in the city, even those forbidden to Jews, at any time, day or night.

I went back to Schrodula frequently to see what the others

99

were doing and to learn if there were any new rumors. Though we knew that they would be quietly wondering where we were hiding, we also knew we had nothing to fear from our own people or from the people whose silence we could buy.

So the days and nights passed. It was confining and uncomfortable, but it was safe.

We crept out to the old unused horse trough at night to wash and get water and to use the primitive sanitary facilities nearby. Those who could not leave the tower day or night watched the activity in the street below through cracks in the boards of the old building.

At the end of the second week we had become accustomed to the precautions we had to take and adjusted as much as possible to the cramped quarters and the whispered conversation. Life had fallen into a pattern.

I started up the perpendicular ladder of the tower one night with the usual rucksack of supplies strapped to my back and this time with a pot of hot soup in my left hand. The food was always divided in two before I left the Polish woman's house—some for the hayloft, some for the tower. I had left a supply in the hayloft already. It was almost eight o'clock when I began to climb, using my free hand to grasp the rungs one at a time. Halfway up the ladder I lost my balance, grabbed for the rung, missed, and fell backward to the ground.

At the base of the tower were stored large glass containers of the caustic disinfectant acid once used to sterilize the floors of the stable. In falling I struck one, which fell over and broke, spilling its contents over the floor and me. I quickly took off the rucksack, which had broken my fall, and ran into the yard in agony, not daring to make a sound for fear it would lead to the discovery of our hiding place. Fumes and smoke poured from my clothing as the acid spread, consuming the fabric and the skin of my left leg.

The noise aroused a Volksdeutsche across the street, the man who worked as assistant to the man in charge of the stable. He came running, and when he saw me and the broken container he knew immediately what had happened. He grabbed me and helped me across the street and into the office of the warehouse.

I was writhing in agony as he stripped off my clothes. Another man came in with a blanket to cover me.

I kept asking if anyone had been attracted to the street. "Are there any soldiers out there?" I begged him to go out and see.

I knew that the people in the tower and hayloft must have heard the noise and looked out. What would they think when they saw the acid fumes and my packages lying strewn on the ground? They must be frantic. I didn't want them coming out of hiding to find me.

At my insistence the Volksdeutsche helped me out to the street with the blanket wrapped around me. I looked for the slightest sign that I had betrayed our presence by the accident. The street was empty and quiet.

The other man came back to the warehouse with a pair of his own pants and shoes for me. By now the acid had already eaten deeply into the flesh of my left thigh and was still spreading.

"I'm going to take you to the hospital," the Volksdeutsche said.

"No," I pleaded. "It's too dangerous for you. You know they don't allow Jews there. They'll ask questions, and you'll be in serious trouble if they find out where I came from and how I got hurt."

He wouldn't listen to me, and, risking his own life, he took me to the hospital.

"I'll tell them you hurt yourself working and that you're a valuable employee."

The chief surgeon was still on duty, a Polish doctor my family knew, because he had treated Sala many years before.

He helped me onto a table and did what he could as fast as he could. He was afraid for his own life. He cut away the corroded flesh where the acid had burned deeply into my leg and put a simple dressing on the wound and bandaged the thigh. When he was finished I got up and thanked him. There was nothing more I could say.

The Volksdeutsche helped me out of the hospital, got me back to the hayloft, and left. He would not accept any thanks for the risk he had taken for me and the others.

When my head showed through the hayloft floor the others

gathered around and pulled me up into the straw. I was in terrible pain but relieved to see that everyone was still safe.

Ruschka had gone up to the tower to tell them what had happened, then she and Franya Gold had come back down. Now they tried to ease my pain and I tried to calm them and reassure them that everything would be all right, that I felt fine.

The night went by, and the pain was constant and excruciating.

I got up and reported to work as usual in the morning. Every step, every move I made was sheer agony. One of the other boys in the hayloft made a fast trip into the fire tower, retrieved my rucksack and basket and carried them to the women.

I could not bear to stand on my leg, and it was difficult riding my bicycle, so I used every pretext I could to loiter around the warehouse and office.

I continued like this for several days and nights until the pain became so unbearable that I began to grow dizzy and weak. The German who had helped me before now risked his life again and took me back to the hospital. Again the Polish doctor cleaned the raw wound and bandaged it.

"You need surgery and bed rest, but I can't do this for you, you know that," he told me. "This will get worse unless it's treated properly and you stay off your feet for a long time."

There wasn't a place in the city where a Jew could get medical aid or drugs, much less a hospital that would treat or care for a Jew in any condition. I made up my mind I would have to endure it.

It would be a terrible sacrifice if this accident destroyed our last chance. The second or third day I started to ride the bicycle again, to go for food, and each movement of my leg sent waves of pain shooting through my entire body. I came back to the hayloft that night, shaking with exhaustion. The others could see the dangerous condition of my leg and the pain I was suffering. Out of their compassion they insisted on returning to Schrodula, where there was a Jewish infirmary and where I would not have to continue my efforts to provide for them. In vain I begged and pleaded with them to remain, but I was unable to convince them.

When I saw that they had made up their minds I arranged for a sanitation truck to be made available to us. This time we climbed aboard openly. We were afraid to go back by night. If we were stopped and interrogated, we could offer no valid explanation for our journey.

We returned to the houses we had left almost three weeks before, and I began receiving medical attention. First, the family doctor of the Koplowich family, Dr. Plawner, an internist long famous in our city, looked at me, but there was very little he could do. He too said that only surgery and hospitalization would help.

The wound began to fester, and the infection spread deeper into my leg. My people, my friends, who had already done more for me than would have seemed humanly possible, were so concerned that one night they even persuaded the Polish surgeon who had treated me to come into the ghetto and operate on my leg. This he did under the most primitive conditions. Dr. Plawner came by every other day to change the dressing on the wound.

The pain went on unabated. I could scarcely walk or ride a bicycle, so I asked Schmidt and a few other German contacts to get me permission to ride the streetcar from Schrodula to the place where we assembled each day for work. Through Schmidt's efforts, I got the necessary permit and went back to work.

I was not required to do any physical work or travel through the town, so I walked around the warehouse area all day. I wanted to be there, still on my feet. I felt my presence might give the people around me a little more confidence and hope. I went to work every day.

At night my group and I tried to think of what we could do next. It was inevitable that unless some miracle happened and happened fast, it would be only a matter of days or weeks until we faced the final horror. From the pattern of events and the almost total winnowing out of the young people, no reassurance by the Kultusgemeinde could make us believe the Germans had any real need of those who remained.

Chapter
16

FROM TRAVELERS AND REFUGEES we heard news of the outside world. The rest of Europe was becoming almost completely *Judenrein*. The Germans were losing on all fronts, but they offered to Hitler, as a pacifier, the killing and burning of more and more Jews. The Jewish populations of Belgium, Holland, France, Czechoslovakia, and of all other occupied countries had been decimated.

The bunker device we had discarded as foolish and a last resort became our principal endeavor. We decided to build one for ourselves. The activity itself helped push the inevitable from our minds.

We divided the basement of our little house with a false wooden partition, creating a secret chamber behind the artificial wall. We left the existing trap door exposed, as always, but over the hidden area we cut a second, concealed, trap door which we covered with a movable cabinet. We knew that our efforts would probably turn out to be in vain, but we had exhausted all other ideas.

Someone said that Jews in other countries had been able to

buy an escape through the Red Cross and get into Switzerland. If we could have contacted the Red Cross, possibly many of our problems might have been resolved. But what means had we, isolated as we were, with no direct contact with the outside world, to get in touch with any person or group of people who might put out a hand to help us, even for a price?

So we talked, but as we talked we dug. It was very difficult because we could work only at night and we had but a few makeshift tools. Apart from the actual digging, the sand, earth and rock we removed had to be carried out and spread carefully through the garden so that it wouldn't be noticed by the patrols. The slightest sign of fresh earth lying around would have given our plan away.

We knew that in the houses around us bunkers were also being worked on, or had already been constructed, although there was little outright exchange of information. Each household could barely provide enough space for its own. Those who lived in apartment houses were less fortunate. They had no basements they could burrow into.

We worked in shifts of three, with Franya and her sister, Chaba and the Gold twins helping. As soon as darkness fell, one man would go down the hidden opening to the secret chamber and dig into the hard-packed earth. Another would wait above him to pull up the dirt-filled buckets and carry them out to the garden, spreading the dirt among the trees and plants. A third young man or girl would lie prone in the garden next to the wall, listening for the patrols or any sign of detection.

We began on a Thursday night, a few days after our return from the fire tower, and worked again on Friday night. It was slow, back-breaking work. Those of us young enough to dig had already put in a long day in the city. Now we had to work throughout the night as well, with little or no rest. We needed more help.

I sounded out two Jewish men who worked on the sanitation trucks, men who had been given their jobs because of their great physical strength. Both of them agreed, but only one succeeded in getting to us that night before the curfew.

During my rest period I heard voices in the Koplowich room and got up. "What's the matter?" I asked them. Everyone was up and very agitated.

Mr. Koplowich said, "I buried some boxes in the basement when we moved in here. I removed them before that man came to dig. But I forgot one box, a small, black one. It's still down there. It's full of valuables. There's no telling what can happen if he finds it."

I tried to calm him down. "Where was the box buried? Tell me and I'll get it. I know the man. I can talk to him and handle him if there's any trouble."

He told me the location of the box, and I went back and dropped down into the basement alongside the man. He was powerfully built and sweating from his labor. He grunted at me and kept digging.

I chatted with him for a moment, asking how the work was coming along.

"All right, I guess; it's pretty hard going," he answered, but he kept his face turned away.

Then I asked him, "Did you find a box down here?"

He laughed and said, "What kind of box do you mean?"

"Please give it to me," I said, not knowing what to expect.

He straightened up and reached into his pocket, pulling out a small, dark container. He handed it to me and remarked simply, "I know what's in it, my friend." And he went back to his digging.

I clambered back up to the floor above and took the box to Koplowich. He opened it immediately. Nothing was missing. The man had taken nothing from it, and nothing more was said between us about the small fortune that had been buried beneath our feet.

Saturday night Franya was on duty as lookout in the garden, and I was taking my turn carrying dirt to the yard. An uneasy feeling gripped us. No patrol had come through our area for the past few hours, which was very unusual. Until that night two or three soldiers had come every hour in groups, either on foot, announcing their approach with the familiar pounding of their boots, or roaring by on motorcycles.

I eased my way back into the house and called down to the two men digging. "Will you be all right if I run down the hill to the Kohans and see if they know why the patrols have stopped?" I asked them. I had the only permit to move about at night, so there was less danger for me.

"Go ahead, Natan," they whispered back. "Find out what's happened and hurry back."

I went over the garden wall and trotted down the hill through the back alleys until I reached the Kohan apartment.

Ruschka opened the door, calling out quietly, "Who is it? Ah, Natan. Come in quickly. What's wrong? Did something happen at your house?" She and her sister, who worked on the sewing machines in the factory in Schrodula, shared one room of the apartment, and the rest of the family was asleep in the other room.

"Nothing has happened that I know of," I replied. "I came to find out if you knew why there haven't been any patrols tonight."

She shook her head. "I haven't been outside since curfew, and my sister isn't home yet from work at the factory. What do you think it means?"

She was frightened, and I was sorry I had upset her.

"It probably doesn't mean anything, Ruschka. Don't worry; they must have changed the schedule or something."

I tried to calm her, but at that moment her sister came through the door, and even in the semi-darkness we could see that her face was white and drawn. She stood for a second inside the door and then said to us, "Have you heard the news? Schrodula is encircled!"

Just as we had always feared it would happen—in a moment, with no warning.

I ran out and back up the hill as fast as I could.

When I got to the house everyone was up. They had already heard the news. It was official.

By twelve-thirty Sunday morning, in total darkness, Schrodula was completely surrounded by troops.

Ruschka had followed me back to our house with her brother to see if anything could be done. Soon we could hear the noises in the streets, the sound of tanks rumbling by and pounding boots, and over them the sound of screaming and weeping. We knew our final hour had come.

The brutal barking of "*Juden, heraus*" began, and we heard it again and again. There was no time left to decide what to do. The decision was foregone.

All of us, including Ruschka and her brother, who had cut themselves off from their family when they followed me back, dropped down through the concealed trap door into the unfinished basement and moved the cabinet over the opening. It was pitch-black, and the little house above us was empty and quiet. We prayed to God that if the Germans came and found nobody there they would leave without searching further.

There we all stayed, cramped behind the partition for the rest of that Sunday, through Sunday night, Monday, and on through Monday afternoon. Whenever it was quiet outside one of us would go up for a minute to look out into the street.

The ghetto had turned into a scene of madness. Soldiers herded Jews along the streets at bayonet point, and every few minutes we could hear the crackle of machine-gun fire. The silence over our heads was broken periodically by the sound of heavy boots tramping in from the streets and through the rooms. We would stop breathing and pray the child would not cry. The German voices cut through the darkness: "*Juden, heraus.*"

We stayed on in this cramped space, not more than five feet wide by ten feet long, without food or water, until Tuesday morning. We realized we had to get food and water or die, so we decided to go up together, all of us.

A knock came at the door, and our hearts sank in terror.

Gold's brother-in-law, Weinstock, came in. "The soldiers are knocking through the floors and breaking into the bunkers. They know all about them. It's the end, the end." He went on talking, almost babbling in his hysteria and shock.

Even at the last minute we reached for wisps of hope. "How could he be sure?" Our lives, geared to sanity and decency, would not let us cut the fine threads that still bound us to our last glimmer of hope or curb our indomitable will to live, even in this hell.

"No, it's true," he said. "They are taking all the families, but they're going to keep each family intact in camps. The young people will work and the children and the old ones will be interned." In his desperation he was clutching at straws. "We are going. You had better come now while there's still time." He left us in silence. We knew it could not be true, and I pitied the man and his desperate need to hold onto a fiction even in this final hour.

There was no purpose in descending into the bunker again. Sooner or later they would come for us, and we could at least spend these last moments in the light, standing erect like human beings. Ruschka ran down the hill and was back in minutes. Her family was gone.

I stood to one side of the group, looking from one to the other, trying to memorize these beloved faces. I wanted to scream at God, "Take me, please, let them live. I am alone; no one needs me any more. Please take me and let them live."

But no words passed my lips. The women and children were in a bad enough state without a demonstration of emotion from me. We had said everything we had to say to one another many times. The bond of love and devotion that held us together spoke for us. Not one of us would have hesitated to give his or her life for the others. We had had a time of fulfillment and friendship that grew out of death and destruction, and if I was to spend my last moments on earth here in this little house in Schrodula, no finer human beings could be found anywhere in the world to share my final breath.

"Natan."

I heard my name and came out of my reverie. Mr. Koplowich motioned to me to follow him. His wife, Mr. and Mrs. Gold and their sons, Max and Schejack, came after us with Mr. Chaba, out into the garden in back of the house. Franya and her sister soon joined us. We gathered around Mr. Koplowich like a flock of small children around the rabbi.

He began to speak to us. "All of you listen to me and what I have to say to you. We are going very soon to an unknown destiny. Maybe all of us, maybe only some, will survive, God willing. We have buried most of our valuables in different places in this garden. There are boxes and containers of currency, diamonds and gold, spread out where we are now standing. Mr. Gold and I want you, all of you, to know exactly where they are." He stopped for a moment to regain his control.

"Now, if we all survive, whatever is here belongs to all of us equally. If some of us survive, it will be shared equally by them. And if none of us survive, it will belong to the earth where it lies."

This wonderful man in his wisdom and enormous love still had thoughts of the future. He knew that he and the older people would probably not come back, but he wanted us younger ones to have something to come back to, if we lived to carry on their memory. In the midst of the hate that surrounded us, this blessed man still found it in his heart to love and plan for us.

Quickly, the hiding places were pointed out. A box lay buried near the bench, another container between the trees, the others here and there near some identifiable landmark. I had one piece of gold, and I buried it there, too, as the Schapelski family's contribution and monument.

Koplowich spoke again to us. "Quickly, go into the house, fill up some rucksacks and prepare yourselves. It's almost time to go."

We packed clothing and stuffed bread and pieces of meat and cheese into our pockets and suitcases. We even secreted some small stones, diamonds and pieces of gold, just in case there was still something to be bought at the end of the journey—if not our lives, then possibly a crust of bread.

We walked out together into the street. Gestapo with snarling shepherd dogs drove us toward the open field where thousands were already massed. Every few hours they cut off a group and marched them away on foot. We had banded together in a group of sixty-four, all friends and relatives, determined to stay together if possible.

I couldn't speak anymore. In my mind the refrain went around. "We are lost—it's the end." Since my mother had gone, I had often wished that I were dead. My life didn't really matter, but my heart ached for the women and children. They were so helpless and so innocent. I could not cry or feel anything beyond this pain.

At a given signal the Gestapo divided the crowd again, and this time we were in the group to go. They started us down the road to the railroad station near Bedzin, where my mother and Rochelle had gone with the thousands taken in the first encirclement. Those few kilometers from Schrodula to the station were a horror beyond description. The soldiers pushed and prodded us, striking the people on the fringes to keep them in line. A man fell; they shot him immediately. A woman screamed for her child; a bullet pierced her head. An old man gasped for breath and slowed for a minute only to have his face smashed by a gun barrel. I saw, through disbelieving eyes, Poles—men, women, and children—lined up along the road and searched their faces for—for what? Horror? Sympathy? Would I never learn? I saw instead smiles and even laughter. On the few serious faces no sign of emotion was displayed. People darted out and snatched the parcels and bundles dropped by the dead and wounded.

A man I didn't know lay wounded and bleeding ahead of us. Mr. Gold, old and tired, was ordered to pick him up and carry him on his back. We started to help him, to relieve him of the weight, but the soldiers knocked us back. Many died on the march, but no bodies were left behind. They made us pick them up and carry them with us. We had seen no bodies from the earlier transports and now we knew why.

The column approached the entrance to the station. A train was standing there made up of freight cars. There was no sign of those who had gone before.

For some never-to-be-explained reason the SS troops suddenly stopped our column and screamed at us to lie down in the dirt alongside the chain-link fence by the roadside.

We lay prone in the dirt for almost an hour, and the next column from Schrodula came past us. I saw Dr. Plawner go by, dazed, his family at his side. The Germans took this later group and loaded them directly onto the train.

We watched from the ground as they were loaded into the freight cars, screaming from the beatings of the guards and the attacks of the vicious dogs goaded on by the soldiers.

We were still lying in the dirt when the train moved out of the station. It began to look as if there would be no other transport leaving that night.

Finally we were ordered to get up and march to a ghetto near Bedzin that had been emptied by previous transports, when the province had been made *Judenrein*. We walked the half mile to the ghetto, still carrying the dead and wounded.

We were locked up for the night, inside what seemed to be a huge shed. There were some rough tables and benches, but most of us sat on the floor so the sick and elderly and the children might lie down to sleep or rest, if they could.

There was no water or plumbing still functioning. We tried to eat a little from our small supply of food, but it was impossible. We were all in a state of shock.

The following day, after a night without water, we were called out to form a column four abreast, and at noon we were marched again the half mile to the same railroad station, where another train stood waiting. There, a further insanity occurred, a madness still difficult for me to believe, even having lived through it.

The SS men formed a corridor, and as we marched between their ranks four abreast they beat us with their clubs and urged their dogs to attack us. My people, my friends, the elderly, the children, bloody, screaming, stumbling, falling, ran this gauntlet of vicious, depraved animals and men, until, having had their sadistic orgy, the SS loaded us into the freight cars of the waiting train.

"Fast, fast, *schnell, schnell,*" they barked and ordered and cursed.

Faces moved past me and around me. I saw Franya, Mr. Gold, other friends, and with them the bodies of the dead. We stumbled into the freight cars, our pitiful packages and suitcases still clutched in our hands. We stood crushed together, heads turned toward the daylight. The next moment the doors slammed shut and all was darkness.

I was still with my friends. We were packed in so tightly that those who died on the journey could not fall. Without water, food, or sufficient air to breathe, we made the trip in just a few hours to our destination.

The train stopped; nothing happened. The doors remained closed. A few minutes passed and we could hear the familiar order—"*Heraus*, everybody out!"—coming nearer.

The doors rolled back to reveal SS men at each side with clubs already beating at our legs.

"*Heraus, schnell, schnell!*"

The welcome set the pattern. We stumbled out onto the platform and into a weird landscape where there was not a tree or bird or water. The bodies of the dead lay between our feet.

"Hurry up now. Pile all your suitcases and all your things in one stack. Take nothing with you. Quickly, fast, into a column. Now, march!"

They screamed at us, using beatings for emphasis. Hundreds of SS and Gestapo stood waiting for us. I could see the same SS faces that had put us on the train near Bedzin.

Off to one side a caravan of trucks was parked, and—a spark of hope—a few panel trucks had Red Cross markings. A short distance away a group of high-ranking officers stood watching us, their SS emblems all over their uniforms.

We were welcomed to Auschwitz–Birkenau by the man I soon came to know as "Dr. Mengele, the Butcher," a notorious Nazi second only to Adolf Eichmann, if not his equal.

As the column approached the officers it funneled down to a single line past this inhuman monster, who stood with a few others on a small platform above us, raising his hand with the thumb extended and moving it back and forth. They herded us past him, beating us to make us move faster and faster. We did not, at that moment, know what the movement of his finger meant, but as the stream of people passed it soon became apparent.

I was shunted off to the left by his thumb movement. Another stream went to the right about twenty feet away. When we looked back we could see that this other line was made up of children and the middle-aged and older men and women. Our line was almost all young men and girls, eighteen to thirty-five years of age, more or less. It happened so fast that some went to the wrong line, but this mistake was soon rectified, not by sending back the young people who were included by haste with the expendable women, infants and elderly but by weeding out only those expendable ones who had gotten into our line in the frantic rush.

All of the young men from our original group were with us, as well as Ruschka Kohan and her brother. I looked back in horror and saw the Golds, the Koplowiches, except for their sons who stood by me, and Mrs. Chaba and her child, all on the other side. Franya and her sister had started toward us, but when they saw their mother going the other way they went back and spoke to Dr. Mengele, asking if they could stay with her. He smiled and said, "Yes, of course." They went to the other side.

The selection was completed quickly, and the group on the other side, weeping and calling out to their sons, husbands and fathers, was herded to the trucks.

Mr. Weinstock began to thrash about and scream. His wife and child were being taken away. We hadn't noticed that he had concealed a flask of vodka on him and, to ease the strain, had been drinking steadily. The liquor had given him such brute strength that it took several of us to hold him down and quiet his cries. "They're going to kill them. My God, they're going to kill my babies and my wife." We surrounded him until he quieted down, still weeping.

The caravan began to roll, with one Red Cross car in the front and one in back of the line.

Again, a little flicker of hope. We dared to think, at the brink of hell, dear God, maybe something will protect them.

Our group had been pinned to the ground while the others were being taken away. When they were gone, we were told to get up, and they marched us away four abreast again.

114

The soldiers then separated the men from the women and took them off in another direction. We began passing barbed-wire fences and could see huge barracks and guard towers. As we came closer we could see the Haeftlinge (prisoners) behind the wires.

The SS herded us inside a huge shed, and there we met our first Haeftling. He took charge of the group.

We were now in the heart of Auschwitz–Birkenau.

The Haeftlinge—trustee inmates—were to be our new guards. "Fast, off with your clothes. That's right, strip all the way down. Just throw everything on the floor. You're going to take a nice shower bath. Fast. Don't try to hold out on us."

One man tried to hold onto his valuables. The Haeftling struck him. "Now run, *schnell!*"

I tried to find some trace of humanity in one of the faces of these men. I could hear unfamiliar accents speaking German, and there were strange markings and colors on their uniforms, if the ragged outfits they wore could be called uniforms. But there was very little humanity left in any of them. They had long since emptied their faces and souls of any human quality, and they treated us like the animals they had become in order to survive.

Most of them refused to acknowledge our questions as we ran past. One shouted, "Do you think you came here to vacation?"

We ran through the showers and out the other door naked, then into another barracks, where we were handed a shirt and a pair of pants; our own clothes were already gone. Out the other door again, with just a moment to pull on the ragged garments. I had a pair of pants with one leg ripped off and the other in shreds, nothing else. My watch, everything, was gone. And in the showers I had torn the bandage from my infected leg.

"Now, lie down," they screamed at us.

Most of the SS had left. Only a few remained to watch the Haeftlinge take over.

I turned to a Haeftling and asked, "What did they do with the other people who came in our transport?"

He faced me and said, "Do you see over there, see those chimneys burning? That's where they are, over there."

I said, "That's impossible. There were Red Cross cars accompanying the trucks!"

"Do you know what those Red Cross cars were carrying?" he asked. "They carried the gas they use on the people at the end of the ride."

He said this with no expression on his face, and I knew he spoke the truth.

I was herded with the others back into the first barracks we had entered. No trace of our clothes remained. Only a number of tables lined the shed. They drove us past the Haeftlinge seated at the tables.

I could hear them asking the men in front of me, "What is your profession? What is your trade?" Someone in front of me said, "I am a carpenter."

When my turn came I answered that I, too, was a carpenter.

The next stop was the tattoo line, where a filthy needle, jammed into my arm, erased Natan Schapelski from the human race and brought into being Haeftling 134138.

When everyone had been registered by trade and tattooed, we were pinned down on the ground again.

We had had no food, no water and no sanitation for all these horrible past days. It was hot, August of 1943, a month they bragged about in Auschwitz later on. It was the biggest and busiest month they'd had. In that one month they had emptied out all of Zaglebie Province and had killed more people than in any month to date.

Hundreds of thousands had gone directly from the platform to the trucks to the chimneys into eternity.

Finally, with the few remaining SS men and their dogs helping, the Haeftlinge beat us to our feet, and, snarling like their dogs, they marched us through the gates and into the compounds.

The last thing I heard outside the gates was a Haeftling screaming over and over again, "Nobody has ever come out of here alive. Don't think you will be the first!"

Looking back into those horrifying times, I still marvel at what had happened that day as we lay in the dirt at the station near Bedzin.

The transport that had been loaded onto the cars as we lay by the fence had passed through Auschwitz the previous night while we were imprisoned in the ghetto near the station. Everyone on that transport had gone directly to the ovens. Why we were passed over I'll never know. I have asked myself many times why my life should have been spared.

There were sixty-four people, all relatives and friends, in that single transport from Schrodula. I do not have to count that high today. There are two of us left: Ruschka Kohan and myself.

Chapter
17

By the summer of 1943 Birkenau consisted of nothing but camps. There were no people living there, no houses and no industry. The only structures were those of the concentration camps themselves, identified by letters of the alphabet, "A" through "Z," and then sub-lettered "AX" and so on. Each camp had a huge compound surrounded by a high barbed-wire fence, electrically charged, with watch towers every few hundred feet.

Naked, except for the rags we wore, our heads shaven, our names taken from us, identified only by the raw blue numbers cut into our flesh, we shuffled into Lager (Camp) "B," which had previously been emptied to receive us. There were sixteen large barracks (or blocks) in the camp. These were lined up perpendicular to the rear of the compound, with open spaces in between and more open space along the back, between them and the barbed wire separating them from the camp behind, and an enormous hard-packed dirt field in front. One by one the blocks were quickly filled as the SS and their dogs drove the men at a run. We were driven into Block 13.

The huge barracks had endless rows of bunks stacked three tiers high in every foot of space. There was a clearing in the center, divided by a low cement trough, intended for feeding animals. There were no water or sanitary facilities, except for a few primitive holes that had been dug by the former inmates. On each side of the main door was a tiny room, and between these two rooms hung a single light bulb, the only illumination for the entire block.

In the general panic, as we ran through the doors into Block 13, I had become separated from my few remaining friends. Young Kohan and I found ourselves isolated at one side of the barracks, unable to see the others in the frantic crush. The beatings we had received from the SS guards outside were continued inside by a man I soon learned was the block senior, a Pole named Mietech, and his assistant. It was they who occupied the two little rooms. "Get up in those bunks and lie down!" they screamed at us as soon as our block was filled. We scrambled into the nearest opening and lay across narrow strips of wood with no covering, each man jammed against the next. Soon there were no Haeftlinge left standing, and only a few SS men with dogs strutted back and forth down the center of the block.

The block senior stepped up on the divider. Turning from one side to the other, he began to scream at us in the filthiest, most obscene language I had ever heard. "Do you know where you are, you ——?" There was silence. He continued to revile us. "You thought you were going to survive because you came here late. I promise you—you're wrong. If any of you think you will walk out of here alive, I can assure you this will not be the case." He walked up and down the divider swinging a wooden club he had fashioned from a pick handle with a pointed piece of wood nailed to the end. As a screamed at us, he punctuated his threats and curses with blows to the nearest heads. "You will get no food tonight. In the morning, when the bells ring, you will have two minutes to empty the barracks and get outside. Anyone who disobeys will be killed. Whenever you hear the bell, get out of the building immediately, do you hear?" The silence was broken only by the groans of those he struck in passing and left with blood streaming down their faces. The tirade of filth finally ended and the guards left, closing the doors behind them. Mietech and his assistant went into their private cubicles and turned out the little light.

Plunged into darkness, the barracks became a tomb. It seemed that all of us, hundreds and hundreds who lay there stacked like so much firewood on shelves, were afraid or unable to move or break the silence. Kohan lay rigid on one side of me and a stranger on the other side. If I had wanted to speak to Kohan I could not have uttered a sound; my throat was dry and paralyzed. I had no way of knowing where the Golds were. We lay on those shelves, row upon row, crushed together, hungry, thirsty, physically and emotionally exhausted, incapable of feeling anything but blind horror. The Birkenau night was icy cold. And every part of my body not pressed against another body was numb. I lost count of time.

We had lain there for minutes or perhaps for hours when I became aware of a growing sound in the distance. A whisper passed among the men: "What is it? What is it? Do you hear that noise?" Within seconds the question was answered as the heart-rending screams and weeping of frightened women came closer and closer, high-pitched and shrill. The barracks was still except for the whispers. Two boys lying near the front door slipped off their bunks and risked looking toward the road. Horrified at what they saw, they climbed back into their bunks and passed a whisper on. A caravan of trucks loaded with naked young girls and women was rolling past our camp in the direction of the gas chambers.

When the last shrieks of those young women had faded in the distance, I could still hear them echoing in my head. Whatever rumors we had heard, whatever horrors we had imagined, we now knew that the reality was worse, far beyond any evil we could possibly comprehend. Depraved men had constructed at Auschwitz and Birkenau a scientifically planned death factory, organized to kill as expediently as possible, devoting trained minds and technical know-how to creating and refining new methods of reducing us to something less than animals and eventually to ashes. So passed our first night in Birkenau.

A bell rang; it was morning, not much past four o'clock, dark and cold. We scrambled from the bunks still in the ragged shirts and pants we had received the day before and ran outside at the first cries of *"Heraus,"* mindful of the previous night's threats. We were again speeded on our way by men who ran in with clubs to drive us out. Not knowing where to go or what to do, we stood shivering in small groups in the spaces between the blocks, huddled together, back to back, for body warmth. This was the first time we saw the Sonderkommando with whom we were soon to become so familiar as they came daily to collect the dead. Someone in our group asked one of them who the women were we had heard the night before and where they had gone. "Oh, they went straight to the ovens," he replied, "all of them." There were no other questions asked.

After almost two hours the Lager camp chief screamed, *"Zaehlappell—roll call!"* They lined us up in rows of eight, and we stood for hours while they counted. Six o'clock, seven, eight, nine o'clock, and still we stood, unable even to touch one another for warmth. The block senior came out again and again just to repeat in vile screams his threat that if anyone still had any thoughts of surviving what lay ahead, he would personally guarantee we would not. "If you think this is the worst that can happen to you, get it out of your—— heads. This is only a sample of what is coming to you, you —— ," he roared, and as he walked by he punctuated his obscenities with vicious blows from his club.

By the middle of the morning the heat, which at first had felt good, began to burn us. We soon learned that at Birkenau the days could be as unbearably hot as the nights were frigid. When the SS came to check the count, the block senior stood out in front of our lines to make his report, so many Haeftlinge alive and so many dead. What the actual figures were that morning I do not know, but from that day on the number of living diminished with each count as more and more dead were carted out of the barracks by the Sonderkommando with each succeeding dawn.

After the first count we remained in line, sometimes at attention and sometimes at ease, while they recounted us again and again. It became hotter and hotter, until we could hardly bear it anymore. We had had no food or water for more than two days but the slightest movement only brought on a beating, twenty or thirty blows, with a club and, for those who dropped, a few well-placed kicks to revive them. Some time during the morning we were ordered to pass a barrel containing a vile, cold blue liquid they called "tea" and were forced to swallow a mouthful. Some spit it up, revolted by the taste, and were immediately beaten by the guards. If any was found spilled on the ground, everyone in the immediate vicinity was beaten. At noon they brought a "soup," a thin, watery concoction made mostly of thistles. We passed before a huge kettle and got a dipper of it. This, too, we had to swallow or be beaten. Finally we were permitted to go back into the barracks and made to lie down again.

In the evening, about six o'clock, we were forced to stand roll call again, and it lasted until almost eight o'clock. Then we were marched back into the barracks and received our other meal, a morsel of bread. The distribution of the bread was so carefully handled and the pieces counted out so exactly that there was not even the remotest possibility of getting more than one small crust. I could not swallow even that for lack of water.

That night some of the men in the outlying bunks got their heads bashed by the block senior on his rounds. Each barracks was run by a block senior and his clerk, the Schreiber, with some ten orderlies, "Stubendienste," they had chosen from the group of Haeftlinge prisoners to help them. Our shirts had the red diamond marking of political prisoners over the heart, and those who were imprisoned for criminal reasons, non-Jews, had a green diamond. There were very few green diamond markings except for the Lageraelteste, the Lagerkapo, a few of the Blochaeltesten and some of the Haeftlinge who worked in the kitchens. All of the trustee Haeftlinge were under the supervision of the SS guards, whose brutality some exceeded to keep their positions and privileges. Some of them had been there since the first arrivals in Auschwitz–Birkenau, having earned their right to survive by the torture they inflicted on their fellow prisoners. They had killed and tortured so many hundreds of their fellow inmates that they had long since lost their own humanity.

The second night passed. And on the second day our condition was even worse. My body was wracked with pain; the strength and will that had kept me going were almost exhausted. When the roll call went on for hours my dizziness increased, until I could no longer stand alone. When we were allowed to stand at ease, my friends gathered around me and made me sit on the ground, where I could not be seen, until it was time to stand at attention again. When anyone walked near they helped me up.

And so it went, each day worse than the day before—a nightmare of starvation, humiliation, and beatings. If one of us moved and caught the eye of a guard or trustee, they had special methods of showing their displeasure. One was to hang a man by his wrists tied behind his back from the rafters inside the block, where we could watch him die as an object lesson and see his body sway there until they decided to cut him down and drag the corpse away. Some were subjected to this during the first days in camp to acquaint us with what the future had in store for us.

When most of the blocks were filled we heard that our part of Poland, Oberschlesien (Upper Silesia), was now *Judenrein* except for small groups of Jews kept back to help the Nazis clean out the ghettos. Later these few also came to join us and told us of the days after we had been taken. For a while they had lived well on the remaining food and supplies we had left behind, while the Nazis were using them to pack our belongings and valuables for shipment into the Third Reich, and then when they had served their purpose they were loaded on the freight cars to follow us.

Now that most of Europe was *Judenrein*, Dr. Mengele and his gang, the same beasts who had welcomed us to the camp at the station, returned to Birkenau, and their infamous "selections" began. At roll call we were now forced to strip naked and stand for inspection as they passed before us. The first time we did not know what it meant when the doctor moved his finger one way or the other, right or left. But when he was through it became apparent. Those who were shunted to the right were mostly the thinnest and weakest. They were immediately surrounded by SS guards and marched into the empty barracks of Block 4 and locked in. We on the left were marched back into our original blocks. I saw Weinstein, the first of our friends to go, taken in the first selection.

Often the men in a selection were locked in the barracks for four or five days if trucks were not standing by ready to take them away immediately. For all this time they were kept without food or water so that when the doors were opened they staggered out wild with pain and fear, crazed and starved. The bestiality of the guards was unbelievable. As they drove one group onto the trucks I heard one say, "Look, that man is bleeding. Someone put a bandage on him quick!" Another: "That man is going to catch cold without a shirt. Someone put a blanket around him!" The horror was such that we almost felt a sense of relief for those of our friends who had gone directly to the ovens and had escaped the torture, suffering, and humiliation we faced.

The selections went on regularly. If they wanted three hundred from our compound, they selected three blocks to stand roll call. Only those who held a position—a Schreiber, a Stubendienst, or those working in the kitchen or building an outhouse—were excused. In this way they emptied whole barracks, one after another, usually using Block 4 to imprison the selected ones until they were transported to the ovens. After Weinstein was taken there remained of our family and friends only the Gold twins, the two Chaba brothers, Kohan, and myself.

After the first week, when I started to recover from my weakened condition, I made a pact with myself. I determined that if there was even the smallest chance of survival I would not permit myself to be the cause of my own death either by giving up my will to live or permitting myself to be dehumanized. I still could not digest the soup, but when I received my morsel of bread at night I wolfed it down as soon as possible. Many of the others tried to make it last by doling it out crumb by crumb throughout the night to stave off their continuing hunger. By so doing, they only became obsessed with the thought of when next they could allow themselves to eat, so that they were unable to sleep. Soon they became what the SS called *Musselmänner,* walking skeletons. After one or two beatings, if they were not taken in the selection, they died from their wounds or simply because their ebbing life force had left them helpless to resist. Death came to some through the ministrations of the doctors and the so-called laboratory assistants who aided them.

Days and nights went by in the same hideous routine. Up and out of the barracks at three or four o'clock in the morning, roll call at six, twelve, and six. Counted and recounted. The ghastly soup at noon, the morsel of bread at six or whenever we were permitted back into the barracks, and the repeated selections, which had started out once every two weeks but became more frequent as our numbers dropped down and down. We did nothing else day in and day out. One day, however, several barracks were taken out for work. SS guards, with dogs at their heels, marched us to a location and ordered us to load our shirt fronts with sand and to carry it to another location. We did this all day long, stumbling back and forth from one location to another. The next day we carried the same dirt back to where we had brought it from. They kept up this humiliating game for days until they grew tired of it.

Weeks passed. I watched the Stubendienste, men who had come on the same transport with us, lose their minds. As time went on they began to forget their relatives and friends. All they could think of was their own survival. Let the others suffer and die. On Yom Kippur night some of the more religious men slipped out of their bunks in the darkness and began to pray with a tattered blanket drawn over their heads. Two brothers who had come from Bedzin with us, and were now Stubendienste, heard them, jumped out of their bunks, and beat them until they returned to their shelves.

Then, one day in early September 1943, we were standing roll call when the most incredible sight passed us in the road. A transport came past—men, women and children carrying luggage and packages, whole families walking on the road where only those destined for the gas chamber had passed before. Even the Blochaeltesten and the Lagerfuhrers were amazed. None of them had seen such a sight in Birkenau before. We thought a miracle had come to pass. These people were well dressed and did not appear to have been subjected to any mistreatment. Their faces seemed cheerful compared to what they must have seen looking back at them. The SS had emptied out Lager C, directly in back of ours, where all of these four thousand or so people were to be interned. Consumed with curiosity, we watched them through the barbed-wire fences that separated us by only twenty-five feet or so. And when we felt we were unobserved we stood within the doorway and talked to those who came near enough to hear us.

They were Czech Jews, attractive people; the young girls looked especially beautiful to us. They seemed to be a select group, prosperous, well dressed. They asked us what was going on and why we were there. We told them that they were the special ones, not we, and enlightened them with the facts. They could not believe what they heard and told us that they were merely going to be resettled. We could almost believe them from the way they were treated. Each day nurses and doctors came to their camp, and they and their children were given special care. They stood roll call briefly and were free to stroll around and to play with their children. Not only were they well fed, but the SS brought the children candy and fresh fruit.

We could not comprehend it. Our daily torture and deprivation continued unchanged, while a few feet away a whole other life was enacted. They could not understand what we were talking about, and we could not believe that they were real. There wasn't a day when cars did not pull up outside their camp, civilian and SS and Gestapo groups going through on inspection. Who they were we did not know, but we speculated they were from the Red Cross or Switzerland or another neutral country. Maybe it meant the beginning of the end. But each day on our side of the camp the beatings went on as before. Each morning the Sonderkommando still came with their covered carts and dragged out the bodies of the dead. The selections never stopped.

Months went by, and the good life continued on one side of the fence and the nightmare continued on the other. Romances sprang up across the wires, and I heard rumors that somewhere a tunnel existed, making it possible for young lovers to meet and touch in the midst of death. Then, one night in March 1944, six months after these people had brought a glimmer of hope to the hopeless by their special treatment at the hands of the SS, the myth was exploded and the dream came to an end. In that one night every man, woman and child was loaded onto a truck and taken back down the road they had walked so confidently the day they had arrived. Starting at eight or nine o'clock in the evening and ending in early morning, they were moved out and sent straight to the gas chambers. The next day it was as if they had never been there at all. All that remained were the belongings they had left behind, and even those were quickly removed. Now we knew the truth. They were window dressing, used to prove that the ghastly rumors were not true. Those who had come to inspect had seen well-treated families humanely interned. If they asked about the wretched ones across the fence they were probably told that we were criminals, special cases requiring special control. When they had left to return to their own countries, satisfied to proclaim that the rumors they had heard about the extermination of men, women and children were untrue, the Nazis had simply erased the specimens they had used.

The death of this one little ray of hope broke the will to live for thousands, and many of the borderline cases went over the edge. The old-timers took it the hardest of all. Some of the men ran to the barbed wire and threw themselves against it, welcoming the electricity that purged them of life. There were times when I too thought the wire was the only answer. Kohan was taken in a selection and Chaba in another. When they were locked up in Block 4 and I knew there was nothing I could do to help them, suicide beckoned; but something inside, the innate will to live, held me back each time.

Later, a small group of gypsies were broght into Birkenau, and the process was repeated. They were kept together, families intact, receiving fairly decent treatment until they too had served their purpose; then extermination. By that time we no longer felt anything but desperation and futility. It wasn't long until many of the barracks were emptied. When there were only a few left in one barracks, the inmates were transferred to another. Block 7 was almost empty. This meant that there were fewer mouths to share their rations. Food had become an obsession. I, like the others, was racked with constant hunger pains. A friend, Mr. Cuker, took me into 7 for a bowl of soup, and to my surprise I found only a small skeleton crew. Cuker knew the Blochaelteste. He also knew the Kapo who supervised the work in the kitchen and introduced me to him. One day Cuker told me that if I was willing to take a chance and smuggle some raw potatoes out of the kitchen, the Kapo would look the other way. In exchange they would share the extra food with me in Block 7. I had absolutely nothing to lose. It was death if I didn't get some nourishment or death if I was caught.

Block 7 was a clothing warehouse. It was stocked with piles of beautiful furs and the garments of men and women taken from a recent transport of French Jews. Only the crew of eleven men and the Blochaelteste Jews who guarded the warehouse occupied the building. I put on a short, fur-collared jacket with the red cross on the back. I tore the lining open on one side and picked up a bucket. It was winter already and bitterly cold; heavy snow lay on the ground. Roll call was over, and although I was supposed to be in my own block I was ready to make a try for the potatoes. I walked through the dusk to Block 1, where the supplies and food were stored. The kitchen Kapo looked the other way as I filled the bucket and the torn lining of my jacket with potatoes. Back safely in Block 7, I turned over the bucket of potatoes to the crew and received some of their extra soup and a few of the potatoes for myself. I went back to my own block with my hunger satisfied for the first time and shared with my friends the potatoes hidden in the jacket. It had worked well, so I made a deal with the men in Block 7. I would take a chance and fill the bucket with potatoes for them whenever possible in exchange for a bowl of soup. Also, since they had a fire in their block, I asked for permission to roast some of the potatoes once in a while, and they agreed.

The men in 7 were decent human beings, old-timers mostly, brought from another camp where they had spent the years from 1940. One of them was a young man, Max Weisbrot, whom I came to know quite well. He cooked for the Blochaelteste. There were a few others from his same home town, Litzmannstadt. We got away with the smuggling for quite a while until one evening, on the way to Block 7, I was caught with a full bucket by the Lagerkapo. He was a direct and brutal man who was known to knock prisoners down and beat them across the spine with his cane. It was his specialty to break spines with a few carefully placed blows on the back. When he caught me I felt that it was surely the end. "Where are you going? What do you have in that bucket?" I knew he had already seen what I carried. I said, "It's potatoes for Block 7." I knew he visited Block 7 because I had seen him there twice and thought perhaps he knew the Blochaelteste, a Czech Jew. To my amazement he marched me to 7, and at the door he kicked me, slapped me twice across the face with his hand, and told me to disappear! Had I been bringing the potatoes to another block the game would have ended right there, and the lives of my friends would have been endangered. I found out from Max that the Lagerkapo went to Block 7 several times a week for the potato pancakes Max cooked for the Blochaelteste. He did not want to risk involving himself or lose a supply of food he himself enjoyed illegally.

With the additional food, my strength returned and with it

a clearer mind. Miraculously, the infection in my leg had healed. It had been treated the first days in camp by a daub of black salve administered by the camp "doctor" with a paper bandage and an accompanying blow on the side. Whatever the salve was, and they used it for everything, it had worked. The wound was now just a numb hole in my thigh. I began to be concerned about my few remaining friends. One of the Chaba brothers was gone, and the two Golds had begun to fail rapidly. I shared everything I had with them. And I began to spend more and more time with the men in Block 7, determined to use my contacts to the limit to get food for them and for myself. My friends had sustained me during the first days when my strength had weakened. It was now my turn to try to keep up theirs. I was deeply indebted to Cuker and the Blochaelteste. They continued to share their surplus food with me, even meat occasionally, and the margarine they had traded for cigarettes with the other Lagers.

The men in 7 had worked out a bearable existence for themselves, and as they came to know me better they made me feel part of their group. Life was easier for them because they had no prisoners to supervise until a new transport would arrive. When one finally did arrive, contrary to expectations, it made things better. Supplies increased.

The transport finally brought into Block 7 included Polish non-Jewish political prisoners who had been taken as hostages by the Germans now that the war was turning ever more rapidly against them. There were cabinet ministers, government officials, and other prominent Poles as well as Jews from France. They were to be interned to quell any uprisings. They wore fine clothing and were allowed to keep their luggage. Only five men were assigned to a bunk, and only the SS were allowed to administer punishment. No Haeftlinge could touch them. Only the Poles stood roll call and then only once a day, and they were allowed to receive packages of food and supplies once a month, up to ten kilograms. The packages were filled with delicacies, tinned margarine, even cake, and because they had plenty of food they shared it with us. Block 7 became a privileged and unusual barracks. One of the highly placed officials, a general, who befriended me was a relative of the French Premier, Léon Blum. Surrounded by such advantages, I became very active in 7, spending every spare minute with them, though they no longer needed the potatoes I had previously been bringing them.

In their new circumstances they tried to secure more luxuries for the Blochaelteste, whom we genuinely respected and liked. He was a remarkable man, still decent and human. Months later he was to display the only expression of humanity that broke through the defense I had built up against feeling anything but contempt for the Haeftlinge who administered the camp under the SS. Several days after a selection in Block 7, the men locked up in Block 4 were taken away on the trucks. To our amazement two men came back from the gas chamber. A last-minute order had come through that if any of the men had Aryan wives, they would be withheld from the ovens and kept as prisoners only. Those two had had the good fortune to have Aryan wives, so they were permitted to live, where hundreds of others died. The Blochaelteste went wild when they returned because of the criminal unfairness of this new rule; it was more than he could stomach, and he began to beat the two men unmercifully, as though they were to blame. We grabbed him and finally restrained him until he calmed down. It was not an act of brutality on his part but rather the instinctive reaction of a still decent human being, overwhelmed by senseless injustice he could no longer endure.

Any surplus food and margarine the men in 7 could not use was set aside for trade with other compounds. Since I was obligated for all they were doing for me and through me for my remaining friends in Block 13, I volunteered to go to the fence and try to trade for cigarettes with the Haeftlinge of Lager D. Lager D was the work camp. The Haeftlinge marched out every morning accompanied by music, in an almost comical procession, to work in the world outside. There they came into contact with civilians who sold them cigarettes. I went to the electrified fence and stood there at the already traditional trading place, careful to stay far enough back so that I could not be seen from the watchtowers. Eventually someone from D came over, and after we had made a deal I tossed across my package and received back a few cigarettes.

This went on for several days until I was finally caught, not by the SS but by my own people. As I walked back to Block 7 along the backs of the barracks, I passed Block 13, where the Schreiber and the new Blochaelteste who had replaced Mietech were waiting for me. They must have observed my previous trips and already knew what I was doing and for whom I was doing it, or else they would not have given me a chance to explain. They dragged me into 13 and asked what I had on me. They found the cigarettes and began beating me. "You must have money," they said. "Hand it over." But I denied it. Over and over I told them, "I don't have any money." When they finally left me lying there, I got up and ran to Block 7, still bleeding. The Blochaelteste in 7 asked me what happened. When he heard the story he said nothing, but he must have taken his revenge because he later got the cigarettes back. He also promised that he would do everything he could to get me transferred into Block 7 permanently, for my safety, and he did. I never questioned how he managed it.

I continued to bring food from 7 to 13, keeping a supply under Blum's pallet on his bunk. The high French officials, approximately twenty or thirty men, mostly Jews, some generals and other military men of rank, were of an age where they would have been sent directly to the ovens had an exception not been made. The Germans were only concerned that the world would demand an accounting of their disappearance and hoped besides to control the partisans by keeping them as hostages. During the same period a few gypsies brought into 7 were quickly taken on selections and were soon gone.

Of the almost four thousand who had come in the same transport with us, at least half were dead, some from starvation, some from beatings and the rest taken to the gas chambers. Our numbers grew smaller every day. There were rumors of escapes, usually ending in death. One was a

Blochaelteste from Block 11 who had tried to make a deal with an SS man who brought supplies into camp. He was a French Jew who had probably accumulated money and other valuables from less fortunate prisoners during his years in camp. Realizing that the end was near for everyone, no matter what their position or power, he was desperate enough to believe an SS man's promise of help. They let him act out his escape one morning with sadistic precision, like cats toying with a mouse. Then at the last moment, when in the insanity of his newfound freedom he must have thought he was going to live, they pounced. They brought his bullet-ridden body to roll call that morning and hung it on a scaffold before us as an object lesson. There it stayed for three days, contributing to the final mental disintegration of many of the borderline prisoners. More of them became walking dead, but I wanted more than ever to live now that I had nourishment.

I prepared myself for more months in the camp, using every means at my disposal to find food for myself and friends. I was determined to live to see justice done when the war ended, as it had to some day. And while I knew that my mother and father were surely dead and that Rochelle, too, was gone, I still had some hope that Sala, David, and Yadja might be alive. As long as I didn't actually know of their deaths, I could go on hoping. The more pain I experienced, the more I wanted to live. I was prepared to die by any method but starvation, so there was no gamble or risk I wouldn't take for soup, bread, or any type of food. I stood to lose nothing I would not lose anyway if I failed to stop the hunger pains.

As the winter of 1944 began the last transports trickled into camp, and we heard that Stalingrad had become the downfall of the German armies in Russia. Although the news should have cheered us, it seemed unlikely that the war would end soon enough to save any of us. Then one evening the SS came to Lager B with our numbers, and for the first time our names were called out, too. Every man who had registered as a carpenter was ordered to report to Lager D for "work." Not only would I be betrayed by my ignorance of the carpentry trade but my instinct warned me that Lager D would be liquidated in a matter of time. Besides, it meant leaving the men in Block 7 and the relative security and nourishment they had shared with me. In another compound there would be no chance to start over. I told myself that if I had to go through the pains of hunger again, I would rather die here in Lager B than give myself up, so I made up my mind that when my number was called I would not answer. I slipped into Block 17 and hid in the toilet. I could hear my name and number blasting out over the loudspeakers. "134138—Schapelski, report to Block 7!" Over and over they screamed it, and I huddled there determined that the only way they would take me would be if they found me and dragged me out. They held the transport for two hours while they searched the camp. Finally they gave up and the transport left without me.

Now I was faced with another task. How was I to get back in? My name and number were listed as a missing prisoner, unaccounted for as dead. I turned to my friends in Block 7, to the Blochaelteste, the Lager Schreiber, the barber, and my friend Max, who had helped me so often before, and to their everlasting credit they performed a miracle for me. Somehow the Schreiber got my name taken off the list, and through his influence and the power of the Blochaelteste from 7 and of Max and my other friends, I was no longer to be searched for. To my knowledge, I was the only one lucky enough to escape like this, and to all of those men I owe a debt. They held my life in their hands and placed their own lives in danger by helping me. There was decency and brotherhood left in the world after all.

As I had feared, many of the men who had been moved to Lager D were soon taken in selections. They had gone there hopefully, remembering an earlier work transport that had left Block 11 in late September and had actually gone to a work camp. Many had tried to join it and failed, including me. So they had gone this time hoping to have the same miracle happen again, but it did not.

As the winter of 1944 progressed it became increasingly

obvious to the Germans that the tide of war had turned irrevocably against them. They had to do more and more to placate the Fuehrer. So one day, without warning, the SS marched into each and every camp, simultaneously, and issued a general call for assembly. When the bell rang we knew it was not a regular roll call. We had just come in from one. No one was excused for any reason, on pain of instant death. Each prisoner had to be accounted for as present or as dead by the Blochaelteste. This was the final clean-up. We stood for hours and hours in lines, chilled by the falling snow that covered the ground and drifted over the tops of the SS cars. Nothing was done until everyone was accounted for. Finally, when they were ready, they took two blocks and sent everyone else back into the barracks. We were herded to one side of the block in Number 7. The few non-Jewish Poles among us were told to get into their bunks. The SS officers then took a position on the other side of the barracks and ordered the rest of us to strip and march across the low divider so as to pass naked before them. The Poles watched with horror as the selection started and progressed. They took nine out of ten of those left this time without regard to who was thinner than another. A few of us were shunted to one side—why I will never know—and Max and I found ourselves crammed into the Blochaelteste's little room. We stayed there for hours, watching furtively while the selection went on and on.

We saw one man try to hide under the lowest row of bunks. An SS guard stepped back and sprayed the area with his machine gun. When they were through they marched those selected into the empty barracks and locked them up.

When at last we were permitted to stumble out of the cramped space we were almost alone. Virtually everyone had been taken and imprisoned for transport to the ovens. The last of my friends who had come with me from home were now gone. I was the only one left. The ultimate had happened.

In that one night thousands were murdered. Only a few escaped. At the final hour of liquidation someone decided they could use a few of the victims for work. They selected a barracks at random and took about sixty men whose qualifications matched the list of jobs they wanted filled, so many printers, so many engravers, or specialists in some field. Everyone tried to volunteer but only a few lucky ones were taken, including the two Hollander boys. Although I did not know where they had disappeared to that night, I later learned that they had been taken outside the gates almost immediately and transported across Poland to a forest somewhere in the heart of Germany where they were put to work in a secret printing plant that was counterfeiting the currency of other countries and other valuable documents. When we learned that these few men had been saved we hoped that in the Germans' desperation for workers we too might find a temporary refuge. The Blochaelteste called us together and advised us that "If they come here and ask for workers of any kind, whatever it is, accept. Go if you can. Get out any way you can. There is no hope here—not for any of us."

Chapter
18

AFTER THIS LAST SELECTION Block 7 was almost empty. Cuker
and I were the only two left from Sosnowiec, and he, Max, and
I were almost alone in the block. The Blochaelteste's warning
words stayed with us, and we determined to try at the very first
chance to join a labor transport. By now the Germans were in
desperate need of labor to work the coal mines and complete the
projects they had begun in the countries they had occupied.
Their own labor force had dwindled as they were forced to send
more and more replacements to the fronts. Labor commissions
began coming into the camp, and the first group they picked
was taken to mine coal. Among those who left were a well-
known cantor and a famous violinist who had been a native of
Auschwitz. The next commission had a much smaller number
from which to choose, so they took nearly all of us, including
Zeppel, the Blochaelteste from Lager B, the Stubendiensteleute
and Kapos, together with the Schreiber and the barber, all now
forced to accompany us.

The SS loaded us onto covered trucks, and we left Birkenau

apprehensive but resigned. Whatever lay ahead could not be any worse than what we were leaving behind. At the end of a few hours' journey the trucks stopped and we clambered out. We were in Gintergruber in Upper Silesia, assigned to be the first inmates of a small, brand-new camp. Although we arrived at night, we were fed and given a blanket apiece. The barracks were well constructed, and each man had a bunk space sectioned off from the next. For the first time in many months I could turn at night without forcing the men on either side to roll with me.

We lay quietly in the dark that first night, waiting for something to disrupt the quiet, but no boots pounded into the rooms and no tortured screams came from outside as they had that first night in Birkenau. The night passed silently and uneventfully. In the morning we stood roll call and were assigned work in the camp. Max, Cuker, and I were selected as carpenters and taken to a small workroom next to the camp kitchen. I was still classified under the occupation of carpenter, although I could scarcely hit a nail on the head, but Cuker was an expert and with his guidance Max and I helped repair gates and other parts of the camp and put up shelves and cabinets. The Kapo assigned to supervise us, a short, nervous German with the green insignia of a criminal, yelled at us constantly. He was determined to make life as miserable as he could, but even with his ravings conditions in Gintergruber were immeasurably better than we had known before.

Blocks 1, 2, and 3 were set up with a Blochaelteste and a Stubendienst from Birkenau in each one. Max, Cuker, and I were assigned to Block 1, where Zeppel was again in charge. The tactics of the SS guards and their dogs were the same, but we experienced no violence or abuse in the first few days to compare with the recent past, and we were fed a digestible and fairly nourishing soup and a bread ration almost double that of Auschwitz. Several days after we arrived two work groups were formed, No. 1 and No. 2, under the supervision of the SS. The Germans planned to mine the coal, plentiful in this part of Poland, and to construct a huge complex of factories to convert it into by-products and synthetics they desperately needed. The men assigned to Group 1 were put to work alongside civilian workmen constucting the tremendous factory and refining plants. Group 2 began the job of building a completely new camp to house the permanent slave labor that would be needed to run them. Once the factory was finished, it seemed they planned at least to keep us alive.

The scope of the industrial complex was so vast that it was planned to run freight trains right through the finished factories once they were in production. Our carpentry crew, with the addition of a young man from Max's home town, continued to work within the camp for a few days. The others who went outside returned at night to report that they were not badly treated by the SS and though the work was hard there was little beating or abuse. Finally, it seemed they really needed us for work. When they came back in the evening, each group described the work they were doing. Group 1 was working on the construction of a twenty-story concrete refinery tower, unloading sacks of gravel and cement. Group 2 was hauling bricks from the loading dock at the rail line to the site of the new camp about a kilometer away.

After a few more days in camp Max and I were assigned to outside work. I went with Group 2 and Max went with 1. Some of the men dug foundations for the new camp, while others hauled the loads of brick in coal cars. The tracks ran uphill and downhill, so that we had to push them up grades and then race after until they rolled to a stop and had to be pushed on up again. A corps of German civil engineers and foremen had been left behind to supervise the construction. Some of the key mechanics were German civilians, most of them middle-aged and older men from Upper Silesia who spoke both Polish and German. When we left the camp in the morning after roll call they counted us, and when we reassembled in the evening they counted us again. The same number that left in the morning had to be accounted for at night, alive or dead, but accounted for. We had SS guards armed with machine guns and with vicious dogs at their heels all day long to make sure.

One evening at the end of the first count there was one man missing. They counted again and then again—still one missing. The list was brought out, and they began to call our numbers and check us off. Our friend the Schreiber from Block 7 in Birkenau was the missing man. None of us had seen him since morning. The SS was in an uproar; it was impossible for anyone to slip away unnoticed. They kept us bunched together and brought out more SS to search the fields and the areas where we had been hauling bricks. After several hours, when it was too dark to continue, they marched us back to camp. There we were kept in the yard while they sent for a special detachment of SS with bloodhounds to surround the entire area and continue the manhunt. The SS Sturmbahnfuehrer, an infamous brute from Birkenau, came out himself to supervise.

We remained standing for hours without food, unable to return to our barracks. We were questioned time and time again, especially those of us who had been working near the missing man. Finally it was announced that they had caught him and killed him on the spot and that we would all be punished because someone must have seen him try to run away and had not turned him in. They let us return to our rooms, and although we had been threatened with the loss of our evening rations, we were fed. In the morning we realized they must have been lying, for we were kept in camp that day and for the rest of the week. We gloated quietly over their hysterical attempt to deceive us, knowing they would have put us back to work immediately if he were dead.

On the following Sunday afternoon Group 2 was ordered out to roll call. We stood for hours. Finally the SS Lagerfuehrer came out of the offices, accompanied by the Sturmbahnfuehrer and a group of his officer cronies. This monster mounted a platform and delivered a cold-blooded and brutal edict. We were told that although they had caught the Schreiber and shot him, they would have to make an example of us since no one would admit to having knowledge of the disappearance and no report had been volunteered by any of us. There were some two hundred of us lined up four deep.

They counted down the front line, and every fifth man was taken until they had ten lined up before us. I was in the front row, and once again fate guided the counting finger past me. We were forced to stand there and watch while they executed our friends and by so doing closed the case of the missing man in the only way they could. We knew definitely that they had lied. If they had had his body, they would have displayed it for us all to see as a warning to any other would-be escapees. I can still see in my mind's eye the SS in their long raincoats making the count—one, two, three, four, step forward—and hear the shots ring out again and again and again.

On Monday we returned to work but under tighter SS control. Until then there had merely been a cordon of SS around the perimeter of our work area. Now the guards stood among us and work was immediately begun to construct watchtowers in the fields so that they could post machine guns and sentries to scan the entire site. They realized they now had reason to fear us. Most of us were young men whose health had rapidly improved under the conditions of Gintergruber, and we outnumbered them.

The escape was our main topic of conversation for a long time, and we speculated on how it had been managed. Had he contacted the partisans or had an SS guard been bribed somehow to look the other way? Where had he found refuge? His freedom had been bought at a terrible price. Would he survive the war? I found out years later that he did.

New transports of men came into Gintergruber. Hungarians caught up in the last Hungarian *Judenrein* had been taken to Auschwitz, and those not immediately selected for extermination had been shipped directly to Gintergruber. They plagued us with the same questions we too had asked in the beginning. What happened to the others kept at Auschwitz? We had the sad task of informing them. Their ignorance of the truth bore out our belief that as yet no one had succeeded in convincing a skeptical world of what was going on. The camp became a little more crowded, but conditions continued to be bearable. Soon more men came—Dutch from the last clean-up in Holland. All these new arrivals were in small groups, the very last ones left in whatever area they came from. The Nazis were careful now about burning the young ones; they needed us.

A third work group was formed to work in the coal mines, which were operated on two shifts from early morning to midnight. Civilians supervised the technical part of the operation. The work was much harder than for Groups 1 and 2 because the men worked in darkness with water up to their knees most of the time. But they received special rations of better food to keep up their strength, and while the rest of us received clean clothing once a week, they were given a change of uniform more frequently. The new camp boasted showers with hot and cold water, and the miners were compelled to bathe when they returned from work each day, an unbelievably luxurious discipline.

Now that they needed our labor they actually cared about our state of health. We had a small hospital in the camp staffed by two Czechs, both doctors brought from other camps, and a small infirmary to dispense medication. And as the new camp was completed we moved into new quarters. The conditions became even more livable than before and the death rate even lower. At least whatever deaths occurred did not result from beatings or torture.

I continued working in Group 2 until one day while pushing the coal car up the grades and jumping on the front to ride it to the bottom, I saw too late that the brick-laden car was going to collide with another one stopped on the track ahead. Thoughtlessly, I assumed that the coupling connections on the cars would protrude enough to take the impact, and I held my leg out to brace against the shock. The cars struck almost flush again each other and my trapped foot was crushed. The SS ordered two Haeftlinge to help me to the equipment warehouse. I tore off a piece of my shirt to stop the gushing blood and bandaged the wound as best I could. I had to sit there until the end of the work day, and then, helped by two friends, I limped back to camp and to the hospital. The doctors cleaned the wound and bandaged it. It was severe enough for them to allow me three days off work to recuperate. But wounded or not, no one could be in camp without working, so I limped around doing odd jobs, cleaning the barracks, helping clean the SS quarters, along with other men who had similar temporary injuries. In the back of my mind for some time had been the desire to get transferred to Group 1, because the men there had contact with people from the outside. But for the time being I could do nothing about it. With the three days of my recuperation period over, I was sent back to work. Since my foot was still quite painful, I was assigned other work. I couldn't have gone back to hauling the bricks.

Morale was surprisingly high in the camp as the improved nourishment and sanitary living conditions brought us back to an almost normal state of health, but we could not delude ourselves that even in defeat the Germans would let us survive. We talked of escape and of the Schreiber's miraculous disappearance and waited to see what would happen next.

One morning I awakened feeling feverish and ill. I considered going to the infirmary after roll call but decided I had only a cold. At work I began alternately to shiver and flush with recurring waves of fever. By the end of the day I could barely stand. Dimly I realized that I must be seriously ill, although I had experienced little actual illness in my life. I had made a terrible mistake in not going directly to the hospital and asking for treatment. Now it was too late. When my friends saw how weak I had become, they put me in a hole we had dug to shield ourselves from the wind. Fortunately, the Kapo was a man from Bedzin, an illiterate bull of a man who had made a living in the marketplace by lifting and carrying heavy crates and boxes of produce at the unloading docks. His physical appearance spelled out killer, but despite the insults he continually screamed at us his heart was even bigger than his muscled frame. He never struck out at any of us. He was a simple man, ashamed of his lack of education. When he had to make his morning report and forgot the count his Schreiber had given him, he would scream, "I have sixteen clerks and I still don't know the number." He and the Schreiber saw my condition and let me stay there. When we returned to camp I could not eat my rations but went straight to the hospital. While I stood in line with the thermometer under my arm, as was the custom, the young man next to me glanced at the reading and remarked how terribly high the mercury had risen. When the doctor checked it he too was obviously shocked, although he would not tell me what it showed. He sent me immediately to the infirmary, afraid whatever I had might be contagious. I crawled between the sheets on the bunk and within minutes I was delirious.

The hospital was only a larger room in back of the infirmary. It had a double layer of bunks filled with patients. Since there were no selections for the gas chambers and ovens from the roll calls, the hospital was the only place in Gintergruber that received the attention of Mengele and his fellow physicians from Auschwitz. Everyone knew by the end of the first few weeks in camp that Mengele came with his associates every Tuesday to inspect the patients in the hospital. Any sick man unfortunate enough to be still lying in a bunk one week later became an immediate candidate for the gas chamber. Many a pitiful, helpless patient had been taken naked, wrapped only in a blanket, placed on a stretcher and loaded into the infamous black van. That was the end for them.

I lay there for days shivering with cold and burning with fever, unable to eat my bread. I gave it to the two orderlies and to Cuker when he and Max came to see me. Tuesday came, and I looked up to see Dr. Mengele and one of the Czech doctors standing over me, discussing my case. The doctor told him about the abnormally high fever I had been running for an unusually long period and how baffled he was by the cause or nature of the illness. Mengele, intrigued by the uniqueness of the case, asked to be kept personally informed of my progress; he wanted to know from a medical point of view the reason for the fever. They ordered the seven or eight patients who had been there since the previous Tuesday taken out to be killed and then left.

In the days that followed Max and Cuker begged the doctors

to hide me or get me out of the hospital before Mengele's next visit, but the doctors didn't dare now that he had taken an interest in my case. Another Tuesday came, and Mengele again made his appearance. When he found I was still there and still running fever, he discussed my case again with the doctor and lifted the sheet to examine me himself. Obviously still intrigued, he left instructions with the doctor to keep my case history for him. I would last another week! This time they emptied the hospital of everyone other than me. They had all been there a week. I was alone. After the loaded black van left, the Czech doctor told me that I was incredibly lucky, but he didn't know how long Mengele's curiosity would last. I could not eat any of the food they brought me, although my body screamed for some kind of nourishment. Each time my food rations accumulated in the locker, I asked Cuker to take them and share them with our friends. The only treatment I received was to be encased in icy wet sheets three times a day by the orderlies. Still the fever did not drop. Occasionally, I took a sip of water from the bucket in which they soaked the sheets. I could see the end approaching. Either I would die before the next Tuesday from fever, or Tuesday would bring the black van and the gas chamber at the end of the ride.

After Mengele had come and gone for the third time, still leaving me behind, I knew I dared not take the risk of being there another Tuesday. The only hope I had was for the fever to drop and to get released before that day. Next time they came to take my temperature, I waited until they had left the room, then took the thermometer from under my arm and placed it on my bare chest until just before they returned to read it. Each day I did this for longer and longer periods, and although the instrument still registered a fever, it was far from the abnormally high degree previously shown. By Tuesday the temperature appeared to have dropped considerably. Mengele arrived. The Czech doctor told him that he thought they were at last getting through to finding the cause of the original fever and that I was improving. I was again spared, but it was time to make a move. On the following Sunday Cuker and Max finally prevailed on the doctors to discharge me. They let me leave, very weak and still very sick. The doctor instructed me to tell the Lagerschreiber that he was sending me to rest in the barracks. This only served to confuse the Kapo. To his knowledge few had ever survived a full week in the hospital and fewer still had ever been assigned a recovery period. So he sent me out to work, and I had no choice; it was either work or back to Mengele. I returned to Group 2 and was handed a pick. It was dead winter of 1944, and the ground was frozen hard. I was to use the pick to break up the frozen soil. I was too weak to lift the pick head from the ground much less pierce the crust of ice. The Kapo and my friends helped me again and saw that I did as little work as possible. On our return to the camp I reported back to the doctor, and this time he gave me a note to the Kapo and Lageraelteste insisting that I be allowed to rest for a few days. They allowed me four.

During this time I got more friendly with the Blochaelteste and asked Max and Cuker to help me get transferred to Group 1. They convinced the Blochaelteste that I was a carpenter and would be much more useful at the factory site than doing simple labor. I started working on Group 1 loading sacks of cement and carrying them from the train platform to the warehouse. When the pains of illness gave way to hunger pains I knew I was getting better. My appetite returned tenfold, and the usual ration of bread and soup could not satisfy me. Though I was still very weak, I went to the Blochaelteste and asked him if I could do some extra work to earn more food. He was taken aback but agreed to let me take on additional chores. I rose early, long before the others, to wash floors in the rooms before we left for work and when we returned at night I helped distribute the bread ration. I was allotted more soup and bread and by working in "bread supply" was even able to get a little extra. Gradually, my hunger was appeased and my health returned.

I continued toting the cement sacks for weeks. It was very hard work, but as my health improved I did not mind it. Then there was finally an opening as a carpenter with a group of men

146

building concrete forms story by story in the twenty-story tower, and I was reassigned. Each day we removed the forms from the cast and reassembled them on the next floor for the concrete to be poured. The foreman of our five-man crew was a Volksdeutsche. For the first time in many months I had contact with someone not a prisoner and not a Nazi. He seemed friendly. We conversed easily in Polish and German, and he occasionally brought an extra piece of bread and a cigarette or two for me. If the SS guards were not watching too closely, he showed little concern about how hard we worked. He lived in the workers' quarters in Glywitz and went home on weekends. He was a source of news about the war and the world outside, and every day I became more convinced of his sincere and decent attitude toward us. Taking a calculated risk, I approached him in confidence one day at the job. "I want to ask you a question," I whispered as we pretended to work. "If I make you a rich man, will you bring food to us? I promise you will be able to afford to buy the food and still have a substantial amount for yourself and your family. Are you interested?"

He looked at me suspiciously for a moment and then answered, "Yes. What do I have to do?"

Having every reason to believe that I was the last one left alive of our original group in Schrodula, I told him about the house and described the location of one of the smaller boxes we had buried, containing, as I remembered, a bar of gold and some other valuables. "I will give you the address of the house if you will promise to bring back food every time you return from your weekend at home," I told him. "You may use the rest of whatever you find for yourself; that's all I ask in return. I assume there is somebody living in the house now, so you will probably have to share with them."

"All right," he agreed, "I'll do it. Give me the address and tell me what you want me to bring." "Some fresh bread and some meat or salami, if possible, something substantial. And, yes, some cigarettes, too." I wanted cigarettes for the Blochaelteste.

"You know from what I have done for you and your friends up to now that you can trust me," he said. "I will go this weekend." I had no reason to distrust him. He had already shown generosity with no prospect of reward. I told only Max about it, and we waited out one of the longest weekends I had known. He could dig up the box, keep the money for himself and bring nothing back and there would be nothing I could do about it. And maybe the taste he would get of the fortune we had left behind would lead him to look for more. I had no other choice but to trust him. The food we might get was far more valuable to me and my friends than what lay buried in Schrodula.

Monday morning I went to work and saw him there. The first thing I said to him was "Were you there?"

He answered, "Yes."

I asked, "Was everything all right?"

He said "yes" again. "I had to share quite a bit with the people, but I kept my bargain."

My curiosity drove me to ask him, "Did you try to dig any place else?"

He evaded my question and did not answer. He told me he had come to work early and had hidden a package in the lumber below. "Go down," he told me, "and see."

I went to the hiding place and found a package stuffed with surprises—bread, salami, butter, and cigarettes. I shared the food with five or six friends and took what was left back to camp hidden in my clothing, including the cigarettes for the Blochaelteste. My judgment of the Volksdeutsche had been right. He could have told the SS I tried to bribe him, and I would have been dead in an instant. But he kept his promise. Almost every day he brought a package that supplemented our diet tremendously, and my strength surged back. He told me that Schrodula had been reoccupied by the former residents and that Sosnowiec, as I well knew, was completely *Judenrein*. Zaglebie was as empty of Jews as Sosnowiec except for those hidden here or there. No one but Max knew my source of supply, but with these riches to share, my friends, Cuker, Max, and I became even closer, and I was pleased I could help them in return for all they had done for me. Max especially gained favor with the Blochaelteste, which made life easier for Max, which in turn made life easier for all of us.

My new friend brought us the news of Stalingrad and the pressure the Russians were putting on the Allies to open a second front. He admitted there was considerable talk among the Germans that they were losing the war. But he did pass along a rumor that was being circulated among the high-ranking officers about a secret weapon Hitler was getting ready to unleash—not the V-2 rockets which were already being used against England. I questioned him about it as closely as I could, but it was obvious he knew only what he had heard. We had constant, daily discussions about the latest news, and he brought packages regularly every few days after each trip home. Life had become so bearable that we started to hear some of the men actually singing at night, together and alone. Hunger pains were forgotten for a while.

Still more people were brought in, mostly from Hungary, and added to Group 3. About the same time the Lageraelteste was replaced. His successor was new to Gintergruber and took us by surprise. He was a German political prisoner wearing a red insignia. This had been unheard of in Birkenau and here. We could not figure out how he had gained such an important position when his very reason for being imprisoned had to have been his opposition to the Nazis. We could only conclude that the Germans, now facing an almost certain defeat, were trying too late to conceal their guilt by elevating men with humane qualities regardless of their background. The new Lageraelteste was a man in his early forties with a quiet strength about him. He first appeared at roll call one evening, on our return from work, and introduced himself to us. He issued his orders and regulations without obscenity or abuse and in a tone of voice we had been unaccustomed to hearing from those in power over us. He placed great emphasis on the cleanliness and orderliness of the rooms. The beds were to be kept made and we were to keep ourselves and our quarters clean. He made the Stubendienste personally responsible for any lapses. An immediate change was felt throughout the camp, reflecting his apparent concern for our welfare. He checked into the food situation and issued orders that the soup should be made as palatable and nourishing as possible and that the kitchen facilities were to be kept clean. He looked into our clothing supply to see that everyone had decent, warm clothing and adequate shoes. The roll calls no longer took one or two hours. As soon as the count was completed, we were released. And he made it clear to the Kapos and Blochaelteste that he would tolerate no brutality or beatings. He really took control over us, and the atmosphere in the camp improved from what we had already considered to be fairly good to even better. He soon gathered around him a group of decent men like the Schreiber, the man from Bedzin, the two Czech doctors and a few others to be the Haeftlinge leaders of the camp. Under his authority they quietly worked out how best they could watch over us and still keep an eye out for trouble. The German Kapo was finally brought under control, and in doing so the Lageraelteste probably saved many of us from death at the Kapo's hands.

When we left for work in the morning we each received a dipper of ersatz "coffee" and on alternate days a portion of hot, thinly sweetened farina. Then at the job at noontime we received our soup ration, which was edible and had some degree of real nourishment. We needed something substantial to sustain us for the hard work we did. Each day the Kapo selected ten men to return to the camp kitchen and get the soup ration for our crew. He appointed me the group leader. I had to report in at the gate, stating who we were, go to the kitchen and announce how many men were working (for instance, three hundred), and wait there until the soup pots were filled. Then the ten of us would balance the heavy soup pots on long poles and carry them back to the job site for distribution, checking out again at the camp gate on our way. For most of the men who had no access to outside sources of supply, this noonday soup was their major nourishment. They lined up holding their tin dishes they carried to work while the head Kapo played God. A decent human being would have seen to it that those most in need would come first in line; instead he took care of his friends first, already privileged men, and if by chance there was any soup left over he and his favorites ate that, too. But the cruelest thing he did was not to stir the soup in serving it to the Haeftlinge. He would deliberately let the nutrients settle to the bottom and skim the clear liquid off the top. When his own turn came, all the ingredients and solids lay at the bottom of the pot.

This had gone on from the first day I joined the group and continued long after the new Lageraelteste took over. One day in camp the Lageraelteste sent for me. I had never had any direct contact with him before and I was puzzled. "I know you come into camp most of the time to pick up the soup for your group. As of tomorrow I want you to distribute the soup as well. Do it alone if you can, and, if not, use your own judgment about picking helpers. And if there is anything left after everyone has had a fair share, I leave it to your judgment also to decide to whom it should be given." I was moved by his concern and knew that he understood only too well the tricks the Kapos played in buying favors with extra portions. He went on to reassure me, "I will instruct the Kapo that he is not to touch the food, and if you have any problems come directly to me." I promised to do my best to see that everyone would get a fair share.

The next day I stood at the pot while the men formed the line. I sent those I knew had outside sources of food to the end of the line because if we ran short, as sometimes happened, they would suffer the least. I gave the Kapo his double portion in his special bowl first, because I did not want him on my back. And after that I stirred the soup; every four dippers I pumped the ladle up and down to keep the mixture as rich as possible. I also sent the men who went to the kitchen with me to the end of the line, because while in camp they always managed to find extra food for themselves. In the kitchen I argued with the cook foreman to get as big a portion as I could. If we were entitled to four and a half pots, I yelled at him that I needed five. And on the outside when *repeta* (second helpings) were possible, I fought to keep those who did not need them from getting any.

I was determined to follow the Lageraelteste's wishes to the letter whatever they involved. During all this time, for some strange reason that we were never able to understand, they weighed us every week in the camp. Perhaps it was their way of deciding whether or not we were still fit for work.

In the evenings I still helped Max distribute the bread. On alternate evenings we got either an entire small loaf or half a larger loaf. Sanitation was good, and there was little disease because of the shower facilities. Because the camp was so clean, we joked among ourselves that if a louse was found in the camp, the finder would get extra bread. However, despite the improved conditions, thoughts of escape still went through our minds. There was always the fear that in the actual moment of defeat the Germans would have us killed rather than leave us to expose them to the world.

As the weather grew colder we were issued heavier clothes and more blankets. The specialists in the camp received tickets for extra food. Living conditions continued at an acceptable standard, but a gradual change in behavior had started to come over the Lageraelteste. He became very nervous and occasionally struck out at us, although his blows were not directed to any vital area. He came into our room one morning and found fault with the way a few of the beds were made up. To our surprise he started to beat the men responsible. It was a great shock because the change was so radical. He seemed to have lost his confidence in the inevitable end of the war and with it his patience. The pressures under which he functioned had become too much for him, and he continued to change, never approaching the deliberate viciousness of the others, but any cruelty at his hand was twice as disturbing because it was so totally unexpected.

The ground froze solid under the heavy snow. We began to hear planes in the night and even the very low sound of heavy guns in the distance. We knew from our outside contacts that the Russians were well inside Poland and still driving westward. The Allies had opened a second front by landing in Normandy, but despite the pressure on both fronts the Germans still talked about the miracle weapon which would turn the tide for them. The gunfire became more frequent and louder. The SS stopped taking us out to work in fog or heavy snowstorms or at night. We noticed an air of confusion and nervousness among them. Then, even when the weather was good they still kept us in camp. The civilians we saw occasionally told us there was talk of an evacuation to the west. But nobody could tell us of our proposed fate. Would they evacuate us along with their own troops or would we be left to be liberated by the Russians? Or were they planning to kill us all before they left?

The guards were strengthened with more SS. Then late one night the bell rang unexpectedly, and we were all assembled. The sound of shooting had come much closer. The Lagerfuhrer mounted his platform, and when he was satisfied that everyone was accounted for he made his announcement. "We are evacuating Gintergruber tonight. You have two hours to propare yourselves for a march. Take a blanket and whatever else you can carry. If you line up at the kitchen, a food ration will be given you. But remember, you must be back at roll call in two hours."

Chaos broke loose, and everyone who was able to move ran around the camp. We broke into the warehouse where the SS stored its own supplies and grabbed whatever we could. The line at the kitchen was a failure before it began. Max and I stuffed whatever we could into our clothing and grabbed a blanket we took turns carrying. We managed to get some tobacco, a piece of salami and a little margarine, and any extra piece of clothing we found we pulled on top of what we already wore. Luckily, I had good shoes. The two hours passed in complete panic until we were lined up again and marched out. Cuker, Max, Weinstock (a man with the same name as the friend I had lost in Auschwitz), and I managed to stay together.

The SS told us we were going to Glywitz, where we would be transferred to another camp in the west. We walked through snow and ice, through daylight and darkness, hour after hour without stopping, always west, away from the oncoming Russian troops whose guns we had heard before we left camp. When the guards said "Rest" or "Lie down," we dropped wherever we stopped, in the snow or, if we were lucky, in barns, where we took temporary refuge. The sound of the guns followed us. As we marched, the old viciousness returned. They wouldn't need us any longer for work, so the beatings and wanton shooting started again. They shot out of their own fear and nervousness, for any excuse, real or imagined, and for no excuse at all. Our line of march was marked by bodies left behind us in the snow. After a time I could no longer remember how long we had been marching. Finally we reached the station at Glywitz, where columns from other camps converged with ours at the depot. They packed us into the station, thousands and thousands, so that the different columns intermingled, losing their identity. Guards encircled the station on the outside, but we were free to walk around and talk to one another inside. Columns continued to arrive until men lay on the snow outside the depot.

Then the trains were ready to load. We four had managed to stay together, and as they herded us toward the open cattle cars it became obvious that the trains could take only a small part of this huge throng. As I stood waiting to board I heard an SS officer say to the Obersturmbahnfuehrer, "We'll never be able to get them all into these cars."

He answered, "I think more can be taken on board if they are laid out flat." His men understood and immediately began to strafe those already inside the cattle cars with their machine guns. As each layer of dead fell to the floor, more men were forced on board and shot on top of them. Only when the top layer stood on hundreds of dead and dying bodies did the strafing stop. They could have made the men lie down without killing them, but it would not have offered them the same sadistic pleasure. After the shooting stopped, instead of moving the trains out, they suddenly unloaded the live ones again and marched us frantically out of the station and back on the road. Either they had never had any real intention of transporting us or they discovered the rails were so badly bombed that the trains would not have gotten very far. They were very frightened by now and drove us relentlessly. Our numbers diminished as they continued shooting without provocation, leaving more and more dead by the roadside every day. We were demented men, including the SS guards and officers, the Haeftlinge and the Kapos. We had had no food for days, and no water. Every second or third day if we happened to pass by a town or city and if the SS could find some spare bread somewhere, they threw it to us as if we were animals. At every opportunity men ran away. One night we stayed in a brick factory, and some of the men hid themselves in the stacks of bricks before we left. Whenever we spent the night in a barn, a few of the men usually burrowed into the straw, and if they lived through the SS's machine-gunning of the hay and straw the next morning, then they survived the march.

My good friend Cuker disappeared on the march from Glywitz. We were stumbling through deep snow with a dark forest on either side when a burst of gunfire came from behind us and someone whispered, "It's the partisans." A few of the deluded Haeftlinge began to run toward the woods. Cuker was among them. The SS, looking like creatures from another world in their winter snow gear of dead white, simply lifted their machine guns and sprayed the snow until all the dark, moving figures lay still. Later, we realized the SS must have started the rumor themselves to get some of us to run so they would have an excuse to shoot.

Another time a young boy in our line saw some acorns on the ground. Starved, he bent over to pick them up. An SS guard swathed in his white snow garb raised his machine gun and sprayed him with bullets. On the other side of the road two German women walking by spat at the guard. He cursed at them, "If you don't get away immediately, you'll get what he got." He lifted his gun menacingly. The women screamed back insults: "You cursed dog; you murderer!" He lifted his gun again but did not shoot. It was the first time I saw a German show any feeling toward us or defy an SS man.

One night they took us into the bombed-out basement of

Schloss Frankenstein, an ancient castle. It was a huge cavern filled with water, and some of the Kapos built a fire for a little warmth. The smoke filled the basement. Another boy and I wedged ourselves near a slit window for air and were almost frozen in that position when morning came. I could hardly straighten up or walk. Half the men were dead from asphyxiation, and we had to step across their bodies to get out.

Every foot of the way was excruciatingly painful to me. I was starved, thirsty, and numb with cold. We came to another camp—Reichenbach. They marched us into a section of the camp that had been evacuated and left us there fenced in with barbed wire to keep us away from the regular prisoners. I had lost count of how long we had been walking and how far we had come. Out of several thousands who had begun the march only a few hundred were left. The others lay behind us, at Glywitz, and strewn along the roads. We began to talk to the other prisoners through the barbed wire that separated our barracks. One of the men asked my name and where I was from. "Schapelski," I said, "from Sosnowiec in Oberschlesien." I could not believe my ears when he yelled back, "There's a Sala Schapelski in the women's camp. Is she related to you?" "Yes, yes," I yelled back. "She's my sister." In the midst of the nightmare I found for the first time that I was no longer alone in the world; two of us had survived. They got word to her somehow, and while I never got to see her, she managed by some miracle to send bread and soup to us every day from her own ration by washing floors and working in the kitchen to get a little extra. We were being given soup only once a day, and very little at that, so what she sent helped to keep me alive.

A day came when the order to march was given again. The prospect of more days and nights of aimless walking, locked in barns at night if we were lucky enough to find one, not knowing how it would all end, was too much to contemplate. After leaving Reichenbach, when darkness came I said to Max and Weinstock, "This is the end for me. The first chance I get I am going to make a run for it." I could bear it no longer; I was desperate. "It's up to you," I told them. "You do whatever you

156

want to do, but the minute it gets dark enough I'm going." I moved to the outside of the column. Max and Weinstock followed. "We're going with you." We were walking through a blacked-out city. Occasionally we could see cars and horses in the dark. Though the SS guards were very close, I made my break. I ran as fast as my worn-out legs could carry me. I heard the sound of running footsteps in the street behind me, but I did not turn around. Every second I expected the crackle of the first shots, but there was only the pounding of my own heart and the sound of my breath whistling in my throat. When the running feet caught up with me, it was Max and Weinstock. We kept going until suddenly our feet flew away from under us in the dark and we fell down an unseen flight of stairs. We had run into the courtyard of an apartment building and had fallen into the basement where the tenants had their food lockers and storage bins. We lay there all night, exhausted and still unnerved by our escape.

When morning came several German women came down to the basement to get supplies from their lockers, and when they found us they were as frightened as we were. We tried to tell them that we were Poles and that we had missed our transport. They seemed sympathetic and told us kindly that we were in Waldenburg. Then some of the men came down. One older man even brought a slice of bread for each of us and something hot to drink. But it wasn't long before we saw a man in the uniform of the Home Guard looking down into the basement, and we were listening to the dread words, "Hands up! Outside, all of you." Three policemen wearing double-billed hats and carrying drawn guns took us to the local police station. As we were marched through the streets we saw civilians running panic-stricken, pushing baby carriages loaded with belongings and children. At the station we were questioned hurriedly. "Where are your papers? Where are you from? How did you get into that basement? If you are really Poles, prove it." It was evident from their confusion that the police were preparing to evacuate. Even while being questioned they were moving papers and everyone seemed on edge. We could not convince them we were Poles. They guessed we had to be from the transport of Jews that had come through the night before. Unable to cope with us in their own panic, they assigned one older policeman to conduct us to the Kriminalpolizei. He took us to the fifth floor of their headquarters and went from officer to officer, trying to get someone to take custody of us. But they were packing, too, throwing documents and records into boxes. The Kriminalpolizei sent us to the Gestapo. We begged the old policeman to let us go. He refused and said he would be shot if we were permitted to escape again. At Gestapo headquarters we were again turned away; they were in the same state of confusion and panic. At last one Gestapo agent told the old man to take us to the concentration camp outside of Waldenburg. And there the SS finally relieved him of his three tired, starved, and hopeless charges. We could have killed the old man easily at any time; he was too advanced in years to have resisted us. But what would have been the use? For myself, I could not go on another step; I only wanted to lie down, even if it meant death. And if we had killed him, perhaps others who had escaped would be punished for it in our stead. We were at the end of our road.

Chapter
19

HAVING SURVIVED AUSCHWITZ–BIRKENAU, Gintergruber and the death marches, it seemed too much to hope that our luck would hold at Waldenburg. When Max and I were marched into the compound with the others we noticed that no air could enter or escape. Since it was a labor camp with no special installations for murder, we could only assume that if the Germans had to dispose of us in a hurry, the barracks could be quickly converted into gas chambers. We immediately inquired if there were any others there from Sosnowiec and found that the Scharnocha brothers, Baruch and Max, Potok and Topol and Victor Weistuch had also made it alive to Waldenburg.

Life was hard in the camp and food scarce, but it was bearable, and as in Gintergruber we could survive from day to day if it got no worse. The Germans needed our labor to construct crude tank barriers in the open fields around the town, though they must have known the stacks of wood they had us construct would splinter like matchsticks under the weight of a tank. We went out in the morning in small groups of four to ten guarded by SS as before, but now the men were noticeably older; the younger men were at the front. We cut logs and piled them across the roads, braced with rocks and stones from the fields.

There were small farms dotted about the countryside, and as I worked I could see the people tending the fields nearby. They didn't look unfriendly or hostile, and since food was uppermost in our minds all the time I took a chance. I asked one of the guards if we could borrow an ax from one of the farmers to help us with our work. He agreed and escorted me to the nearest farmhouse. When the people came to see what we wanted, I asked the farmer for an ax and then led the conversation carefully around to food. The guard knew what I was doing but was only too happy to share what he dared not ask for himself. The food shortage had hit the German military severely, too, but it would have meant harsh punishment for him if he had asked for or taken food and been reported. I went back time after time to the same farmhouse and others in the area, sometimes with the same guard and later with others. We always came away with something. With what food the farmers supplied during the day and what we were later able to steal from the potato bin at night, with the help of a crudely fashioned key, we were able to sustain ourselves.

The SS leader of Waldenburg, SS Fuehrer Schramel, had earned a reputation for sadism unique even in the SS. From the first day in the camp we learned how much he deserved his reputation. One of his favorite methods of amusing himself was to have the guards round us up and force us with jeers and insults to run around the camp, beating those who were too slow and kicking those who fell. For added entertainment, as soon as his guards got us moving he would order us, every few yards or so, to hurl ourselves forward to the ground, then rise and run again. Later, a new assistant from another camp introduced an innovation. We ran as before, but now instead of dropping forward to the ground on order we had to throw ourselves backward. Then with bones cracking and spines numb from impact after impact, we were forced to struggle back to our feet and continue the mad charade—that is, those of us who could still get up. At other times, on some perverted whim, they would order a few Haeftlinge dragged out at night and tied to trees with their arms pulled back and their wrists tied together. In the morning they were cut loose, and those who survived marched straight to work. There were many who did not.

At night we talked about the end of the war and the probability that we would be gassed at the last minute if the Germans had to evacuate their quarters. Schramel would see to it. One day he had us brought out where he could look down on us from his platform. He raised his fist and shook it as he screamed, "Don't think for one moment that Germany will be beaten or that you will leave here alive. Not one of you will live to see us defeated, I promise you." He cursed and threatened, but these were his last ravings in what he must have known at the time were the last minutes of the war for him.

On the morning of May 8, 1945, no guards came to take us to the fields or to count us. We saw a fire near the offiers' quarters, and a surge of excitement went through us. All the Haeftlinge poured into the yard, and we speculated more and more optimistically on what this meant, not daring to believe it. On that day in May, sometime around three o'clock in the afternoon, SS Fuehrer Schramel rode out through the gates of Waldenburg camp, stopped his car while the gates were locked behind him, and, with a last blazing look of hatred, tossed the keys of the camp over the gates and rode away with his SS gang.

We were stunned, frozen momentarily—and then two or three men moved toward the gate incredulously and picked up the keys. One pushed his arm through the bars to the other side, and in a moment the gates parted. We were free, really free! All the guards were gone and we were alone. We stared at one another or into space with unbelieving eyes. Something in which we had long since ceased to believe had finally happened, the miracle of freedom. The months and years of pain and suffering were over. We went wild. Men shrieked and screamed, calling out God's name, sobbing and laughing hysterically at the same time. We grabbed one another and embraced, pressing our gaunt faces together. We were alive and free!

The gates of the camp swung wide, and those of us with enough strength surged forward and passed through. We ran into the streets of the town, deserted now by German civilians, who had not even waited to lock their homes and stores. There was gunfire all around, but it didn't stop us. We had been so close to death so many times before. All I could think of was finding food; nothing else mattered. I found a bakery stripped bare except for a sack of dry bread. With that we started back to the camp. The town was still the scene of active fighting. There were Russian soldiers in the streets, driving the last resisting Germans back to the west. Some of them startled us; they were women in full battle gear. There were bodies of German and Russian soldiers everywhere. Troops loaded on trucks moved into and through Waldenburg, battle-tired, strong-faced Russian men and women—our liberators. We talked to some of the women. "Who are you?" they asked. "Where are you from?" "We're from the camp outside of town, just two miles away." They were very kind and understanding; they made no attempt to stop us from taking supplies and food. We went on our way unmolested while they continued checking the streets and houses for German soldiers. Perhaps the camp uniforms with their stripes gave us some immunity from the bullets that flew all around.

We walked back to the camp, carrying whatever we had found, looking without any special reaction at the bodies of the German soldiers we passed on the way. I felt nothing, no satisfaction, no hatred. Most emotion had long since been drained out of me and the others as well. To survive, we had schooled ourselves not to feel, and for some of us this would be a lesson that would take a lifetime to unlearn.

The camp was in an uproar, wilder than when we had left it. Some had never returned once they got outside the gates. Others were crying, singing and dancing, alone and together, arms around one another, two and three or more. By the time

162

we got back it was the middle of the night, and we could really begin to believe that the gates would indeed stay open; it wasn't a dream. All through that miraculous night we talked and ate. The guards' and officers' quarters were ransacked, and the potato bin in the basement. Everything that was edible, wearable or usable we dragged into the barracks to store against an uncertain tomorrow. Time lost its meaning.

Sometime during the next day or the day after, Russian soldiers came into the camp, and we rushed to greet them. They called out happily to us, and their words started a roar racing through the crowd. "The war is over. The Germans have surrendered!" "Yes, it's true, it's all over. The war is ended!" Jew embraced Jew and Jew embraced Russian; we danced around yelling the words back and forth. For them the fighting was over; for us, the long nightmare had ended. They brought food for us, and we gorged ourselves, unable to stop, as though the craving of years had created an appetite impossible to satisfy. The excitement and frantic activity combined with the excessive eating finally took its toll. Many of the Haeftlinge became desperately ill or went into convulsions, and some who had lived through indescribable suffering and deprivation actually died in the first few days of freedom.

As the camp quieted down in the next two days, the eight of of who had become friends—Rudofsky, Max Weisbrot, Baruch and Max Scharnocha, Potok, Topol, and Victor Weistuch and I—together with a few others, discussed our immediate future. There was unanimous agreement that we should leave the camp as soon as possible and find temporary shelter in the area, some place where we would have access to food and could continue to build up our strength. I suggested the small farm where I had secured the ax, and it was decided that it would be our destination. We left Waldenburg's barbed wire and barracks and the scene of so many horrible memories behind us and moved to the farm. It was deserted but unharmed. And so for the first time in so long we had a decent shelter.

The town was wide open and safe now that the fighting was over. The Russian soldiers took us into deserted houses, opened

163

closets and said, "Go ahead, take whatever you want. Put on the clothes, help yourselves." We needed little encouragement to tear off the demeaning rags of a prisoner and feel like human beings again in trousers and real shoes and boots. Some of the Russians had seen the extermination camps of Maidanek and Auschwitz and expressed compassion and sympathy for what we had experienced. We were grateful to them and felt safe and secure knowing that they were in complete control of the area as the German civilians began to drift back.

Now that we were free the first thought in the minds of all of us was of finding our own people. We were some thirty kilometers from the camp near Reichenbach where I had discovered Sala was still alive. If she had survived these last few months, she might still be there. Three days after liberation, Max Weisbrot and I set out for Reichenbach. We walked for miles and occasionally got a ride from German civilians in horse-drawn wagons. We found the camp still full of excited people tasting the first hours of freedom. Everyone seemed to know everyone else. Almost immediately someone told us Sala was still alive and where in the camp we could find her.

At last Sala and I faced each other across the barracks. We both broke down completely. Someone else in the family was alive; we weren't alone. She had been certain I was dead. News had reached her that the transport from which Max and I had escaped after leaving Reichenbach had been marched to an unfinished tunnel in the mountainside nearby and all the men locked in behind iron doors and left to die. A friend, Silbergold, one of the few who lived to tell the story, later described how the men inside had actually choked each other to death, suffocating in agony in the darkness of the tunnel, as with each breath they drew they exhausted the available air.

She asked me every terrible question I had dreaded. Where was the rest of the family? What had happened to the others? One after the other I had to answer, "I don't know. I don't know, Sala." "No, after you left, after you were taken, we never heard again from David or Yadja. Papa was gone already before you were taken away. Remember, Sala? You know what happened at Wolbrom?" And I had to tell her as briefly as I could that Rochelle and Mother had vanished in the raid on Schrodula.

Before Max and I undertook the trip back to the farm with Sala we had to warn her of a new danger that had suddenly and forcefully made itself known to us on the road, just before entering the camp. Three young Russians in civilian clothes had accosted us. When we stopped, expecting some friendly questions, they gathered around us and demanded, "Take everything out of your pockets and hand it over." "But we are Haeftlinge. We're from the camp at Waldenburg," we explained, thinking they had made some mistake. "Never mind who you are. Just empty your pockets or we'll empty them for you." We had very little—a knife, perhaps, and some cigarettes—but they took everything. Max and I couldn't believe it. Were these the same Russians who had liberated us in Waldenburg? Perhaps they were hoodlums, not regular army. But we had to face facts. If they were robbing former camp inmates, then they would have little respect for women, so we made the trip back to Waldenburg carefully, keeping our distance from anyone who looked unfriendly.

Later, we were to find out that it was unsafe to leave a woman alone with most Russian soldiers, and we saw to it that a woman had a man's protection at all times. Within a short period our liberators were to become more distant and less cooperative and friendly. Very soon we had to be concerned about our position with them and our safety. A marked contrast developed between the treatment we had received from the first troops and the treatment later shown.

Back at the farm, clothed, fed, and sheltered, we began to enjoy the semblance of a home with the care and warmth of Sala and the other women who soon joined us. As the days passed we found more survivors we had known and took them in. Soon we were a family of twelve.

Sala and I spent hours going over the experiences of the past years and weeping together over our lost loved ones. During those days all of us became increasingly preoccupied with thoughts of the ones we could not account for and dared to hope and wanted to believe had survived. I became obsessed with thoughts of my mother, Rochelle, Yadja, David, our many aunts, uncles and cousins, nephews and nieces. Every day we saw joyful reunions or heard stories of family members and friends who had found one another, and in the end I knew I would have to go back to Sosnowiec to search for any possible survivors or I would never rest. The others felt we were all too weak to undertake such a dangerous trip so soon, and Sala agreed. I listened, knowing they were right, but I could wait no longer. "No," I finally told them, "I cannot wait another day. What if someone comes back to Sosnowiec looking for us and leaves never knowing we are alive? We might never find each other again. I'm going now and I'll take my chances."

Perhaps I felt a little stronger than the others; but whatever it was, I knew I had to go, alone if necessary. Baruch came to me as I made my preparations to leave. "You know, Natan, my girlfriend, Regina, is alive." He had heard the wonderful news from someone who had known her in the camps. "Will you look for her in Sosnowiec and, if you find her, bring her back with you?" I promised, of course, to search for her and for all our relatives and friends. I would look for everyone and bring back whomever I found.

The railroad station at Waldenburg was in chaos; there were almost no lines of communication. The rails had been bombed and all traffic confined to one set of tracks the Russians had repaired. The few trains that were operating ran without schedule and with no control of passengers or fares. There were only boxcars and freight cars to ride in. The station was jammed with people of all types: Germans, Russian soldiers, and every nationality of refugee, all trying to get somewhere at the same time. Every face I saw showed the ravages of five years of war. We waited for hours, sleeping in the station, until a train of freight cars came through and I clambered on board, packed in tightly with the others. The train moved slowly across a wasteland. It seemed nothing had been left untouched by the war. Each time it slowed at another station, more people tried to jump on board. Often we waited for hours on sidings to let other trains pass in the opposite direction. It was indescribably depressing. I felt incredibly alone and anxious about the answers I would find at the end of the trip.

Finally, the journey ended. I had returned to Sosnowiec! The impact of my homecoming was shattering. From the railroad station I walked down Mungeyofska about a mile and a half, through streets familiar from my youth, streets where I had seen daily the faces of my playmates, the boys and girls of my neighborhood, the faces of their mothers and fathers, and our family friends, the storekeepers, the students, the young and the old. I saw no one I knew, not one. I felt my heart pound as the realization came over me that I was in a city inhabited by ghosts. When I came to Descartes, where the two synagogues had been, my gorge rose in my throat and I thrust my clenched fists deep into the pockets of my trousers. I turned the corner onto Schklarnastrasse and approached the entrance to the building I had once called home, walking more slowly, waiting to be greeted by someone, anyone. No one, not a voice I knew. I walked into the corridor, but I could not make myself go directly to our old apartment. My feet stopped in front of the caretaker's door and I knocked. She was still there, old Mrs. Budsin. Her face showed her shock and she screamed, "It's you, my God, Natan Schapelski!"

"Where is everybody?" I asked. "Where are all the others?"

"You're the first one to come back, Natan," she said. "So far—only you."

Her words hit me like blows. I stood there leaning against the wall. Her husband come to the door behind her, and his face showed shock and surprise. "Schapelski," he said, "you've come back. I guess you know you are the first one. I'm afraid every apartment here is filled," he continued. "But not one of them by the same family who lived here before, not one. In fact, there is only one Jew living here, a young girl, and she didn't live here before the war. I'm very sorry, Schapelski," he mumbled, "very sorry."

I walked past them through the corridor and stopped. From

the hall I looked through the window into the kitchen of my former home. A Polish family moved around inside the walls that had once held everything I had ever loved. My grief welled up inside me, and I went out into the courtyard and cried uncontrollably. All the emotion I had buried was suddenly released in a torrent of bitter tears. The very courtyard around me was crowded with the memories and sounds of a hundred a thousand nights, when families met to talk and gossip. Where mothers sat cradling sleeping babies in their arms while their men talked of profound and simple things. Where children ran laughing and calling out to one another in a dozen ancient games. Where once a baby cried and someone called a child into the house. They were real. I could see their faces and hear their voices through the tears. Where were they all, these people who had been so close—my people? Where were they all, the girls, the young children, the old people, the babies? Dear God, I began to count them in my head. Regina's family—eight people; Sucha's family; Uncle Chaim; my own family—five missing; Mother's family—aunts, uncles, cousins; the Koplowiches; the Golds; the Kohans; the Chabas; the Weinstocks. I could not stop. Each recollection brought another person to mind and the numbers grew and grew. If any of them were still alive, wouldn't they have come back by now?

Until that moment, alone, in the courtyard of the house on Schklarnastrasse, I still had hope, an impossible dream that there would be some kind of magical reunion, perhaps that the father lost in Wolbrom would be here again or that my sisters and my brother would come home. And the biggest fantasy of all—that my mother, my wonderful mother, would be waiting for our return. Now I had to face reality. Barring miracles, Sala and I would have to carry on the family alone.

I left the courtyard and crossed the street to the house of the Polish woman who had befriended me and helped so much in the past. She was overjoyed to see me and called her family in to welcome me back. But the tears she saw in my eyes overcame her instant joy and she sat and cried with me in my distress. When I had regained control I tried to eat the food she set before me while we talked of the days before the final *Judenrein*. She related how she had been questioned by the Gestapo. Someone had informed on her and accused her of giving food to Jews. She had been severely beaten for one of the few acts of kindness I had experienced from Poles in those dark days. Still undaunted, she had gone to Schrodula to look for me the moment they let people back in after the *Judenrein*, and she told me of the horrible shock she had, walking through the ghetto and finding it completely deserted. There was no end to the despair and tragedy that every memory and each name evoked.

I finally became restless. I wanted to be in the street again, not knowing what I hoped to find. They insisted I come back and stay with them as long as I remained in the city. I promised them I would and went out. It was all too clear now. In those streets which had once been entirely or at least partially occupied by Jewish families, almost none of the thousands had come back. Numbers began mounting again in my mind. If the thirty to forty thousand Jews who had once lived here had disappeared from this one city, then what must have happened all over Europe? The thought was awesome. Then, as I walked down Mungeyofska I saw the first familiar Jewish face. It was a man who had been close to Koplowich and Gold, a neighbor of the Koplowich family. I was shaken just to see him. He called out as we neared each other, "I know you. You are Schapelski. Do you remember me?"

"Yes, I do, yes," I answered. "Tell me, did Gold or Koplowich come back? Have you seen any of them?"

He shook his head sadly. No one had come back, and he had heard nothing about any of them. I told him where I had come from, and he told me how he had been hidden by a Polish family in the city all through the war. "Let me help you, Natan. Why don't you stay at my place? You are welcome to come and live with us and stay as long as you wish. Please say you will," he asked warmly and gently. I thanked him and declined, explaining that I already had living quarters and a place to eat. "Then there is one other thing you must do," he said. "I am the chairman of the Jewish community, and we have a center set up at Mungeyofska Five. You must go there right away and look over all our lists. Almost everybody who has come to the city is registered there. See if you can find anyone from your family or your friends. And you must register yourself and the names of everyone else you know about and leave an address where you can be found, so if others come later they will know where to look for you."

His firm and positive attitude rekindled a spark of hope, and I went straight to the center. There were lists and lists and lists, and I went over each of them with care. Not one familiar name appeared. The center was full of others like myself. It had become the gathering place for refugee Jews. A kitchen had been set up to provide food, and I waited there like the others, hoping someone would walk through the door and back into our lives. Hours passed, and we consumed cup after cup of coffee. A few familiar faces finally appeared—two brothers I had met in Birkenau and some others I had met in other camps—but they were the only ones I recognized.

In my search I had found the name of the girl Baruch had asked me to locate, and her address showed she was living here in Sosnowiec. When I left the center hours later, I went to her apartment and knocked on the door. "Who is it?" a woman's voice inquired through the door.

"You don't know me, Regina. I'm a friend of Baruch Scharnocha's. He's alive and well and asked me to come and talk to you."

"There was a short silence, and then I could hear her say, "Oh, my God." The door opened and two young girls stood white-faced, looking at me. I introduced myself to both of them, and one stepped closer to me and put out her hand. "I'm Regina and very, very happy to see you." She introduced her friend as Yadja Fuchs. "What wonderful news you bring. Please tell me about Baruch. Where is he? Is he all right?" I told them about the small group of survivors on the farm in Waldenburg and how much Baruch would like her to come back with me. She was stunned and thrilled at the prospect of being with him again so soon. "When can we go?" she asked. "Of course, my girlfriend will have to come with us; she's all alone and I won't leave her here."

I advised them that I thought I would be ready to go back in a few days, but I warned them, "You ought to know right now that it's a dangerous trip for anyone, even a man, and twice as dangerous for young women. There are no regular trains; you take whatever comes along, and they often stop for hours along the way. It means sleeping in open box cars crammed with people. It might not be too dangerous for one man and one woman together, but one man with two women will be risky." I had to tell them what they faced without sparing them. "You may as well know that Russian soldiers are everywhere along the tracks and roads, and they have been assaulting unprotected women."

Regina turned to her friend, Yadja, and asked if she would be willing to take the risk. They both agreed they had nothing to keep them in Sosnowiec and would rather face the danger of the trip than stay behind, alone and friendless. It was settled then. I told them that I was staying with the Polish family if they wanted to find me and that I would be coming to see them every day until we left.

I went back to the center on the second of many trips. As I went over the lists time after time, I started counting again. There was no trace of our entire family. Every uncle, aunt, cousin, from every branch of our family, was gone. And all those who had started on the last trip from Schrodula in the freight cars were gone, too. The sense of bereavement was overwhelming. It was hard to watch the occasional joyful reunions that took place at the center without envying them.

A week of desperation passed. I went from the center to the girls, back to the center, visited with some of the other young Jewish men and women living in rooms around the center, then back to my temporary quarters with the Polish family and started the cycle all over again. I knew that back in Waldenburg Sala especially must be worried and anxious by now. It was pointless to stay on. I said goodbye to the family who had sheltered me and left Sosnowiec with Regina and Yadja. My friends had given us all the food they could spare, and we had additional supplies from the Russians who occupied the city and from the Kultusgemeinde. It seemed strange that a Jewish Council was once again operating in Sosnowiec. Secretly I hoped that perhaps Yadja and David had crossed my path and were already in Waldenburg waiting for my return.

The trip back was as rough and frightening as I had predicted. We finally managed to board a jammed freight car, but it soon stopped. We spent nights on the ground beside the halted train or in the shelter of nearby trees, not daring to go too far in case it suddenly started again. Russian soldiers approached and questioned us. I told them both girls were my sisters and I was taking them home. It worked and we were not molested.

More than two weeks had passed since I left Waldenburg, but no miracles were waiting to surprise me. Sala was frantic, terribly afraid something had happened to me. There had been stories of Jews who had been robbed and beaten upon their return to the places of their birth. They had been followed by Poles, Germans, natives of their homeland who knew that many Jews had buried their valuables. When they recovered them they had been murdered or beaten and robbed. No one protected them. It was tragic and frightening, but in the light of everything else that had happened to us it was no surprise. I brought Sala and the others no good news and no hope, but at least we had the satisfaction and pleasure of seeing Baruch and Regina reunited and later married, and Yadja became one of our family also.

The farmhouse was overcrowded now. Potok had found his girlfriend's young sister Helen, and she too joined us. But when she heard through the grapevine that her sister Edda had returned to Sosnowiec, all she could talk of was going back for her.

We had endless discussions of what to do next. The farm was only a temporary shelter, and we had been forced to find additional quarters on an adjoining farm for some of the girls.

Some began to speak of going back to Sosnowiec to stay. I tried to argue them out of what I felt would be a disastrous decision. "If you go back now, you return unwelcome," I told them. "Don't think for a minute that you are going back to your own country. You don't have a country, and, what is more, you *never* had one. I can tell you after being there that it was never our home and it never will be." I suggested we go west, to the American zone, and finally they all agreed, provided that we go to Sosnowiec first. I knew it would be a terrible mistake, particularly if some of them were eventually misled and decided to stay. But their minds were fixed on going, desperately hoping to find somebody, and I couldn't blame them. After all, I had felt compelled to make that journey myself. One point we all agreed on was that we would stay together.

We decided it was almost impossible to go by train and keep from being separated, so, since we had two horses strong enough to pull a wagon loaded with people and luggage, we packed and set off on the road east. When we had traveled four or five hours from the farm we were stopped by Russian soldiers. "We need your horses; we'll have to take them," they said. We begged them in vain until, fortunately, one of the infantry officers made himself known to us as a Jew and he convinced them to let us pass. But our reprieve was short-lived; a few hours later we were stopped again, and this time, although we argued, begged and pleaded, we succeeded in saving only one horse. We had gone only a few miles and without both horses it was unthinkable to continue. We turned the wagon around and made our way back to the comparative safety of the farm.

Our situation became more and more tense. We felt trapped because we could not move east, and the others did not want to go west unless and until they had made that one last trip. We were particularly concerned for the girls. In the nearby farmhouse, where Sala lived with two others, a Russian lieutenant had taken rooms. He was a mature man in his late forties and acted as a protector and friend, generous with food and information. But he frequently held parties for his fellow officers. One night while several of us were visiting their door burst open and the lieutenant came in with two colonels, carrying bottles of vodka. They were drunk and boisterous, insisting we drink with them. Not daring to refuse, we swallowed the raw liquor, hoping it would satisfy them. But the colonels began to grab at the girls and struggle with them. It was rapidly getting out of hand. The other men and I managed to distract them while the girls left the room and crawled out a ground-floor window, running across the fields to our house. It was a tense night spent in fear of a reprisal for their injured vanity. But in the morning, to our surprise, the lieutenant volunteered his apologies for their behavior, and the tension eased.

The Russians were our liberators. They had made tremendous sacrifices in the war; but on the other hand the whole situation was becoming electric with unresolved and enormous problems which needed immediate decisions. By now we all firmly agreed we would go west to the American zone. None of us wanted to live under communism; it represented to us a dictatorship and a totalitarian form of government under another name. But now I was the one who felt I could not leave without making at least one more trip back to Sosnowiec. When I informed the others Max Weisbrot asked to join me. I was glad of his company. Weeks had passed since my first trip, and I was going back with renewed hope. Surely somone would have turned up in the meantime.

Max and I went straight to Mungeyofska 5. As I checked the lists my heart almost stopped. I had been letting myself believe that this time I would find some of the names I searched for. But when I reached the end there was none, not one. I tried to explain to Max why I was so distraught, and for the first time I told someone beside Sala the story of Schrodula and of the people who had spent the last days there, including the fortune that lay buried in the garden. He offered to accompany me back there to recover the buried boxes and jars. I refused. "If none of the others came back then I am not here either. If not one of them survived, then neither did I. I don't want to take anything," I answered. But I wasn't ready to give up yet. I took

Max to my Polish friends, and they opened their home to us for as long as we stayed in the city. When I wasn't at the center searching the lists we went from house to house visiting among the pitifully few Jews who had returned, asking them questions. Maybe somebody saw somebody and maybe somebody forgot a name they should have registered and maybe there was someone in the camps still too weak to travel back. I exhausted myself and Max, too. If this was to be my last trip back I had to be absolutely sure I had left no stone unturned. I wanted just one person to say he had known one of them in the camps and remembered.

At night we relived the past. Yablonska told Max about the people I had hidden in the fire tower and how she had helped me provide them with food. She spoke tenderly of my mother and what a wonderful and loved woman she had been. Until I heard her tell Max I had not known she had watched me unload my mother still alive from among the corpses from Punkt Targowa. She spoke of my whole family and how well she had known them through the years we had been neighbors and friends—and now I was never to see them again. A whole world vanished.

Max tried to reason with me about my refusal to go back to Schrodula. He argued logically that if I did not want to use the buried fortune for myself, then why not use it to help the others? He felt I had an obligation, but he could not alter my convictions. "No, Max, I could never face it now, not as the only one," I told him. "I never wanted to be the only one of all who had been there to come back. What special right had I to live?" Deep down, I knew that it really was because I did not want to admit to myself I was the only one who survived. As long as the legacy lay buried there in Schrodula, I could still hope perhaps some day Franya or the Chabas' little boy or Mrs. Gold might come back to claim it. I would go back then gladly. But not alone, never alone.

One night my emotions overflowed. I raged to my friends at the indifference of our fellow Poles. "You have seen the stories and pictures the Russians published of Auschwitz and the other camps. I tell you one day history will judge the Germans and the Polish people as well for what they have done and for what they could have done and did not do. The world is not just going to forget it. Some day when the history of this is written, it will be almost impossible for people to believe that such atrocities were committed in the twentieth century and that most of our fellow Poles did nothing to stop it. Look at the Danes. When they refused to obey the Germans and refused to allow their Jewish neighbors to be taken and murdered, the Germans stopped. Not so our fellow Poles. For this reason and many others, but mainly for this reason, I will never in my life want to see this city or these people again!"

In this one long talk I poured out every ounce of hatred and truth that had built up inside me to the few Poles who had befriended me. They recognized that truth and understood. Finally, drained and exhausted, I told them, "I am leaving tomorrow and I'm never coming back."

Max and I spent our last night in the makeshift beds on the floor of their apartment, and in the morning, after a last, futile trip to the center at Mungeyofska 5, we made our farewells. The warm, courageous woman came with us to the station. She pressed food parcels on us and an envelope of photographs of herself and her family. "Please, Natan, take these and remember us. I don't know how, but perhaps one day you will find it in your heart to forgive and come back." I thanked her again for everything she had done and turned my face away from Sosnowiec forever, never once looking back at the land of my birth and the land of the betrayal of my people.

Part II

Chapter

20

WHEN MAX AND I RETURNED to Waldenburg there were already indications that the Poles were going to occupy that part of the country. It made no sense to stay there, for the same reason we had left Sosnowiec behind. Besides it seemed only a matter of time before some new violence might break out. It would be wiser to move on, at least for the time being. All of us would have left Europe immediately, but there was no place to go. At least we would find some temporary shelter under a democratic way of life. That is what the Americans represented to us. Baruch and I decided the time had come to make the move, and we told the others of our plans. Each was to make up his or her own mind—come with us or stay in Waldenburg. Their decision without hesitation and almost unanimously was to go. Only Potok decided to remain to care for the two girls in his charge.

The question now was how to escape, for an escape it had to be. We could not get papers to leave the eastern zone, so we would have to leave illegally and take our chances. Baruch had met a Russian officer in charge of transportation, and we went to see him, prepared to make a deal if we could persuade him to let us get on a westbound train. We had very little of value to offer, but he finally agreed to accept what we had. "All right, I will let you know when the next train leaves; it is on the siding now and I will know tomorrow when it starts for the west. I will see that you board without being bothered or questioned, but after that you're on your own, and I don't know you, understand?" It was done. He sent word as he promised, and that day in late August 1945 our small group boarded a freight train while the Russians looked the other way. It was a closed car; we could slide the door shut, and there was hay spread on the floor on which we could rest. The train started after an eternity of waiting. We were on our way at last.

The journey was very hard, with the train making frequent stops, spending hours and even nights in one place. We left the boxcar for water and to flex our legs but never strayed too far away for very long for fear the train might start unexpectedly and leave some of us behind. One night we slept on the floor of the closed boxcar while the train waited motionless on a siding. We were suddenly awakened by pounding on the door of the car and Russian voices calling, "This is the police. Open up." We had to slide the door back. Four men in civilian clothing confronted us with machine guns in their hands. They instructed us to hand over everything in our possession. We gave them what little money we had; then they began to search each one of us. Frau Citrin had two diamonds she had managed to conceal in her clothing all through the camps. They tore her dress down the front and found them. Our rucksacks were ripped open, and whatever they wanted they took. They left us physically unharmed but mentally distraught. In the morning we reported the robbery to the local Russian police. They deplored the incident, promising to search for the men, but we heard nothing from them, and when the train moved on we went on, too.

At no time did we actually know how close or how far we were from the border between East and West, but finally we reached the end of the line and could go no farther by train. We jumped off and walked west through fields and woods, nervous and excited. Someone whispered, "Down, quick. Russian soldiers." Down we went until they had gone. We hid several times, whenever we saw anyone nearby. Our path led us into a heavy forest. We wandered through it, nervously wondering if we had gone in the right direction and, if we had, if we were across the border yet. Suddenly we noticed chewing-gum wrappers on the ground, then empty cans with labels printed in English. "American. They're American! We've made it; we're across the border." I think we all said a silent prayer.

The first road we followed led us to a small roadside restaurant. Signs along the road were in both English and German. Now we knew for certain we were safe. At the restaurant we laid down our packages and rucksacks. The proprietor came over and greeted us, but when we asked for food he said we had to have ration cards. "Where is the nearest town?" we asked him.

"It's Hof, just a few kilometers to the west," he answered.

"Has it been bombed? What's it like there?" we wanted to know.

"Ach, you'll find it's in good condition. There's a food shortage like in every other city, but otherwise everything is pretty much like normal," he assured us.

We walked on with high spirits into the town and asked the first German policeman we saw if there was a Jewish community where we could get some help as former concentration-camp inmates. He gave us an address and we went directly there.

There was a registration department for survivors, as at Mungeyofska 5 and wherever Jews found themselves after the liberation. In keeping with the European tradition and law, we asked for permission to register. Our fellow Jew said, "We are very sorry but the town is overcrowded with people. We cannot register people who have not lived here before unless we have housing for them, and I'm sorry to say that the American military government has instructed us that for the time being, at least, we must not accept any more registrations because there are already too many displaced persons here." It was the first time I had heard the expression "displaced person" and I asked him to explain. He explained that that was what we were now called, a new term applying to us and to the thousands of others like ourselves, of many nationalities, who did not want to return to their homelands because their families had been wiped out or because their countries were occupied by unfriendly forces that they feared. So we were stateless, belonging nowhere, and our plight was so widespread that they had to invent a new category and title for us—displaced persons, DPs.

His inability to accept us was an unexpected blow, but he softened it by advising us that if we could find living quarters for ourselves, independent of the Jewish community, he would see to it that we got properly registered. Somehow we obtained the name and address of a German minister, and we approached him, asking if he would be willing to share his home with us. Happily, he was willing to take us in, and we immediately went back to the community center to report we had found a place to live. Another blow: We were told that in the interim they had received new instructions from the American military government not to accept any more refugees into the city on any account because the overcrowded conditions were dangerous. The disappointment was like a slap in the face. However, we managed to stay on in the minister's home for a few weeks, getting week-to-week extensions of our temporary permission to remain and of our temporary food ration cards. We told them we did not intend to make Hof our permanent home, only to make it our headquarters while we searched for a more permanent place or found a means to get away entirely. But each time we were warned we would have to move on soon.

It was puzzling, confusing, and shattering for all of us. We had never expected to be received with open arms by the Germans, nor had we expected to be given any special treatment; but we had expected understanding of our background and our very special needs. All we found was a stone wall of rejection. We made a few hurried trips to neighboring towns, hoping to find better conditions, a few of us hitchhiking to Bamberg, the headquarters for Oberfranken (Upper Franconia). Someone suggested we try Lichtenfels, another town untouched by the war. In Lichtenfels we heard the same story. If we found housing independently they would allow us to register. Otherwise, we would have had to have lived there before the war. It was worth another try. We went through the town and saw beautiful villas. We began ringing doorbells, asking for housing without success until one family agreed to take us in.

After this stroke of luck we went back immediately to the registration center. Again, another unexpected hurdle. "Yes, well, you have a place to stay. Good, good. Now you need the approval of the American military government."

"Why didn't you tell us that before instead of letting us waste all this time?"

No answer. Apparently they thought they had seen the last of us, that we would not be able to find or afford private quarters. "Now, don't get upset. We'll take care of it for you. It's just routine. Come back in a day or two," they assured us. We had walked into another roadblock.

The girls were becoming increasingly exhausted. We made other trips, including one to Nuremberg, and the anger began to build up inside me. We confronted them in Lichtenfels again. Again we were told we could not stay because we had not lived there before the war. Incredible! I asked the man in charge of the department for refugees, "Did all of these Germans live here before the war?"

He shrugged and said, "That is not up to us to decide. We only handle refugees like yourselves."

We saw we would not get any further with them. They had to be lying to us; it was impossible for this to be so. We were ineligible for Red Cross or other relief-organization aid because we were not registered and we were unable to find a "permanent" temporary place to stay. Only those displaced persons who had a registered address could receive aid, and there were no Jewish displaced persons in Lichtenfels because at this time the American military governor would not permit them to stay.

We talked and talked among ourselves and finally decided to approach the Americans personally. The next morning we called upon the commanding officer, an American colonel. A German interpreter fed the questions and answers back and forth. "Did you live here before the war?" "No, sir," we replied, "but . . ." "Request denied," he answered curtly, not interested in our explanation or problems.

I was becoming enraged and more desperate. We talked again, and the girls volunteered to visit a higher-ranking officer themselves, hoping to engage his sympathy, but it was no use; they were turned away as coldly and quickly as we had been. If this was justice under a democratic army government, then we were really losing our minds. Everyone seemed to be behaving as if we had invited ourselves willingly to this zone of Germany. There seemed to be some terrible conspiracy between our persecutors and our liberators to make us the scapegoat again. It was outrageously but courteously suggested that we, the unwelcome overflow, take up residence in one of the former slave-labor camps like Felderfink and move into the old barracks. Back to the camps? It was unthinkable. I could not understand it and I could not accept it. How was it possible that only three or four months after their victory the military government of the army which had fought the Nazis was now rejecting the displaced persons who suffered under the Nazi boot?

It has never been explained what caused this attitude on the part of the American military government in that area. Admittedly, nothing could have prepared them for the overwhelming situation they found upon taking responsibility for their section of Germany. Never before in world history had thousands of homeless victims been liberated to wander the face of Europe. But where was the human element that should have made them instinctively want to reach out a helping hand or at least lend a sympathetic ear? Was it a problem in communication, a language barrier, or were the old influences already subtly at work in Germany to close all doors to us? The girls had had to resort to displaying their tattooed arms in a last desperate effort to convince the officer in Lichtenfels that they had a right to shelter. If that was not enough, what would we have to do that was?

We realized we needed an organized plan of action. It was decided to enlarge our search for a town by fanning out, visiting as many towns as possible at the same time. The men split up. Rudofsky headed back to Bamberg, and Baruch and I returned to Hof.

Outside the towns it was sometimes possible to hitch a ride. We would walk along the road until we saw a truck going into low gear at the base of one of the many hills and jump on the back, hoping the driver had not seen us. It was not too dangerous since the trucks burned wood because of the petrol shortage and they had little power, even on level ground. Rudofsky hitched a ride only to find himself stranded halfway between Hof and Bamberg when a tire went flat. It was late, so he went into the little town of Munchberg nearby and inquired at the police station if there was a place they would recommend where he could stay overnight. They sent him to a small hotel where he had no problem registering. In the morning he looked around that little town of Munchberg and saw a community untouched by the war—a beautiful village nestled in the mountains in the best Bavarian tradition. His curiosity aroused, he visited the registration office and asked if there were any displaced persons in Munchberg. They said yes, a few. Instinct told him he had found something important enough to make him turn around and return immediately to Lichtenfels. Not finding us there, he followed Baruch and me to Hof and told us excitedly of his discovery. Leaving Baruch to stay on and search in Hof, because we could not afford to take anything for granted, Rudofsky and I set out immediately over the same road. A truck came along; we jumped on the back and jumped off when it reached Munchberg.

My impression of Munchberg verified everything he had

told us; it was beautiful and intact. We went directly to the registration center and asked for permission to register all our group. They said there would be no problem if we got permission from the American military government for them to accept our registration. The same old story. We asked if there would be any difficulty in finding living quarters if we did get this permission. The German in charge, Herr Banker, impressed me as being a sincere, straightforward person. He replied, "I cannot foresee any problem once you have the American military government's permission. And it's worth a try, at least, isn't it?" We asked whom we had to see at the AMG; he gave us the name of an officer, Captain Rosenbush, and directed us to their offices.

The captain received us, and we made our request to him as usual through an interpreter. I explained briefly and politely who we were and how many there were in our group. At first the captain seemed cold to our request and to me. Now more strongly than before I felt an urgent and pressing need to reach out for understanding. Our small group was being torn by the repeated rejections. Our enthusiasm and hope were dwindling as the feeling grew that we had survived to no purpose if we could not find refuge among the people who had liberated us. After almost a half hour of pleading we seemed to notice a new sympathy in the captain's attitude and a warmth in the tone of his voice even though we did not understand what he was saying until the interpreter repeated it to us in German. Captain Rosenbush asked us through the interpreter if we would be willing to take over a building called the Schuetzenhaus, the "Shooting Range," and fix it up ourselves to make it suitable for occupancy. Since we did not know the extent of the work needed to repair it or its condition, I asked for his permission to inspect the building that afternoon and return the following morning with our answer. He consented, and we left feeling encouraged but still tense.

Our hearts dropped when we found the Schuetzenhaus. It was a huge shed in terrible condition, beyond restoration, and unfit for human habitation. There were gypsies already camped inside when we walked through, and their situation was deplorable. The building that had once been a shooting club for the sportsmen in the town was now a derelict fit only for demolition. To repair it was inconceivable.

I was pushed to the limit of my endurance. We went immediately back to confront Captain Rosenbush, and I struggled to retain my self-control. "Captain, please tell me what's going on here; I don't understand. You offer us this Schuetzenhaus, a building without windows or doors, filthy and beyond repair. Let me tell you what kind of people you want to put into that building. There are eleven of us left from six families. We've had everyone we loved, including our children, taken from us and murdered. We've lost everyone and everything, do you understand? Some of us lost a little and some of us a great deal. And here we are going from one city to another, one town to another, and in each place they tell us there is no room for us, because we did not live here before the war. Whose war? Not ours! Who says this to us? The same people who took away our loved ones and slaughtered them, who stole our belongings and imprisoned us. And you are concerned now that these same people who did this to us might have to live a little less conveniently? What do you want us to do? Where do you want us to go? We haven't the stamina for this treatment; we're too recently out of the concentration camps." I rolled my sleeve up over my tattoo and asked, "Am I just a number here, too?"

I went on to tell him a little more of our history and background and what we had come through these past months and years. I poured out passionately everything I felt until suddenly I saw that tears had come to his eyes and he turned away from us for a moment. The interpreter stopped when I stopped. Then Captain Rosenbush turned back to me and said, "You go to see Mr. Banker tomorrow morning. Tell him I have sent you and tell him to get decent housing for all of you." Suddenly I felt every kind of emotion mixed up inside me—anger mixed with relief, resentment with warmth. For the first time I realized that most of the Americans did not know our real history or the scope of our situation. Captain Rosenbush had not known the full facts, and perhaps we had previously failed by not explaining ourselves to the other officers from whom we had asked assistance. These Americans, soldiers and officers, were not trained for military government. They were fighting men who found themselves suddenly the peacetime governors of an occupied country, faced with problems unique in history.

At last a bridge of understanding had been built at Munchberg, and we crossed over it to a refuge. In the morning Rudofsky and I took the captain's handwritten note to Herr Banker at the center, and by the end of that day we had brought our whole group to Munchberg and settled them in decent, comfortable living quarters, with proper identification papers and ration cards.

Munchberg—a place to begin again.

Chapter

21

THE DREAM THAT HAD BROUGHT US THROUGH the dangerous and rough trip from Waldenburg had finally become reality at almost the very moment when we had begun to lose all hope. We could stop running now and breathe the air easily and quietly. It was good to stop and rest.

The living quarters were decent if not spacious, and the Germans left us to ourselves, not daring to resist the orders of the Americans that had placed us in their homes. We split up. Baruch and Regina, the only married couple, were together. Sala had a room alone not too far from where Max Weisbrot and I shared quarters, and the others made the best of their arrangements, together or separately. We agreed to pool our food and eat our meals together, so Regina Scharnocha and Frau Citrin took charge and prepared the meals in their community kitchen. The intimacy and closeness that had held us together these past months gave us the only real family ties we now knew, and we meant to preserve them. We had no one else in the world but one another at that moment.

Munchberg was exactly what we had hoped it would be. It had none of the war's devastation, and all the buildings were intact. It was a very picturesque and clean town, almost a storybook Alpine village nestled in the Fichtelgeberge, the mountains of Bavaria, in Oberfranken, near the Czech border. As we became more acquainted with the main street, Ludwigstrasse, and the other streets, we explored farther out and asked questions.

Munchberg was the capital of the district, the Landkreis, which bore its name. There were small villages and good-sized towns throughout the lush valley and perched in the mountains. The cool mountain climate and abundance of water made the farms productive, and they were beautifully tended and apparently well run. It was late fall when we settled, and the weather started to become more wintry with each passing day. It was refreshing and invigorating, and having time to think about tomorrow, next week, next month and next year was abundantly satisfying.

I had heard from Herr Banker that there were a few displaced persons in Munchberg prior to our arrival, including a few Germans, who had been concentration-camp inmates. It seemed to me that the wise and friendly thing to do would be to introduce ourselves and pool whatever information or influence we might be able to muster in the coming days. I also thought this was the time to begin forming a basic community relationship with the American military government and the German civilian government.

Baruch and I visited the other group and met with the German who seemed to be their spokesman. We talked extensively about our many common problems, and I suggested for our mutual benefit that we form a committee to represent us in our future contacts. The group included several Jews as well as former concentration-camp inmates of many nationalities and Germans who had been imprisoned by their own people for political philosophies in opposition to the Third Reich.

Their spokesman had qualified for his imprisonment by his deep communistic convictions. He agreed that a committee would be mutually beneficial, since inevitably there would be the common problems of better housing, more food, and eventually employment for all of us. In addition he was looking forward to the day when they would be able to ask for reparations, restoration of businesses, reinstatement in places of employment, when the factories and industry resumed normal operation, and when professional men, attorneys, doctors, educators whose degrees and licenses had been revoked by the Nazis would have their professional standing and rights returned.

I told him I was leaving for Bergen-Belsen the next day but expected to be back in Munchberg soon. Upon my return we would organize our group and apply to the American military government for recognition. I was gratified at his cooperative attitude and even more pleased when he expressed a desire that one of my group hold a position on the committee so we would have a voice in matters of common interest.

The proposed trip to Bergen-Belsen had been brought about by Max Scharnocha discovering that his girlfriend, Chaika, had survived and had been found in Bergen-Belsen in the British zone. He had asked me to accompany him there to ease the unpleasantness of traveling alone. We had learned the gruesome details about Bergen-Belsen when we first reached Hof—and from the few pictures in the Hof newspaper of what the English had found inside the walls of the women's concentration camp—the typhoid epidemic that had killed so many women, the thousands killed by starvation, illness, and brutality. There was always the possibility that Max would find only tragedy. It was better for him not to be alone.

Since we could not leave the Landkreis without permission, we applied at the AMG for interzonal passports to the British zone, "to search for survivors," and received them without difficulty. The trains here, too, were still functioning erratically and were crowded, but there was some semblance of order, and at least we rode inside passenger cars instead of standing up. It took us a few days to get to Bergen-Belsen. We had no difficulty finding the huge camp. The English soldiers guarding the gates let us through; we were only two of many who came on the same search. The camp had been cleaned out and living conditions greatly improved by the English. The women who were ill had been quarantined in emergency hospitals and were receiving medical care. Fewer women occupied each barracks than under the Nazis, and they were fed regularly and were free to leave if they wished. But there they stayed, still in a German concentration camp four months after the war had ended and they had been "liberated." They were still virtually prisoners, for where were they to go?

Bergen-Belsen was too big for all the women to know one another, and none of the girls we asked knew Chaika. Someone directed us to the camp office, and they quickly checked their records. Yes, she was there, alive, and they told us in which barracks. I hung back as Max and she faced each other. Another reunion, painful and wonderful. She had known nothing of Max's survival and believed she was alone. "But why did you stay on in the camp so long?" I asked.

"Some of us did leave," she replied. "We ran out the first day or two. Nobody stopped us from leaving. But it didn't take long to find out that there was nowhere to go. Most of the girls came back in a few days. Even if you could find someone to take you in, you couldn't get food. At least, in the camp the English fed us and we had a place to sleep. I didn't know what I was going to do when the time came finally to leave and I had no place to go."

My sensation of depression returned. I was again troubled by what I saw and heard. Was there no end to this suffering for the survivors?

The office of the British military government gave her permission to leave their zone and cross to the American zone. We left Bergen-Belsen and started back to Munchberg.

On the train I was still disturbed. It was impossible not to become more and more aware of the scope of this tremendous problem. The train was as packed going back as it had been in the other direction. Some were German civilians, of course, and military personnel of the Allied Armies of Occupation. But so many DPs. Where were they going? What did they hope to find at the end of the ride? At one of the many stops we were informed that the train would stay for several hours, so we got off to walk around. It was a cold and windy day, and the faces of the other refugees on the train made a vivid and permanent impression on me. We found shelter from the wind in a large depression in the ground, probably a bomb crater, and joined in the general conversation as the people began talking among themselves. I listened to people tell each other of their aimless drifting from one town to another, from zone to zone, looking for survivors and a place to live outside of a camp barracks, but there was simply no place to go. Everywhere the same rejection and senseless regulations. "If you didn't live here before the war, you can't register," or, "the town is overcrowded and we can't take any more DPs. The military regulations have to be obeyed." Many had been traveling for weeks, back and forth, and every place they had gone they'd been told to leave. "I don't know what we are going to do; we'll just have to keep on going." Some were determined never to re-enter a camp no matter how long they had to keep moving. Others, older and weaker, with less hope and diminishing energy, were beginning to give in.

They had no guidance, no help, and as far as I could tell, no one cared enough about them to lead them in any direction. Several organizations, including the Joint Distribution Committee, had begun to operate in relieving the material needs of those still inside the camps, but they could not offer them any immediate hope for the future outside. They could only promise that plans would be made as soon as possible, whenever that would be.

As usual, everyone asked about the various camps and exchanged names, hoping to find someone who had known a loved one or a friend. And one of the few happy coincidences of those hectic days happened. I saw a familiar face from Waldenburg. It was Victor Weistuch. We greeted each other warmly, and he introduced his wife and called over another familiar face from Waldenburg, Topol. They, too, were among the endless stream of wanderers. "Look," I said. "We have found a fine place to stay. Why don't you come back with us to Munchberg and we'll try to get you registered?" But they were determined to continue on to another city where they had heard by rumor they might find a place. "Schapelski, if we don't have any luck there, we'll come to Munchberg and get in touch with you." I told them where Munchberg was located and how we could be found. The call came to reboard the train, and the crowd dispersed through the chill, as hopeless as when they had descended.

I was a depressed and puzzled young man. I could not block out the confusion and unanswered questions this whole trip had rekindled in my mind. I looked long and intently at the faces of the others in the same coach with us and tried to reconstruct their lives. Who were these men and women, mostly young, for few of the older Jews had survived the gas chambers or the punishment of the camps? They had been average human beings on September 1, 1939, living in cities, towns, and villages all over Europe, where their families had lived for generations. They had grown up in homes ranging from poor to middle class to wealthy, their parents working hard to care for them and loving them as all parents do. Perhaps that young man's father had been a tradesman of some kind, and the handsome older man might have been a doctor or a successful businessman. They were from every walk of life, just as our community had been in Sosnowiec. They had gone to *cheder* as children, as I had done, received as much education as a Jew could get in their society. Their children had played and laughed and cried as all children do. The memories that had tortured me in the courtyard of the house on Schklarnastrasse returned as the train moved slowly through the night. Why had this happened to us? Why were we chosen for the role of victim? A nation declared war on us. Announced clearly in advance that they planned to exterminate us, and no one believed them then or later. They had carried out their intentions without resistance or protest of any effectual degree with almost total success. Six million Jews, six million men, women and children; and all that remained, a pitiful few, were in the same hopeless condition as those I sat among now. I asked myself, "Where are mankind and society failing? They failed before in not standing up against Hitler, in not halting the slaughter. Are they going to fail again with what's left?" Somehow the world must be made to assume some responsibility for our future, but right now, at this moment, we needed more than anything else a place to live, until the gates opened to other lands and we could leave.

When all hope had ended for me at Sosnowiec, I, like so many others, had promised myself that I would live the rest of my life alone and make the best of it. Except for Sala, I had no desire to involve myself with anyone. The wounds and scars were still too raw. But I could no longer ignore what was happening. I thought of Munchberg where Germans lived comfortably, relatively unscarred by the devastation and death they had brought to millions and millions of other human beings. There, in that cold train filled with numb and hopeless, forgotten people, I made a new commitment to myself. When I returned to Munchberg I would use every means in my power to find room for as many as possible, no matter what I had to do. If there was no other way to find justice in this world, we would fight for it and create it for ourselves. Max and I agreed. If we must wait here in Germany, we would make it the obligation of the Germans and the duty of the Allied Armies of Occupation to make it as easy as they could for these people; and those of us who were able to help one another would start to do it right now.

I sat back exhausted while Max and Chaika talked. The future seemed very dark. I did not know what I could achieve, but it had to be better than doing nothing.

Chapter

22

WE WERE WELCOMED back to Munchberg joyfully. Chaika's discovery, after all these months, brought renewed hope to us. If she still waited in a camp to be found, maybe there could still be others.

Almost immediately I raised the question of proceeding with the committee we had talked over with the German and the other displaced persons before our departure. To my amazement I heard from Baruch that in my absence the committee had been formed—and we were not represented on it. It was unthinkable that any committee should exist in so small a town unless all of us had a voice in it. I went directly to the man who had given me his promise and reminded him of our conversations. "There is a lot of work to be done by all of us," I told him, "and we want to share the responsibility and the benefits. These people need every kind of rehabilitation and they deserve to get all the assistance they are entitled to from the Germans." He agreed that the committee be expanded and suggested that

I join as vice-president. "In fact, let's go tomorrow to the American military government and see Captain Metzger," he said, explaining that Captain Metzger was the officer in charge of political affairs in our area and would have to give his approval.

The captain was attentive to our plans and gave us an opportunity to explain our whole situation to him. When we concluded he gave his approval and expressed his personal feeling that the representation had been well set up.

The committee held several immediate meetings to deal with the most pressing problems—identification cards, housing, medical care for those in need, and the very important matter of ration cards. The Americans had fixed the allowed caloric intake at some point when they first occupied the Western zone, and displaced persons and former concentration-camp inmates were permitted more food than the Germans. Even with the additional several hundred calories it was barely enough. I was dissatisfied with the lack of progress the committee was making. The memory of the train ride still haunted me. More, much more, had to be done and quickly.

Captain Rosenbush received me alone this time, and I felt more at ease speaking to him through a new Lithuanian interpreter, Vladimiroff. I could be certain now that there would be no misinterpretation, careless or deliberate, in the translation. With the captain's encouragement I told him still more about our background and described our recent experiences on the trip to Bergen-Belsen and back. "There are so many of us homeless, wandering the roads or existing in camps, Captain. And here in this town where the war passed them by, the German people are going on with their lives as if nothing had happened. They pretend not to know who we are, and not one of them will admit to a share of the guilt. But you know as well as I that there was a concentration camp so close to Munchberg none of them could avoid seeing it." I went on, "We were forced to come here. We did not choose to live among people we have every reason to hate. And aren't all of the other homeless victims entitled to a decent place to stay at least until the day comes when they will be able to leave this country gladly? They owe it to us. I can't see that this is too much to ask."

He heard me out patiently and then replied, "I am personally very sympathetic to your cause, Mr. Schapelski, but in order to bring more DPs or refugees into Munchberg, I will have to discuss the situation with my commanding officer, Major Abbott. Come back in a day or two and I'll try to have an answer for you."

I thanked him for his understanding and courtesy and left, confident I had made the correct decision in bypassing the committee.

In the next few days I tried to do as much groundwork as I could. Vladimiroff had impressed me as being sympathetic since he, too, was a refugee. I visited him several times alone in his rooms and we spoke freely in German. His position as interpreter gave him tremendous influence with the American officers, and his work placed him in close contact with Captain Rosenbush. In our conversations I had more time to elaborate on the suffering and hardships that could be eased by making more room in Munchberg and towns like it, and it seemed that it met with a warm response.

When I returned to Captain Rosenbush as he had asked, he greeted me with the words I had hoped to hear.

"Mr. Schapelski, Major Abbott has considered your request favorably in view of the background I have given him. You have our permission to go to Mr. Banker at the housing office and arrange to bring more people into Munchberg." He then dictated a note to Mr. Banker in English, signed it, and passed it over to me.

"We look to you to conduct this in an orderly manner, Mr. Schapelski, and we expect you to accept full responsibility."

I assured him he would have no reason to regret his action and asked him to express my gratitude to Major Abbott. Vladimiroff seemed pleased, and I sensed he had done a most effective job in preparing the way for us. It was an almost overwhelming responsibility. To my knowledge, no one else in that area had been given such an opportunity by the American military government.

Neither Captain Rosenbush nor the note said how many was "more," and I was not prepared to limit it. With that note, the wall came down once and for all. I went to Banker with the official backing of the Americans and with open instructions: "If there is room in Munchberg, take in more people." With Banker's list of all known Nazis and their party rank and details of their living quarters, we began to canvas Munchberg. From this first moment on, once the registration office had these instructions, I never went back to the AMG for permission to bring in more people.

Almost every day, sometimes past sundown, Banker and I went through Munchberg with his list to see how much living space we could find. It was difficult to realize that while thousands of homeless people had no place to rest, former Nazis lived comfortably and in some cases luxuriously, not in the least inconvenienced by the war they had caused or their defeat. Wherever we found a family with sufficient living quarters, we asked that they vacate certain rooms and at times that they share the kitchen and bathroom facilities. When we met with hostility or resistance, as we did many times, I would leave and Banker would notify the AMG. Very soon the family would receive an official requisition ordering a certain number of rooms to be made available immediately. A few tried to argue that they needed all their living quarters and could not spare the space. It was my job to persuade them, if possible, that it was wiser to share without resistance. It was a long time before they realized it was useless to resist.

As if by magic the word went out: Munchberg had opened its doors and refugees began to trickle, then pour into town as the news spread. We needed some central location to handle the growing work and a place where the people could come for help. The Americans turned over to us the lower floor of a spacious house on Ludwigstrasse, and we set up a four-room office. Captain Rosenbush had given me the privilege of choosing an assistant, and Baruch jumped in gladly to take over the office, since most of my time in those early weeks and months was spent searching for more housing.

In the first few weeks almost forty DPs found homes among us. By word of mouth our name and reputation spread first in our own area and soon all through the Western zone. Hungarians, Poles, Czechs, Lithuanians, Rumanians and other DPs who had been looking for a place to live came to us and we took them in. They heard about us in other communities where no room could be found except in camps like Lichtenfels. And these other communities sent them to us. Each day more came, searching, suspicious, afraid to believe this was a place of welcome. And we took them in. In the other towns they said, "Go to Munchberg." In Munchberg we could say, "Yes, there is a place for you here. Here you are welcome."

Banker, convinced that I was using the authority I had been given wisely and armed with his instructions from the AMG, cooperated fully and spent most of his time helping me.

We formed a Jewish community to give us unity and organization, and I had the honor of becoming its leader. Each moment was filled with an intense awareness of the enormous needs of these people. But hour after hour and day after day I saw our accomplishments grow and had the desperately needed satisfaction of knowing that I was helping to create something good out of all the horror. The days spun by, crowded with excitement and achievement. The challenge of meeting the needs of those who came to our office each day drove me on to checking and rechecking the lists. All I could think of was "How many can I get in here?" and then rush back to the office to learn the number of new arrivals and to greet them. Tomorrow, their problems would have to be solved.

Early in October, Captain Rosenbush called me into his office. I had come to him of my own accord many times in the past weeks to report on our activities and problems, and we had established a fine relationship with good communication and understanding. His summons was disturbing, but he soon put me at ease. "We have been observing with great interest and, I might say, even greater satisfaction the manner in which you are accomplishing the integration of your people into the town. You have done a great deal without creating any problems for us and with far less friction than they are experiencing in other places between DPs and Germans." I was relieved to hear this expression of confidence from him, for the AMG held absolute authority over all civilians.

However, he went on to convey to me their concern that the situation, while now under control, might eventually get out of hand because of the number of DPs still coming into Munchberg, bringing additional problems and pressures for them as well as for us.

"We feel this is the time to provide some official leadership and organization for your people, and I would like to appoint you the authorized representative for all the Jewish displaced persons who come here. How do you feel about this?" he asked me.

It was an unexpected honor, and I accepted gratefully. On October 5, 1945, I received my first official letter from the American military government reading:

HEADQUARTERS
MILITARY GOVERNMENT DETACHMENT H 256
Co "B," 3d MG Regt
APO 403

5 October 1945

SUBJECT: Employment of Civilians
TO: Landrat, Munchberg.

1. The bearer, Natan SCHAPELSKI, is appointed leader of the Jewish former concentration camp inmates in Munchberg.

He will discuss with you the possibilities of jobs for those people under his leadership.

By Order of the Military Government Officer:
Bernard Rosenbush, Jr.
Captain, CAC

With this letter I proceeded to set up a meeting with the Landrat (Chief County Counselor) and discussed with him the conditions of the Jewish immigrants and their temporary needs. He showed a sympathetic attitude, but it was only a surface response. "I am one hundred percent for these people, " he told me after I had explained to him who they were, from where they had come, and what had happened to them.

"I am very glad to hear you say that," I answered, "because we have a moral obligation to help them. It's too early, of course," I explained, "to discuss specific problems and details about jobs and businesses because I don't yet know what the people in our community are trained to do, but Captain Rosenbush and I felt it was necessary to prepare the way."

He assured me that he understood and promised his full cooperation, but his cold, harsh manner left me with the feeling that he could not be depended on and I felt dissatisfied and troubled. In the light of the rumors that he had been a Nazi sympathizer, it seemed probable his words were hypocritical. Fortunately some time later he was removed from his position as head of the Landratsamt, the County Counselor's office, for reasons I personally suspected were political. Perhaps the rumors of his past had finally come to the attention of the AMG, and they had found cause to remove him from this important office.

To our good fortune, they appointed in his place as Landrat a fine and far more humane man, Herr Zietsch, who had been completely cleared by them as an anti-Nazi.

I also met with the newly appointed Burgermeister of Munchberg and found that the AMG had selected a man who had been imprisoned by his fellow Germans for political reasons. Max Specht was a simple, honest man of great sincerity and feeling. We talked for two hours at our first meeting, and he spoke with tears in his eyes of the guilt his people must carry for generations to come. "Herr Schapelski, there is no doubt in my mind that more is preferable to less in whatever we can do to help you. There is no way to make amends for what the Nazis and the German people did to so innocent a people." He had difficulty controlling his tears as he spoke, and when we parted I felt he was on our side. In all the months that followed, he never gave me reason to alter my opinion, and my respect for him grew with time. When free elections were restored, the people of Munchberg re-elected him to the office of Burgermeister for many terms.

Our four-room office hummed with activity day and night. It became the principal gathering place for our community, and in the evenings we held meetings open to all Jews who had settled among us. We talked about individual and community problems and speculated about the future. It was vitally important that we handle our own difficulties and try to function independently of the AMG so they would have no cause to regret the free hand they had given me. There were problems at times that could have erupted into violence, but they were few. Mostly there were disagreements with Germans whose comfort had been lessened by having to share their homes. A few German families left their places and moved elsewhere in the town, but most of them went on living as before, barely acknowledging the presence of the unwelcome strangers. If complaints were made on either side, I settled them as best I could, pleading for patience and control from our own people and insisting that the Germans face up to their responsibility. It was far from easy to ask a man or woman with memories of the past still fresh in his or her mind to treat a reluctant German with politeness and suppress the hate we all could not help but feel in our hearts. But I explained over and over that we had to get along with as little friction as possible. We were completely interdependent. None of us must do anything to harm another or stop the flow of tired, desperate people who came to us. This way we kept our house in order and stayed to ourselves.

Every second or third day I visited the military government headquarters to keep our relationship alive and to make encouraging reports on our progress. Through Vladimiroff I met other officers, Captain Metzger and Lieutenant Bowers, who knew of our work and treated me courteously. Then one day Major Abbott, the military governor in command of Landkreis Munchberg, asked that I come to his office. Major Abbott's position made him all-powerful over every phase of life in the Landkreis, and he carried all the authority and responsibility for every military and civilian act in the district. He was well informed of the condition of the displaced persons throughout the Landkreis and through his interpreter expressed his appreciation for the fine job our Jewish community was doing. The orderly fashion in which we were conducting ourselves was far superior to the friction and disturbances in other Jewish communities. He was pleased he did not have to contend with such problems in his district.

I thanked him, promising we would continue to preserve his high opinion of us. "Your officers have treated us fairly, Major Abbott, and Captain Rosenbush knows I will do everything I can to follow your regulations."

"Now," he said, "I am leading toward something else, Mr. Schapelski. As you know, there is another committee here in Munchberg apart from yours, representing former concentration-camp inmates." I indicated my familiarity with it. "The chairman of that committee has notified us that because of his political beliefs he intends to move to the Russian zone. In view of this, I am asking you to assume responsibility for all former concentration-camp inmates formerly represented by his committee. Help these people get started, also; get them housing, see that they get everything they are entitled to, as you are doing now for your own people." I accepted. It was another important job that had to be done. Another official letter was issued.

HEADQUARTERS
MILITARY GOVERNMENT DETACHMENT H 256
Co. "B," 3cl MG Regt ACA/1s
APO 403

30 October 1945

SUBJECT: Jewish Committee and Supervising Office for
Former Concentration Camp Inmates.

TO: TO WHOM IT MAY CONCERN!

1. The bearer of this letter NATAN SCHAPELSKI is appointed leader of the "Committee of the Jewish former concentration camp members" and of the "Supervising office for former concentration camp inmates" in Landkreis Munchberg.
2. He is authorized to travel within American territory on official business.
3. Any consideration and help given to him by American and civilian authorities will be appreciated.

ARGYLE C. ABBOTT
MAJOR   OAC
Mil Govt Officer

Allied Expeditionary Force
Military Government Office
Official

Captain Rosenbush and I decided after considerable discussion that the most orderly way to keep both offices functioning would be to absorb the other committee and set up a new office solely for former concentration-camp inmates of all nationalities and keep our existing office separate. Banker was instructed by Burgermeister Specht to secure offices for us in the City Hall on the Bergstrasse, a few blocks from the AMG and near the police station and all city departments.

Thus, I found myself at twenty-three, untrained for leadership, with the triple responsibility of being president of the Jewish community of Munchberg, a growing, needy, troubled community; chairman of Jewish former concentration-camp inmates; and now head of the office of all former concentration-camp inmates, with the responsibility of representing and supervising people of all nationalities who had been imprisoned by the Nazis for religious or political reasons, or because they were members of a minority racial group. My authority now covered not only the city of Munchberg but the entire Landkreis of Munchberg, and it was my responsibility to speak for all of them.

So the days formed a pattern. Always the first concern was housing, and in the late afternoon and evening I returned to our office to take care of the day's business and go over the latest problems with Baruch. The second office was efficiently managed by the assistant to the former committee chairman, and he met with us often to resolve difficulties he could not handle alone. There was little or no time for personal life, nor did it matter. My life was full and meaningful once more. Sala and I had finally found a comfortable house in which to live, and she took care of me, trying to make me eat and get enough sleep. Our friends stayed close and gave me much encouragement. I was seldom alone or lonely.

At the suggestion of the AMG, a notice was published in the newspaper instructing all former concentration-camp inmates to report to our office within a specified period of time. This would give us an opportunity to establish a central file, screen the people, issue special ration cards, and, more important, help them re-establish their identities.

Late one October afternoon when I returned to the office, now busier than ever, my secretary informed me that in my absence two young women, one of them an interpreter and secretary for the AMG, had come in quite angry and upset, claiming that we were trying to requisition a room already assigned to them. Fräulein Szenes, the one who worked for the Americans, had made it quite clear she believed we had no authority to do so. I did not want to cause trouble for anyone in the AMG offices, and at the same time I was curious about the position this girl held. I went immediately to the AMG and asked the American guard to announce to Fräulein Szenes that I was there and would like to see her. She came out into the hall and acknowledged my greeting coolly, obviously still angry. I asked for an opportunity to hear the nature of the complaint she had voiced to my secretary. "Yes, I would like to know how you can take living quarters away from another DP?" she asked. For the first time I noticed she wore a Star of David on a chain.

"Are you Jewish?" I asked in turn, astonished.

"Certainly I'm Jewish! You did not know that? Didn't you know I was here in Munchberg?"

I apologized. "No, I did not know you were here. I am sure there has been a misunderstanding about the housing requisition. You may be sure I will take care of it."

"And that's not all," she said icily. "I have been screened and cleared by the Central Intelligence Corps, and I have no intention of registering with your office or anywhere else."

I wanted to explain the necessity of reregistering, but there were too many people passing by. She impressed me as a very intelligent girl, and I wanted to know more about her. I asked if I could call on her later that evening so we could talk in privacy. She agreed, gave me her address, and we parted formally. I immediately canceled the requisition of her room.

Lilly Szenes shared a two-bedroom apartment with the Meyers, a married couple, and when I called on her that evening she gave me a chance to explain that her CIC screening had no bearing on the need for her to register with our office. "We are merely trying to set up proper files for all displaced persons, and this is the only organized way we can do it," I told her. She still did not indicate that she intended to comply, and, hoping to make our work a little clearer, I invited her and her friends to visit our community center so they could observe first hand what we were doing. She did not seem interested, and from the few brief comments she had made about the demands

207

her job made on her time I doubted that she would find the opportunity to come.

"Mr. Schapelski, I appreciate that you are working very hard for these people, but for myself, I am alone, the only one left of my entire family and without friends. I have a very good job here, and I intend to go on working and making a life for myself. I have no desire to become involved," she said.

I repeated my invitation, but her attitude was not encouraging. A day or two later, however, she came into the office in the afternoon and sat to one side for several hours watching and listening to the people coming and going with their problems and, it seemed, observing me. She left with little comment after I invited her back again. To my surprise and pleasure, she returned to attend some of our evening meetings and discussions, some open and some organized.

At these meetings Baruch spoke, and others spoke; sometimes everyone in the community was present. We talked of the need for more housing, the inadequate clothing ration, and other problems. For instance, some married couples who had been liberated in the east early in the spring had come to us with infants who needed plenty of milk and special foods they had not been able to get. And among other things, while the clothing was distributed by the Landkreis without cost, it was tightly rationed. I agreed to approach the Landrat for a more realistic allowance. And always we talked about the future and dreamed aloud about the day we would be able to leave Germany forever.

Lilly came to meetings whenever she could, and slowly it seemed that her natural reserve was melting. When I had gained her confidence and trust, she tried to explain her aloofness and withdrawn attitude. "I don't have to tell you how it was in the camps, Natan. You had to make yourself hard inside to stay alive, and when you've gone through that and find yourself alone, it's very difficult to begin caring about other people again." She told me how demanding her work was. Because she spoke a number of languages fluently—English, German, Hungarian, and French—her services were very much in demand, and she had a position of responsibility and trust with the American military government. "You have to understand that every day, all day long, people come to me asking for special favors. I mean all kinds, Germans, Jews, other nationalities. Because I work for the Americans and have an important job, they expect to get something out of me. Some of them even try to bribe me so that they can get passports to leave the zone or for other things. I don't know which is worse—the Germans who tell me to my face they were never Nazis and knew nothing about the camps and the ovens, or the others, all seeking favors. It's always 'I want this or I need that,' and they just want to use me to get what they want. So why should I care about them?"

I could not contradict her; everything she said was true, but I tried to make her see that these people still needed help. "I don't understand you at all," she said. "Why do you do all this? You know, when I first met you I waited for you to ask me for something, too. But you haven't once mentioned anything you need or want for yourself. There must be some reason you are helping all these people and giving them all your time."

In time she grew to know I was sincere, and our friendship deepened. She was patient, though puzzled, when I called on her at home. Too restless and troubled to sit still, I would unthinkingly leave abruptly and ride around the countryside for a while to relax, then return without explanation. She would ask me, "Are you angry about something? Why did you leave?" As we came to know each other better, my restlessness became a trait she accepted. Whenever a problem arose and I needed help, she came forward willingly. The day Major Abbott appointed me as leader of all former concentration-camp inmates, she prepared and typed the official letter. What had started as a cold, impersonal relationship, as a result of my concern for her solitude, became a mutually trusting and valued friendship.

Late in November the Main Central Committee of Jewish

Communities that had been established, with its main office for Bavaria in Munich, and for Oberfranken in Bamberg, notified all Jewish communities that in order for us to become eligible for aid from the Joint Distribution Committee we had to register with the Central Committee and hold a free election of officers. If we complied it would entitle us to much needed food and clothing from the "Joint," as it soon became known. We conducted our elections in the community center, and Baruch and I ran for vice-president and president respectively and won almost unanimously. On election night we held the first big party to celebrate, and it was wonderful to be surrounded again by our friends and their warmth.

Immediately after the election we gathered the necessary documents and lists of our community members for the trip to Munich to register at the central office. With Gershonovich driving, Lilly, Baruch, and I rode the two hundred and fifty kilometers to Munich over the icy winter roads. It was the first time I had been away from Munchberg since returning from Bergen-Belsen. It had been only a few months, but it seemed like ages.

Munich had been devastated by the Allied bombings, and the city was in ruins. At the central office we filed our documents. Everything was in order, and official recognition was granted. Our community was assigned to Bamberg's jurisdiction, and we were told we would be notified when supplies were available in Bamberg for our needs. They were amazed at the number of people we had registered. I told them proudly we were still growing. "Didn't you have any problems? The other communities are always complaining and asking for our help." I told them how well organized our community was and what a fine relationship we had with the American military government. It seemed that Munchberg was unique in many ways.

During the few days we spent on this trip Lilly finally responded to my questions about her background and early life. It was painful for her to relive the haunting memories of the past, but slowly and with a trembling voice she told me her heart-breaking story.

She had been born in Vienna, the only child of Hungarian-Austrian parents. Her father, a very talented, gifted man, had originally come from Czechoslovakia, and her mother, a beautiful woman, was Hungarian by birth. They had met in Hungary while her father was serving as an officer in the army. They soon married and returned to live in Vienna. At the time of Lilly's birth, her father managed the Heller chocolate and candy factories, the largest in Vienna. A bullet wound in the lungs had made him a partial invalid, and its failure to heal necessitated frequent convalescence in sanitariums. With this chronic illness, he could never fulfill his potential or take advantage of the education he had struggled so hard to achieve. His family had been poor, and he had been educated in an orphanage, but despite this he had mastered seven or eight languages and had had great ambitions which the First World War had destroyed. When Lilly was ten years old, her mother and father traveled to Italy for a short vacation, and there her father had died, a victim of tuberculosis brought on by the wound.

Lilly's mother, left with only a widow's pension, struggled to see that Lilly received a good education. They lived modestly while Lilly finished high school and began her studies at the University of Vienna, majoring in modern languages with the gift she had inherited from her father. Her mother managed to send her to England for almost a year, and while studying in London the rumors and rumbles of war made her decide to return home to be with her mother. When Hitler occupied Austria, they left Vienna with one small suitcase, two women alone on one of the last trains to Hungary. For a time they lived with her mother's family, two married sisters, and then moved to a small apartment. Lilly could not continue her education. No school or college would accept Jews any longer, so she supported her mother and herself by tutoring private pupils and teaching in a Catholic high school, studying in the evenings on her own.

211

The war years went by and life became harder. Hope that the war would soon end was crushed when Hitler occupied Hungary in January 1944. Then everything changed rapidly for the Jews. They had to wear the identifying yellow stars and were issued special ration cards for minute amounts of food. The English and American bombers were flying air raids over Budapest, so they spent their nights in the cellar of their building and their days in fear of arrest. An order had been issued that Jews were to begin moving into ghettos and would no longer be permitted to live in mixed quarters with non-Jews. In the midst of the terror, Lilly had found love and married a young man only to lose him a few months later when he was taken away to clear mine fields for the Germans and to die.

One night, awakened by an air raid, Lilly and her mother ran to the cellar, forgetting to put on their coats with the yellow stars. A Hungarian officer who lived in the same building reported them to the Gestapo, and the next day they were arrested and charged with the crime of being in a public place without the yellow star. Their sentence was ten days in jail. The jail was overcrowded, and they were kept in a basement under terrible conditions, without food or sanitation. Her mother, still a young woman in her early forties, contracted dysentery and became very ill. As soon as the sentence had been served, they were both transferred to an internment camp at Sorokszar. The internment camp had been a brick factory, and there were only empty sheds with no living facilities or shelter. After two horrible weeks in the camp, the Gestapo came and trains pulled up outside. To keep the women quiet, they told them terrible lies. They did not intend to transport them to Auschwitz, they said. The young women would go to work as slave laborers in Germany, and the older women would be kept in Hungary. Lilly parted from her mother believing their lies. "The last time I saw her, Natan," she told me softly, "was when she brought me a piece of bread and a glass of water before they loaded us into the boxcar and she said for me to

take them, that it would be the last thing she could do for me."
Lilly did not know at the time that her mother and all the older
women were merely loaded into separate boxcars on the same
train and that the train would take all of them to Auschwitz-
Birkenau.

She was transported on a freight car jammed with a hundred
people without water or food. On the trip the people had cried
all the way, almost insane, some of them sick and dying and
some already dead. On arrival someone told her that her
mother had already passed the selection point and had been
sent immediately to the other side. She soon learned what it
meant and knew her mother was undoubtedly dead.

From then on her story of torture and humiliation was as
tragic as any of us could tell. Starvation, beatings, heads
shaven, brutalized by German women guards, as sadistic or
even worse than the SS men. She befriended a young woman
whose mind had snapped when her three-year-old boy was
torn from her arms and killed. Lilly comforted the bereaved
and helpless girl until they became separated months later.
Except for this young woman she sealed herself off from the
misery around her and determined to stay alive. In her mind,
she said silently over and over to the beasts guarding them,
"You will perish and I will stay alive." And she held to her
belief through beatings and punishment. In September 1944 in
desperation Lilly obeyed a sudden impulse to stand in a selection for outside labor even though she was not supposed to
appear and was struck by a Kapo for leaving her work. She
managed to get into the line knowing that if she were not
picked for labor it could mean the gas chamber. In this selection the women were ordered to undress before the SS officers
and doctors walked by, pointing with their fingers, either to the
gas chamber or the other side. For once they were truthful and
had actually separated a group for labor.

The girls were loaded on boxcars with food and water and
enough room to sit down. They rode for three days, passing
through a bombed-out Berlin, to Ravensbruck. It had formerly

been a death camp, but now the Germans were short of labor and they had converted it for accumulating and building up selected prisoners so they could be useful. For the first time they were issued prison clothes—blue, white, and gray striped dresses—and a pair of wooden clogs. They had blankets to cover them when they lay on their planks at night, two to a bed. After six weeks of rebuilding their strength, they divided the group, and Lilly together with some four hundred girls were loaded onto freight cars again. In this separation, she became parted from her one friend, the young mother, and never saw her again. This time the train went to Neustadt near Coburg, and the girls were put to work repairing telephone cables for the German Army. They were housed in fairly decent barracks and worked twelve-hour shifts around the clock. Lilly and a few other girls were assigned to test the repaired cables, and the girls, running the risk of being killed if they were detected, managed to sabotage the wires. After first stamping the cable as usable, they would then cut into it so it would be defective.

Winter and spring passed, and they could hear the booming of American guns becoming louder and louder. The Germans did not want to be caught with slave laborers, so they ordered the SS to take the prisoners out. The labor camp was attached to Buchenwald, but there was no way to move them and the Germans were short of manpower in the camps. The French had already occupied the territory nearby, so the only route open was through Germany. The Germans hoped to take them across the Czech border to the camp at Theresienstadt.

In March 1945 they issued each of the girls a little piece of bread and marched them out, four hundred of them. For a week they wandered, guarded by SS and their dogs. Whenever they saw a girl fall ill or faint, they shot her. If anyone tried to escape or wandered away in a daze, they shot her and had a grave dug where she lay. Lilly and four companions, three sisters and another young woman, knew this transport could lead only to certain death. Despite the risk it would be better to try to escape.

The SS marched the dwindling group through Helmbrechts, hoping to leave them in the camp there, but it was already overcrowded, so they marched on. The SS was desperate, trapped on both sides, by Russians on the east and the Americans on the west. While passing through a little town near Munchberg, watched by stony-faced inhabitants, a man approached them. No one else moved a muscle to help them or even offer a glass of water. This man came close to Lilly and whispered, "It won't be long now." She didn't know whether he meant it as encouragement or a warning that their death was near, because the SS officer slapped him and dragged him away. The SS did not want to be captured with concentration-camp inmates, and yet they were afraid to let them go.

The five girls decided to try to make a break the next day. Whenever an air raid sounded, the SS ordered them to lie down under trees, spread out so they could not be easily spotted from the air. When the next air raid order came, Lilly ran into the forest and kept on running with her friends close behind. They hid in the woods for two days, hungry but afraid to ask for food. Eventually they approached a German woman, and Lilly tried to convince her they were foreign workers. The girls had torn a piece of cloth from their rags and covered the yellow Stars of David. The woman seemed to believe them and offered to cook some potatoes. While they waited, desperate for food, her husband returned and said he knew they had escaped from a transport. Frightened, they hurried back into the forest and spent the night hidden in the trunk of a tree, while German soldiers ran past, screaming and shooting, less than a yard away.

In the morning they walked to the edge of the forest and saw American chewing gum and candy wrappers along the road. Suddenly, they saw tanks coming from the direction of the town of Marktredwitz, where a white flag was flying. The first American Lilly saw was a big Negro soldier standing up in the first tank. The five girls must have looked like ghosts to him; they had not eaten for a week. Their clothes were torn in dirty rags and their hair had only started to grow back. Something told him who they were; he started to smile, reached down, and his arm came up with packages which he threw at them. Later, they learned these were K-rations. When the last tank passed, the girls ran up to it, and Lilly asked in English where they had come from and where the girls could go for help. She explained they were concentration-camp escapees and needed food. The American soldiers directed them back down the road to the town and went on their way toward the Czech border in pursuit of the remainder of the German Army.

In Marktredwitz the German civilians shunned them, and they had to find the CIC headquarters by themselves. The Americans didn't know what to do with them, so they locked them in the basement laundry of their makeshift quarters while they made inquiries to verify their story. While the girls waited they found large kettles of water and bathed themselves. An officer came in unexpectedly and left, followed by outraged screams. Finally, after they had been interrogated, the American officers said they would take care of them, at least until further orders. They let them pick out clothes left behind by the former occupants of the house. Lilly picked up a brown velvet hat and pulled it down over her almost bare head! They were taken to the nearby hotel, and under orders from the Americans the innkeeper gave them two rooms and furnished them with food.

The next day two giant American soldiers called for them and said, "Come on, girls." They followed, frightened and bewildered, only to be led into a store. The Counter Intelligence Corps had commanded the Burgermeister of the town to order the shop opened, and the girls were invited to take any clothing they needed. They rested and slept and ate, still very weak. They went for short walks with nobody guarding them, trying to get used to being free again. Often groups of American soldiers and officers would come to their hotel rooms and quietly place boxes of gifts and food by the door.

There were only thirty or forty Jews left in Marktredwitz by the end of May, and the Americans wanted to talk to them and find out what their experiences had been and what the Germans had done to them. Some of the soldiers would come just to look at them, moved by their tragic story. Lilly exhausted herself translating for everyone. Naturally, her first thought was to go home, back to Vienna, to see if her mother had survived by some miracle, or back to Hungary to look for her there. Later, Lilly found that except for one uncle, the rest of her mother's relatives in Hungary were still alive. But her mother was gone. She began to feel stronger and restless for some activity to occupy her time.

While translating for a few Jews who did not trust the German interpreter, Lilly's ability to speak so many languages came to the attention of Colonel Hargrave, the military governor, who came to Marktredwitz once a week from his headquarters in Munchberg to conduct hearings. After the affairs in question were settled, he asked Lilly who she was and she explained her background briefly. He asked her if she would like to go to work for him. Without thinking twice, she accepted. The days were becoming too long and she had too much time to think and remember. He left and a week passed with no further word. Then one morning a jeep pulled up in front of their hotel; they had come for her. Lilly refused to leave her four friends behind, so the officer agreed to take them all. In Munchberg, the American officer took them to the house of the Kreisleiter District Leader who had been interned by them. His wife and daughters were still living in a beautiful, luxurious apartment. The American officer told the women they had ten minutes to leave. When the mother began screaming, he only said, "Your time is running out." He permitted them to remove only their personal clothes, and everything else was left behind. In the afternoon, the officer returned with a supply of food for the five girls, and the next morning Lilly began to work for the American military government in Munchberg.

Colonel Hargrave saw that they were supplied with

everything they needed. Lilly's friends kept house for her and she worked, sometimes seven days a week, as she still did. The summer passed, and Lilly transferred to Wunsiedel with the colonel, but she was lonely without her friends. When she found large enough quarters, the other girls joined her there, but a few weeks later the three sisters and the other woman decided to go home to Czechoslovakia to search for their families. Lilly helped them get their papers and an American truck took them to the Czech border. She parted company with them; they walked across at the checkpoint, and she never heard from them again.

Alone now, the only Jew in Wunsiedel, Lilly rode to Munchberg one afternoon and asked for a job there at the AMG. They were badly in need of a secretary and interpreter to aid Captain Metzger, the Public Safety Officer. They engaged her immediately. When she met Mr. and Mrs. Meyer, they moved together into a larger apartment that had belonged to a high-ranking Nazi official, and she settled down to her life as it was when we met. Now I understood her far better. The trip to Munich had been a wonderful experience for many reasons.

On our return, I plunged back into the never-ending problems. Then, late in the fall, a group of people came to Munchberg from the Russian zone and brought with them unexpected, exciting news. They had come through Sosnowiec a few weeks before and had met David there. I was overjoyed and raced home to tell Sala. It was unbelievable; we had long since given him up for dead, but it seemed miracles could still happen. We had to find him. I knew I dared not cross back into the Russian zone, because I was now too closely connected with the American military government. The Russians would have made it very difficult for me if I were caught. Fortunately, another young man, Jules Fluer, wanted to go back to Poland to search for his people. I asked him to go to Sosnowiec and look for David, and if he didn't find him there to go to Waldenburg, since that was the last address I had left at Mungeyofska 5. If he didn't find him there, I begged him to continue looking for as long as he could, since I knew David must also be looking for Sala and me after finding our names in Sosnowiec.

Jules finally returned to Munchberg without locating him. But he had left messages everywhere telling everyone he knew, including the people in the registration centers, that David was known to be alive and that if news came to them of his whereabouts to inform him his family was waiting for him in Munchberg. The message finally reached David, and he made the long journey west. No words can ever describe our reunion.

Other happy events came to fill our lives and help erase the sad memories. Several months after our arrival in Munchberg, Baruch and Regina Scharnocha became the parents of the first child born in our community. And Sala and our dear friend Max Weisbrot were married.

Among the many occupation personnel who came to Munchberg was an American Army chaplain who had been a rabbi in civilian life. The AMG introduced him to us, and he offered his help. He was especially assigned to displaced-persons affairs and performed religious services and officiated at weddings. We had found a new friend, admired and respected for his knowledge and dedication to our cause. We discussed at length the problems of the displaced persons, particularly in the camps, and his broader experience reaffirmed my personal observations, since he had personally visited many of them. We agreed that those in the camps should be given first consideration and help. He visited often and performed the ancient wedding ritual for Sala and Max when they wed. There were many other marriages, which was understandable in the special circumstances even among those who knew one another only briefly.

The first people who came to us in Munchberg were mostly young and alone, the last few left from their particular families. They were bewildered and without guidance, and it took months before the realization of their plight sank in. They needed more than just a roof over their heads; they needed material, physical, psychological, and moral training to become human again. There were few teachers left among our own people, so they turned to the Allied forces as their friends. After all, they had liberated us. But the armies of France, England, and America had more to do than care for their needs. They had to occupy and control the territories they had conquered. In many areas there were clashes and misunderstandings between Jews, other DPs, and the soldiers of the armies of occupation. And, of course, the clashes between the DPs and the Germans, and these were the most violent. Suddenly, so many Germans anxious to wipe their records clean refused to admit they had been involved in the war crimes; it must have been some other Germans, never they.

The military governments in many instances did not comprehend the true nature of the DP problem. They gave orders bluntly and expected to be obeyed. The DPs, angry, oversensitive, and without guidance, made no attempt to get through to them. Major Abbott and I discussed his concern about these grave problems. "Two parties are involved, Major," I told him. "Perhaps both sides are wrong in their approach. When the war ended your front-line officers and soldiers were perhaps unprepared for peacetime governing and certainly not prepared for the unexpected deluge of displaced persons with whom they were suddenly faced. And who were these people they had liberated? They were those few who by a miracle had stayed alive, those few who were able to fight harder and by their cunning and ingenuity to gain advantages in the camps for food and protection for themselves and their friends. It is not all black and white! There is a long hard job to be done where misunderstandings divide us, and representatives from both sides must work hand in hand so that we will come to understand each other better."

I talked of the long-range problems that we faced. "You are military men with discipline and a chain of command, while we have few leaders. Our strong men are ashes now. Most of those left are so young, with so little education, it will take years for them to unlearn the twisted habits of survival and self-preservation they had to learn in the camps. And this re-education must happen here and now, before we send them on to another land, or I am afraid many of them will never be able to adjust to the normal world again."

Through wave after wave of seemingly insurmountable problems we managed to maintain Munchberg's unique record as the best example there was of a self-sustaining, self-governing community, not only of Jewish refugees but also of former concentration-camp inmates of many nationalities, with an unequaled lack of friction and violence and an unusually close and harmonious relationship with the American military government. It was hard, challenging, and delicate work, but I welcomed it because the rewards were so great. I had only to look at the faces of the people around me.

New difficulties arose. The German mark had no buying power or value, and the only other legitimate currency was the American Army scrip used by the military and their dependents. The remaining means of exchange was barter, which rapidly grew into a black market all over Europe. The AMG had stringent regulations against black-market trafficking, so I tried to watch our community for signs of trouble in this area also.

And old difficulties persisted. Friction between the DPs and the Germans was ever present. Occasionally our people would respond abruptly and hotly to displays of hostility from the Germans, and the atmosphere would grow tense. I tried constantly to instill into them that we could not take the law into our own hands. "Yes," I'd tell them constantly, "there is injustice here, but by the same token we must realize it is not for us to sit in judgment here and now. The Allied forces are the judges, not us. We must let them cope with the Nazis because we have no other choice and because we have more important work before us." I hammered on a theme of rehabilitation and urged them to come back to reality so we could get started on the first priority of fitting ourselves for the day of exodus from this hostile land. It was far from easy, but they listened and tried very hard. And not only did I urge them to try to get along with the Germans, but also I stressed the need for us to get along with each other, despite the many countries and different backgrounds from which we came. "If you have a problem you cannot settle yourselves, come to me," I promised, "and I will take it up with the Americans." We were by no means closing the book on the past, nor would we ever be willing to forget, but we had to live as best we could for the present until we would be in a position to judge those who were responsible for our plight.

At times, keenly aware of my own youth and the enormous responsibilities I had undertaken, I marveled at the trust and confidence they placed in me as I tried to build a bridge between them and our surrounding world, tirelessly interpreting one side to the other and serving to bring about understanding and tolerance. We had a long road to travel back to normal life, and we needed all the help and understanding we could get.

The Alpine winter covered the mountains and the valleys with a deep snow, but still people came to Munchberg and became part of our community life. By the end of December, six months after the war's end, we had taken in almost one hundred and fifty, either rescued from the despair of the crowded camps or released from hospitals and rehabilitation centers or escaped from the new oppression of the Eastern zone. It seemed minute in contrast to actual needs, but each new arrival, man or woman, young or old, was one more rescued life.

The Jewish chaplain from the American Army toured the camps and related to us the anguish and deprivation he still found there. In some camps there was only barely nourishing soups and a little bread, and newborn infants cried for milk and warmth. In one camp a tragic incident occurred that convinced him to ask for his release from the chaplaincy so that he could fight for the rights of the DPs full time. He had gone to offer religious consolation and comfort to the inmates, but in their desperate state all they had seen was his American uniform, not the Star of David that marked him as a rabbi. He had been struck and assaulted by angry, hungry people waiting in long, slow-moving lines for a bowl of thin, watery soup. The shocking realization that these, his fellow Jews, were so shattered and beaten, so driven to striking out blindly against a world that had turned away from them that they would unknowingly commit an act of violence against a rabbi who had come to serve them started him on his mission of mercy. It was heartening for him to come to Munchberg and see real progress and visible rehabilitation. He continually offered us assistance, but I always thanked him deeply and told him with pride that Munchberg could take care of its own needs and whatever he could do for us could be put to far better use in the DP camps.

Lilly and I had become inseparable since our memorable trip to Munich; she spent every hour, when not on duty, at my side. The cold, disinterested, fiery young girl had become an invaluable and trusted friend of our community, willing to help in whatever manner I asked, and I asked often. More and more I contacted her at all hours, needing her gift for languages to interpret in some emergency and calling on her experience and knowledge of the AMG for help in solving a problem that could not wait till morning. She had a gift for organization as well and took such an effective part in my work that it became advisable to appoint her recording secretary of the Jewish community.

Because of the demands of my work I received a priority for a telephone, and the Americans posted "Off Limits" signs on our home, restricting Germans as well as American soldiers from entering, placing it under the protection of the military government.

By the end of 1945 the Allied High Command had finally been

brought to a full awareness of the displaced persons' tragedy, and instructions were issued to the various AMG headquarters to lend us every assistance. The success of Munchberg had spread throughout the Western zone, and it was inspiring to know that other DPs looked to us as an example of progress and self-sufficiency. The Jewish Agency (known also as the Palestine AMT) and the Joint Distribution Committee were impressed by the reputation we were building, and (of tremendous importance to us) the monthly reports filed in Washingon through the military governor's office were looked upon with great favor and interest. We were, after all, a credit to the American officers who had placed their confidence in us.

Having once opened the gates to Munchberg, I could not conceive of turning anyone away, so the search for housing was a daily hunt. But if I discovered that someone had been a Kapo in the camps or had held any other position in the camps and used it for personal benefit at the expense of the other prisoners or had mistreated them in any way, then in no circumstances would he find a place to live in Munchberg.

Occasionally Banker would protest mildly and ask me when I intended to stop. He felt the town had absorbed its limit. And at times my respected and valued friend, Captain Rosenbush, would likewise question the town's ability to shelter any more people. But always my reply would be the same: "They have nowhere else to go; any little inconvenience they create is no great hardship to the Germans. They are lucky to live in a town where no bombs fell. And don't forget that these same Germans sheltered a concentration camp only a few miles away in Helmbrechts. They don't know what suffering is. My people do. It was Germans who taught them."

Each month I made written and oral reports to government headquarters of the current state of the Jewish community and the Committee for Former Concentration Camp Inmates so they could incorporate the information on how many were registered and other data into their confidential report to Washington.

Our office was kept open every night until ten or eleven o'clock and even later if newcomers were directed to our door. Each new arrival performed one act all had in common. We kept in our office the register of those looking for lost loved ones; everyone who came to stay or to visit spent endless minutes turning the pages and scanning the names, hoping to recognize a mother or father or, more realistically, since most of the older folk had gone to the gas chambers, a brother or sister or young friend. At regular intervals we copied the new additions to the register into a report and sent it to central offices in Munich and Bamberg, where at last an attempt to centralize this vital information was proving successful in reuniting many who had given each other up for dead.

In compliance with orders from the Allied High Command, all new residents in Munchberg had to be screened when they registered and they were required to fill out long, detailed questionnaires of their life history. In the first months Germans wanting to register were sent to Herr Banker at the registration office, and we handled the other nationalities. Later, when the overall responsibility was given to me, any new arrival had to be cleared by us.

Soon after the occupation the AMG had prepared a long questionnaire delving into every detail of a person's life, and everyone in the Landkreis who was employed or in business, owned real estate or residences or was practicing a profession had to complete it, including the wives of former Nazis. They had to answer every question and return the completed questionnaire to the AMG to receive identification papers and ration cards. There was a severe penalty for perjury. When the Americans captured Munchberg they had established their headquarters in the hastily deserted offices of the local Nazi party, where they had found the complete records of all party members, their rank and history still intact. So they had files and documents to prove the lie of anyone denying an affiliation with the Nazi party.

From the beginning, by direct order of the AMG, any high-ranking Nazi party member who had actively and openly supported the party was forbidden to hold any job or practice any profession other than unskilled labor. And no member of the party could occupy any public or private position of authority. When this order first went into effect, all known Nazi officials were replaced by the AMG, with men such as Burgermeister Specht appointed to serve until free elections could be restored. However, when the first large group of questionnaires had been screened and checked, I learned to my amazement that a great number of the men still holding positions of power or authority had to be removed and replaced by proven anti-Nazis. Of course, the known "war criminals" who had been captured were interned in prisons and were being prepared for trial by the War Crimes Commission.

The Allies had set up a sliding scale of guilt for members of the Nazi party. A dedicated party member was one who had joined closest to 1923, carried the lowest party number, and participated in crimes against humanity. Every person screened had to be checked in the records of the local Nazi party, if they were available, as they were in Munchberg, and when the central files of the Nazi party were found intact in Berlin, they were checked again. There it was possible to check Germans who had not lived in Munchberg during or before the war.

The Nazi party in Munchberg was considered to have been only of average activity and power. Yet they must have been very certain of the people's support, because the concentration camp near Helmbrechts had unquestionably functioned with their full knowledge. Though they tried, they could not deny knowing of its existence, especially at the end of the war when the SS actually lighted up the camps at night with diabolical cleverness so the Allied planes would drop no bombs on them, thereby guaranteeing their own safety. And I knew from Lilly that her transport as well as many others had passed through Helmbrechts and many of the nearby towns and villages in the last days of the war. Few Germans ever had the courage to admit to our faces that he or she knew, much less condoned, the atrocities and mass murders. Even in the face of irrefutable facts, they still denied their guilty knowledge.

My authority to issue papers to displaced persons extended to and included German nationals imprisoned for political or religious reasons. The identification card bore my signature and was countersigned by the CIC. My office issued these identification cards, and I affixed my signature only when I was satisfied that the applicant had actually been imprisoned by the Nazis as a victim of their persecution.

Many German former concentration-camp inmates came to me and their papers checked out without problems. In one case I was approached by a German man whose application stated that he had been a Nazi prisoner for political reasons, but my intuition warned me that there was something dishonest about him. My inquiries of other camp inmates and his neighbors verified that it was generally agreed among them that he had been in a camp for reasons other than political, but no one knew the truth. Because we were unable to clear him, I refused to issue him papers, time after time, offering to reconsider if he could substantiate his claims. To my surprise and dismay, he reappeared one day and presented me with a letter signed by the Public Safety Officer of the AMG instructing me to issue him official identification papers entitling him to the privileges and rights of a displaced person. I knew the Public Safety Officer of the AMG. I had met him originally through Vladimiroff. In the absence of Allied civilian counsel, he acted as prosecutor for the AMG in cases involving DPs who could not legally be tried by German courts. I was at a loss to understand his action. Why had this particular order originated in the AMG when the normal procedure was for the application to originate in my office and then be presented to the AMG? I went immediately to his office and asked him point-blank, "Sir, why did you issue this letter? Normally, you accept my recommendation. Why is this case different?" He flushed at my words and retorted that he was personally satisfied as to the man's integrity and truthfulness. I was sure the German had some influential connections in the AMG. I could not believe an American officer would voluntarily lend his support to such a man and go against the standard procedure. And I did not propose to let either of them get away with it. Too many people who truly deserved them were waiting for papers. In the course of our heated discussion I stated flatly to him, "Captain, this man should have been thoroughly investigated before getting this letter, and I stand by my prior decision not to issue him official identification papers until I am satisfied he is entitled."

I sent a stream of letters to departments of the German government in search of some record of his past. When no replies were received, I myself drove to Munich, where the remaining documents of the German government were stored. These files contained the records of the German Justice Department from the entire district of Bavaria and covered all court records. I was permitted to search. Finally, in one central office I came across his file, a complete police dossier with his photograph and two pages of criminal history involving arrests and convictions on many charges, including sexual crimes. The authorities furnished me photostatic copies of the entire dossier, and I returned to Munchberg completely confident. I visited the captain again and placed the dossier quietly on his desk. When he had digested the contents I commented simply that I felt this had been a very vital and important matter to many people and that I had made an issue of it only because I felt (and I was certain he would agree) no one with a criminal record should be sheltered by the AMG or my office under the guise of being a displaced person. He immediately recalled the letter and brought charges against the German, who was later tried for perjury for making false statements to the American Military Government.

This was the first clash I had had with an officer or soldier in the American Army or military government, and I found no joy in my victory even though I knew I had done the right thing.

Because of the delicate balance in relationships I had tried to maintain with the AMG, I was particularly disturbed to learn from Lilly sometime later that a German woman employed by the AMG as an interpreter had made several anti-Semitic remarks in her presence, not knowing Lilly to be a Jew. My main concern was the fact that she acted as interpreter to the same captain with whom I had had the earlier problem, and whenever I had met with him she had been the one who had translated for us. From her behavior she either had to have been a member of the Nazi party or a strong supporter. It was unthinkable that we should rely on her to translate on our behalf.

Lilly, Vladimiroff, and I discussed the woman and her background. She was an intelligent, capable woman with a doctorate in economics. She had given her background as a refugee from the Eastern zone and had sworn she had never had any affiliation with the Nazi party. There had to be something wrong with her story. I went searching again in the records in Munich and Berlin, and what I found only served to heighten our suspicions. The situation was serious enough to bring to the attention of the military governor. While having a brief discussion with him on another matter, I mentioned that I had heard on reliable authority that the AMG was employing a former Nazi party member. "Were you aware of this, Major?" I asked.

He was surprised. "It's impossible, Mr. Schapelski. Your source of information must be wrong."

I urged him to check further into the matter, but his attitude gave me the feeling I was stirring up something too delicate for me to pursue. However, her remarks continued, and in the end we were forced to push for an investigation because of the obvious danger she represented to us and to them. They ran a check on her through the Nazi party records and found, as we had, enough to warrant further investigation. The final report came back, damaging beyond belief. It was incredible that she had been able to lie her way into such a sensitive position. The major called me into his office and told me he would take all necessary action.

While all this was going on, word had spread through the military government that I was circulating lies about the captain's secretary. A garbled, twisted version eventually reached the captain himself, and since he was as yet unaware of her true background, he automatically concluded that my actions were malicious. He decided I deserved to be taught a lesson. One Sunday morning I received a call from him to come to AMG offices. Never suspecting any problem, Lilly and I went together. There was an unusually large group of officers at the AMG for a Sunday morning, but the captain had not yet arrived. Another captain called me aside and told me word had leaked out that I was about to be challenged to a duel. I was stunned. Before I could recover, the captain arrived and strode up to me. "How dare you go around spreading vicious rumors about my secretary? You have questioned my trusted friend and my honor as an officer!"

I tried to explain that she had been making insulting remarks openly about Jews, and for the first time I brought Lilly into the situation as a witness.

"Is this true, Miss Szenes?" he asked Lilly.

"Yes, Captain, I'm afraid she really did say those things."

"Well, Miss Szenes, don't you think it would have been more proper to report this to a responsible officer rather than carry the story to Mr. Schapelski?" He was partially right, of course, but as yet he did not know the whole story. "Mr. Schapelski, you tried to destroy this woman, and I intend to defend her honor. I will meet you with pistols and we'll settle this matter once and for all." He was getting angrier by the moment.

The other captains stepped in and tried to quiet him. "Now, Captain, let's look into this a little further before we do anything drastic. Besides, you know you can't duel with a civilian; it would break you as an officer." Slowly, the captain calmed down and then left quietly. The crowd dispersed and we walked away still shaking.

The matter had become too public to suppress any longer, and the captain was presented with the file and all the facts concerning his secretary's background. Confronted with this evidence and convinced that my interference and interest in pursuing the matter had been for his personal benefit as well as that of everyone else involved, he made overtures of apology, and in a very short time we reconciled all our differences. After our two clashes over the German man and the German woman we became very close friends. To protect everyone concerned, his secretary was quietly discharged from her job. With her importance and influence destroyed and the truth revealed, she left Munchberg and we never heard of her again.

Chapter
23

THE NEW YEAR OF 1946 lay before us, holding out little more than the promise that we might one day leave Europe. Some day the soldiers of the Allied armies who had liberated us would go home. It was always thus after a war. But not us. We alone were adrift, all ties severed and all the roads back closed. Munchberg would never be home, but until we found a new road leading out of the past, here we would stay. And so we continued to entrench ourselves and to take pride in our accomplishments and ourselves. And the respect and cooperation of the American officers encouraged me even more in my work.

Early in January I was called to Captain Metzger's office in the Political Affairs Department. This was the department responsible for removing all Nazis from positions of authority and influence, as well as for monitoring the future political life of the Landkreis. Without wasting time, he plunged into an explanation for his summons.

"As you know, Mr. Schapelski, wherever we have found active Nazi party members or supporters guilty of crimes against humanity in public offices we have removed them and replaced them with men we know to have clean records. We have carried this program into the professional and business life also, although, regrettably, we have had to make exceptions in special cases." I was familiar with the work of his department and nodded my understanding. "Naturally, Counterintelligence has picked up all the high-ranking Nazi war criminals we could find and they have been interned. But we are faced with many borderline cases, and Headquarters has instructed all AMGs to establish a Denazification Bureau to examine the records of all people who held positions in the Nazi party and were responsible for crimes against humanity or for looting occupied countries. We are going to set up two basic departments in Munchberg," he explained. "One will consist of five men representing a cross-section of the community who will act as a board to examine the records and files we furnish them and make recommendations based on their findings. The other department will be supervised directly through our office. If the civilian board recommends that a business or farm or other property be placed into custodianship and we accept its recommendation, this second department will appoint a custodian in place of the Nazi owner. You understand?"

I indicated that I followed his explanation, still not sure where I fitted in. "For the five-man board we are appointing leaders of the community who represent a true cross-section of all concerned, and since you have already demonstrated your personal integrity and ability, we would like you to be one of the five. Will you accept?"

I was overwhelmed. To my knowledge, no other displaced person in Germany had been offered such responsibility or recognition. "Captain, I am very moved and very proud that you should choose me. I consider this a privilege and will consider the confidence you have placed in me an honored trust. Of course I accept," I said.

"Good," he answered. "We had hoped that you would. I am very pleased that you will be one of the men on the board."

He then told me that the other four members had already

been appointed. They were the leader of the new Social Democratic party; an attorney who was the leader of the Christian Social Democratic party; the Burgermeister of Helmbrechts, who was the leader of the Free Democratic party; and a representative of the Communist party—someone from every faction of political life permitted under the occupation. I was the only one not a spokesman for a political party.

An indoctrination meeting was scheduled at the AMG for instruction in procedures, duties, and responsibilities. The Political Affairs Department would furnish us with the files they wanted us to review, and they pointed out the sensitive and informative sections of the questionnaires we were to examine and evaluate. When we had reached a conclusion and submitted our recommendation, they would make the final decision and take action accordingly. They stressed that our recommendations would be given very careful consideration but that final judgment would always rest solely with them. They told us, "Offices will be placed at your disposal, so that you will have a central place to meet. You will need secretarial help, and we have provided for that also. We can promise you the cooperation of our office and the CIC whenever you need guidance or information. And we are instructing the Landratsamt and the Burgermeistersamt [the Board of Supervisors of the Landkreis and the Council of Mayors of the Landkreis] and all the various German authorities to give you full cooperation. We want to see to it that these people are completely removed from any position where they can influence the economic and political life here and continue to spread their poison."

After our briefing we met to elect a chairman, and with the leader of the Christian Social Democratic party installed, our Denazification Board began to operate. The AMG supplied us with an accumulation of files they wanted checked. They fell into many categories: teachers, professors, doctors, businessmen, manufacturers, civil servants, small and large property owners, farmers, and ranchers. Before long word leaked out and the people involved knew their histories were being scrutinized and judged. Several times a week, sometimes at night, we met

234

in our special office in the Munchberg City Hall. Each of us had before him a copy of the suspect individual's questionnaire as the chairman announced it, and we took turns analyzing and discussing it. If the man had become a member of the Nazi party before 1933, there was very little doubt about recommending his removal, since he had obviously joined of his own volition. Such people were subject to automatic dismissal anyway. And if the man had belonged to the SS or Gestapo, unquestionably he had to be removed. But not all the decisions were as easily reached or as clear-cut, for we discovered many things had to be taken into consideration that we had not forseen.

The file of a German doctor lay before us, and his record of high-ranking membership in the Nazi party was clearly spelled out. While he had not himself played an active part in any inhumane acts, how could we permit a man of medicine who by the very fact of his party membership had lent his support to the most vicious and anti-human crimes in history continue to serve as chief of staff at the local hospital? We could recommend that he be dismissed and forbidden to practice his profession—but he was a surgeon, and the only one in our area. Could we deprive the community of his services in the name of justice? We could not in all practicality do this, but we could and did vote to recommend that his status be changed and the AMG accepted our recommendation. The doctor was given only temporary clearance and allowed to continue to practice on extensions only; he could obtain no permanent position or clearance.

I voted vehemently against clearing any of the men who had helped create the Nazi party—those who had worn the gold pins so proudly showing they had been among the first to join in the early 1930s. In the beginning our votes were mostly unanimous and were seldom questioned or reversed by the AMG. Many of the cases involved men of wealth and power, some of them owners of vast textile factories which made up the principal industry of Landkreis Munchberg. There were men who had ranked high in the party and had enriched themselves during the war by bringing in machinery looted from occupied countries and the slave labor to operate them. We even visited the factories involved and inspected the machinery to determine the country of its origin so that we could be certain of the facts.

Whenever we recommended placing a Nazi's business or property into custodianship and our recommendation was approved by the AMG, the second board they had established would appoint a custodian in the owner's place. Some of the factories involved were back in operation and giving badly needed employment to the people of the area. It was essential that they be kept in operation and that the farms and ranches involved be kept productive. The custodian took complete charge and received compensation from the business as determined by the AMG. The Nazi owner was barred from any voice in the business and from any control of the finances. He could not enter the premises or interfere with the decisions of the custodian in any way. His only possible access was to take employment in his own factory if permitted to do so. The custodians, mostly Germans, had already been cleared of Nazi affiliation, and some of them were already employed in the very factories and mills of which they assumed control, so they had the knowledge and experience to keep the businesses functioning.

I found the work challenging and exciting. At least in Munchberg (the only place we knew where this had happened), a Jewish displaced person could sit in judgment of his persecutors. It was no small satisfaction to me, my family and friends. I went to each meeting eagerly despite the constant pressure of my other work, and never missed one.

The voice of the board, at first united and clear, began to change—imperceptibly at first; then, later, a radical shift occurred. Where heretofore discussions had been open and intelligent I now found myself listening to sermons from the others as to why we should make exceptions in this case and in that. Suddenly there were excuses. This man had been too young to know what he was doing; and that man did what he did only because he was forced to; he could not help himself.

The discussions became heated when our votes began to split. More often than not I found myself allied with the Communist party leader against the other three, and many cases went to the AMG with a three-to-two vote against any action being taken. But the AMG was not to be easily influenced, and many times when they felt the board's recommendations were too lenient, based on the file, they called us in and questioned our decisions. To my satisfaction and to their credit, they overruled many of the recommendations I had voted against.

I made sure that I was at each meeting even when the Communist leader deserted his political beliefs and became a German among Germans again, leaving me the lone dissenter. In one classic example we examined the case of a small textile manufacturing business in Helmbrechts, operated by a father and his two sons. One of the sons had a gold party pin, and the other had joined the party around 1926. But our examination of the records and their factory failed to indicate that they had used their positions to enrich themselves by taking in looted machinery. The case could have gone to the CIC for handling, but it was a borderline one, so it came to us instead. When the two brothers were questioned, they said it was all a mistake. If there had been any war profiteering, their eighty-year-old father was the guilty one, not they; after all, the business belonged to him, not them, and their ancient father had not been a Nazi, had he? I cast the only vote for turning their factory over to a custodian; the other four men fully accepted their explanation and found them innocent. It was outrageous and unjust, but I stayed on the board, gratified when the AMG overruled the decision.

The troublesome, gradual change in the atmosphere of the Denazification Board was compensated for by the satisfaction I felt at the healthy condition of our people. They were settling down. There were more married couples among us and a slowly increasing number of babies. We were better dressed and better fed than those less fortunate in the camps and even those in other communities where the relationships were strained between the different factions. The new arrivals who came daily to our office were housed as soon as possible, but demand suddenly exceeded supply, and we encountered trouble for the first time.

The Communist regime in Poland and Hungary began to bear down on the people. The Jews who had returned to their homes in those countries or who had been liberated and stayed in the eastern part of Europe found themselves once more oppressed and persecuted. New anti-Semitic violence erupted, and in the Polish town of Kielce a tragic event took place. A new pogrom was under way. The Poles, apparently angry with the less than 5 percent of the Jewish people who had returned, turned on them and committed wanton acts of murder and persecution. Perhaps some of them were concerned that they would have to return to the Jews the personal property they had appropriated after the transports had passed by on their way to the ovens and camps. The news of the pogrom shocked all the decent people in Europe and all over the world. Its immediate result was a new migration from the East. Fleeing Jews crossed over into the Western zone and began to overflow into Bavaria and inevitably into Munchberg. We could not continue to absorb them, but I was determined that they would not be turned away.

I went to Major Abbott with the problem and a proposal. "The suburb of Helmbrechts is only fifteen or twenty minutes away from our city by car. It was also spared any war damage, Major, and even though it's only a little smaller than Munchberg, there's only one Jewish man living there. Because of the terrible pogroms in the Eastern zone, there is a new flood of displaced persons pouring into our zone and we are feeling the pressure here in Munchberg right now." He knew of the pogroms, of course, but was not aware of the size of the migration nor of the speed with which it was taking place. "I think we have proven ourselves to you, Major. In what we have achieved so far you have shown us only the finest cooperation, for which we are very grateful. We have accomplished a lot together, and with your continued help we can do even more."

"What do you propose, Mr. Schapelski?" he asked me.

"I would like your permission to expand our operations into Helmbrechts to find additional housing there. You have my promise if you approve that you will have no reason to regret your decision," I said.

I had no difficulty convincing him, and with Helmbrechts opened up, the pressure eased and the door to Munchberg stayed open.

Chapter
24

As our operation expanded our office space became stretched to its limits. No one could have foreseen when Baruch and I first moved in what those original four small rooms would eventually have to accommodate. Lilly and I had commented on the situation while at the AMG one day, and they had made a note of our increased requirements, promising to get into the matter. A day came when we could no longer wait. Special orders were issued that displaced persons would be taken off German ration cards and would be supplied instead directly by UNRRA. This involved taking delivery of bulk shipments of food and other supplies, and storing and distributing them. Larger quarters and a sizable warehouse had now become essential.

Just when our need was critical a magnificent villa that had been occupied by Allied troops was evacuated, and the American military government graciously turned it over to us. We had only a few days in which to convert it to its new use before the first shipment of UNRAA food was due to arrive. It had obviously once been elaborately and richly furnished, and there were still some Oriental carpets and a few pieces of fine furniture we could use. The basement was large enough to make a fine warehouse, and our people swarmed through it, cleaning and hammering together shelves for the foodstuffs we expected to store. I assigned Tanc and Schutzman as storekeepers and Joachim Komet, a vice-president of our community, as warehouse overseer.

The first shipment arrived, and our system went into gear. The warehouse store was open several days a week. The people came there to receive the weekly rations of flour, potatoes, and other bulk foods that UNRRA had allotted. The storekeepers kept detailed records of the supplies received and distributed. We filed monthly reports with UNRRA, updating the number of people in our community, and they sent monthly shipments based on our requirements.

With the space we now had we could begin to fill other pressing needs. The first floor of the villa had been converted into offices at last adequate for the many activities we had crammed into the old office. And there was sufficient room left over for a recreation area and meeting hall, as well as a little café on the same floor. But the most pressing need was for adequate space to fulfill a spiritual hunger too long unsatisfied. Up to this time we had been holding services regularly on the Sabbath and on our High Holy Days wherever we could, but not everyone could worship together. There was no one place big enough to accommodate all of us. Now at last we had the space to form our own synagogue. Once again we could freely and proudly practice the ancient faith no Nazi hell nor the murder of six million of our people could destroy.

We had our synagogue, our congregation, and our faith, but we had no Torah. The Central Community in Munich and Bamberg were unable to help us. Where in Nazi Germany could there be a Jewish religious object the fanatics had not destroyed? I searched everywhere without success. One day Mr. Weistuch, a member of our community, left for a trip to Nuremberg, and I asked him to look there for a Torah. The Jewish community of Nuremberg could not help him either.

241

All their synagogues had been burned, and the books and religious objects taken from the Jewish homes had been destroyed. He walked through an old temple and went down into the basement of the wrecked building. There he found a charred heap of prayerbooks, menorahs, and other religious objects, almost unrecognizable in the ashes. He searched through them and miraculously found a Torah intact, only slightly charred by the fire, and brought it back to Munchberg. We were overjoyed and inspired by the treasure we had found and placed it with reverent hands on the *bimah* we had built. Our synagogue was complete.

The second floor of the villa was soon made useful, too. The Joint Distribution Committee sent us a doctor and nurse from Bamberg, displaced persons themselves, and they established a dispensary with several beds for patients needing in-house care.

I set aside a storeroom for clothing and shoes from the "Joint," and we watched the monthly distribution of these scarce items closely. Everyone was entitled to a fair share, but since the distribution was left to our local discretion, we had to be careful not to let ourselves become indulgent and find ourselves short in the event of emergencies. Joe Komet supervised this operation also. He and his assistants had a master list of community members, and whenever clothing or shoes were issued it was meticulously recorded. When new shipments came in, we held a committee meeting consisting of Lilly, Joe Komet, Drexler, and myself to determine distribution. We tried to be as impartial as possible, allocating the available clothing and shoes according to need. Joe notified the people selected by card and did an excellent job of resolving the inevitable problems that arose once in a while.

With such great quantities of valuable and scarce supplies warehoused in the building, we needed permanent security and maintenance, so Ignatz Rotter and his brother moved into the villa to provide resident security and to supervise the maintenance workers. In addition, the regular weekly and monthly shipments of commodities like cigarettes, food, and clothing were a constant temptation to black-market operators. Traffic through the villa had become so heavy that we badly needed someone to keep order in the queues. I asked for and received permission from the AMG to form our own police force. No German police officer could arrest a displaced person without the consent of the AMG; only the American military police themselves could perform such an arrest. The permission to form our own police force was another expression of the Americans' confidence in us and our ability to govern our own lives. I appointed Mr. Adler as Chief of Police, and he selected as officers five young men from our community who had had some military training. No German or DP could carry a live weapon, so even our police were armed with only a nightstick for which they thankfully had little use. We obtained appropriate uniforms for them and set aside a small room which we called our "jail." One or two officers were always stationed at the front door of the villa to greet and announce important visitors—ranking American officers, representatives of UNRRA, JDC and other communities, and even German dignitaries and officials. It was a startling sight for many of them as well as a great satisfaction for us to see Jewish police functioning authoritatively in Germany.

On the spacious grounds of the villa we built a playground for the children, few as they were, and an athletic field for the adults. Little did the former Nazi occupants realize when they surrendered this villa to the AMG that one day we would fill each room with the very life and meaning which they and their colleagues had tried and failed to wipe from the face of the earth.

Our community grew and flourished and the new center was in constant use, registering new arrivals, issuing papers, dispensing medical supplies and treatment, distributing food and clothing, meeting to discuss problems, holding wedding ceremonies and naming new babies, conducting our own services with our own rabbi and cantor, and gathering twice a week simply to enjoy ourselves with music, dancing, singing, and food. DPs from other communities in the Landkreis came to visit our center in Munchberg. There was no other place like it, and we were very proud. Our little world, temporary though it was, was sending its roots down deeper.

Through all these weeks and months of excitement, achievement, and frustration, Lilly and I had strengthened our personal bond of understanding and affection. In February we decided to marry. It was a far from easy decision to make and one we knew, once made, would be difficult for us to carry out. It was imperative for me to go on with the work to which I was committed and dedicated and to which there was no end in sight. And Lilly's position with the AMG was too vital to them and to us for her to withdraw. We both had such tremendous obligations to fulfill that there was really no room for a personal life. So we went alone to a rabbi and were married secretly.

Chapter
25

We did our best to provide proper medical attention for the members of our community whom food and rest alone could not cure. For the most part they responded to treatment and gradually found their way back to a state of almost normal health, at least physically. However, early in 1946 we began to discover scattered cases of tuberculosis, and as the number mounted I was very much concerned not only for the care of those already diseased but for the risk to the other members of the community who might be susceptible to infection.

I brought the pressing problem to the attention of the AMG and asked for their aid. They immediately responded and helped me set up a three-point program.

First, those already stricken were taken for treatment and isolation to a sanitarium staffed by German doctors and nurses in Gauting, in the foothills of the Bavarian Alps, that had been taken over by the American occupation forces.

It should be noted as a medical curiosity that while some of the patients had developed tuberculosis only after the liberation, others who had been invalids (with tuberculosis and other diseases) before the war somehow in their fight to survive had experienced a remission while within the camps—only to suffer a relapse after they had been liberated.

The second part of the program was aimed at the protection of the rest of the community by uncovering any latent unsuspected cases among them. For this the AMG provided mobile X-ray units and the necessary vaccine. Fortunately, very few latent cases were discovered, and those few were immediately placed under treatment in the sanitarium.

The third part of the program was a continuous medical observation of the other members of the immediate family of every known patient to see if any evidence of the disease was developing in any one of them.

Because of the rapidity with which these steps were taken and because of the full cooperation and understanding we were given, our friends in the sanitarium recovered and were discharged and soon returned to us with their health restored, and the incidence of new cases rapidly diminished.

Chapter
26

IN THE SPRING of 1946 one of the landholdings in Landkreis Munchberg which had belonged to a high-ranking SS officer was to be placed under custodianship by the AMG. Because of its unusually important function in the food economy of the area, the AMG was faced with the necessity of keeping it at the peak of operation without interruption. Captain Stamates, by now a close and good friend, asked me to take on the responsibility.

The captain explained that the huge ranch was a very complex experimental center where they were performing hybridization projects to develop and grow more and better strains of crops. The scientist in charge of the experiments had been there all through the war, and although they knew him to have been a Nazi of high rank, he had been permitted to continue his work because the center could not be operated without him. The wife and young son of the interned owner lived on the property, but the AMG wanted them excluded from the management and financial side of the business.

Although I protested that I had no experience in farming, much less on such a highly scientific level, the captain prevailed, explaining that I would be concerned only with the business end and that I would be fulfilling a real need of the AMG. I could not refuse. From then on I went to the farm several times a week to check the conditions, look over the books, approve the payment of payroll and and bills, sign checks, and administer the office routine. There were hundreds of people employed both in the laboratories and on the land, so that it was a time-consuming responsibility. However, it was all worth while. The crops and livestock flourished and helped greatly to fill the need for good, fresh food.

The ranch property was quite beautiful, with acres of gardens, flowers, and trees. From time to time I invited friends and dignitaries from the town and out-of-town visitors to join us there on Saturday afternoons for picnics. Mr. Scanes, the UNRRA representative who joined us in Munchberg later in 1946, was especially fond of the place and came there often.

I held the custodianship until 1949, when I returned the responsibility to the American military government. Subsequently, it was returned to the family of the original owner.

During 1946 the Denazification Board continued to deteriorate into complete disharmony. We had reviewed file after file on men who held vast areas of land in farms and ranches and still, in some cases, continued to live on them or control them. For example, in one case that came before us, which clearly illustrated how distorted and useless the board had become, the wife and family of an interned high-ranking SS officer still lived on their farm in Wilmersreut. There was no question as to his guilt. So that when I heard the irrelevant arguments proposed in his defense, I became deeply angered. "Gentlemen," I told them bitterly, "there can be no doubt in any of our minds that not only has this man enriched himself during the war through his criminal position in the SS, but he even took direct part in proven war crimes. What right do we have to let his family operate a project under the government? It's a very clear-cut case!"

"Well," the defense came back, "he's interned in any case, so let's leave everything alone."

I pointed out that this was in direct contradiction to the AMG's instructions.

"But if we interfere with the management of such a big ranch it could affect the production of food," they countered.

"That's not the issue," I replied. "We are not here to make decisions about shortages. We are here to reach a decision about this man's actions and his participation in war crimes. It is our duty to vote on that issue and that issue only. It is the AMG's prerogative to decide what action should be taken. If you are honest with yourselves, you will face this reality." I pursued the argument until the vote was taken and it was recommended that the ranch be placed into custodianship.

Chapter
27

MANY FINE, DEDICATED REPRESENTATIVES of the Joint Distribution Committee, the Palestine AMT (known also as the Jewish Agency for Palestine), and UNRRA came to us expressing their admiration for our well-run community and seeking our assistance on various problems, one of which had become an increasing matter of concern to me also. Some of our people in Munchberg, like others who had settled in different cities all over Germany, were anxious to return to their regular trades, businesses and professions, where the state of their health and finances permitted, and if they were able to secure the necessary licenses. A few who had come from Germany originally were fortunate enough on their return to regain the businesses and properties that had been taken away from them and were already occupied in rebuilding them; but most of our people were just existing on aid. For them there had been little or nothing we could do.

There was one group, however, for whom we saw a possible opportunity: the young boys and girls and young men and women who had been taken into the concentration camps as children and teenagers and came out orphans, with little or no chance of an education or training. At one meeting with the JDC we discussed their special situation. It was disturbing that they should have to continue to live and grow up in the restricted atmosphere of the DP camps, existing from day to day without education, detailed supervision, leadership, or any creative activity. They were unable to plan any concrete future and had no parents to instill in them the proper moral or spiritual values. They were becoming demoralized and slipping into a negative pattern of life, some of them getting involved in petty black-market activities.

As our discussions progressed, the JDC brought representatives of the Palestine AMT to join in, and at one memorable meeting at which Lilly was also present we managed to induce Mr. Scanes, the UNRRA team worker, to join us. We shared our fears for the future of these young people and the condition they would be in if left to themselves when the time eventually came for them to leave, as it surely must one day. "We would like to find a place where they could learn a useful trade for the life ahead—someplace where they could be trained as farmers, so that when and if they emigrate to Palestine, they will have the ability to make lives for themselves and help build their country."

As we talked the idea was expressed that it would be a wonderful solution if we could set up a kibbutz for them. "What do you think?" I asked. Their response was enthusiastic, and ideas began to fly back and forth across the table. "It would keep them occupied while they learned a trade and received an education in agriculture," a young American girl from the JDC said excitedly.

The representative of the Jewish Agency volunteered to do his part. "We can send teachers to get them started. They'll be coming to Palestine anyway."

But where and how to do it? Some of the recent cases involving the custodianship of nearby farms suddenly entered my mind, presenting a possible solution.

"I have an idea," I told them. They listened eagerly as I described the properties that had passed into custodianship through the Denazification Board. "Who could be better entitled?" I asked.

I was so firmly convinced of the rightness of the plan that I approached Major Abbott about it right away. He heard me out courteously. "I can appreciate all that you have said, Mr. Schapelski, but you must realize that we must also consider what effect this would have on the Germans. It may unsettle them and disturb their community."

I had to reassure him, reminding him of our past performance. "Major Abbott, you again have my solemn promise that I will be personally responsible for the entire project. If there should be the slightest problem, you can close it down immediately. Let's do something together to help these young people and to show others that it is possible to rehabilitate them. We have already built such a fine record that this would be one more example of what can be achieved with cooperation and understanding between us."

He gave it more thought and then turned to his telephone and called in some of the other officers. "Gentlemen, Mr. Schapelski has proposed a very complicated and delicate situation to me," he explained. They went into all the ramifications of such a project. It would mean turning over to me houses, land under cultivation, pasture, livestock, and equipment so that a group of young, inexperienced boys and girls could be taught to become farmers. It would be risking the peace of the Landkreis and jeopardizing the output of the land, and if the project failed, it would be a serious reflection on their judgment. "We'll give this serious thought, Mr. Schapelski," Major Abbott concluded. "I'll see you again in a day or so and let you know our decision." I thanked him and left with high hopes.

He was true to his word, as always. In a matter of days he gave me an affirmative answer. As military governor of Landkreis Munchberg, he was prepared to place in my hands a suitable site for the kibbutz. We were jubilant! Now we had to get down to real planning. Everyone had been waiting eagerly for his answer—the JDC, the Palestine AMT, and all our friends. "Now," I cautioned them, "before we go any further, I want you to know that I have made a solemn promise to Major Abbott that I will be personally responsible for every detail. This will have to be set up and controlled so well that he will never have any reason to regret it. On the contrary, we must do everything we can to make him proud. Now, let's get down to work."

We made out a list of the special needs for a kibbutz to accommodate 100 to 150 people. They wanted to start with more, but I was concerned that the housing would be inadequate and it would be purposeless to bring young people from a crowded camp to an equally crowded farm. The farm would have to be as self-contained as possible. There would have to be houses and barns we could convert into dormitories and sufficient fresh water and sanitary facilities. And, ideally, it should have the latest farming equipment in good condition.

When our list was done I returned to Major Abbott's office, and he sent down to the custodianship office for details of the available farms and ranches in our area for us to study. There were several good possibilities but one which sounded ideal. It was the farm of the interned SS officer whose case I had fought so bitterly before the Denazification Board. Major Abbott agreed it was the most logical choice. The next step was to notify the wife and give her time to vacate the property. He assigned two officers to accompany me to the ranch. She reacted angrily to the news, but there was nothing she could do; she had been extremely fortunate to hold on to it for as long as she had. They gave her two weeks to move.

All the plans started rolling along with great speed. As soon as the Germans had left the farm a small staff of our own people, previously selected and trained by the Palestine AMT, moved in to prepare the way. We began to stock the farm with supplies from our own warehouse to meet the needs of the newcomers who would automatically become members of our community and thereby eligible for supplies from the "Joint" and

UNRRA. We had enough space in our building to take care of them. We compensated for the insufficiency of exisiting houseing by erecting sturdy tents. We took care of every detail according to our plan. I had exacted from the JDC and AMT their promise that while the leadership was to come from them, I was to be kept informed of exactly how everything would be set up and controlled, since I was ultimately responsible.

A few days later the first group arrived, and Lilly and I were there to greet them. We were struck by their youth; there were so few people of their age in our community. They looked healthy and vigorous, a colorful mixture of young Jews from every country in Europe—Poland, Russia, Lithuania, Czechoslovakia—and all united in one common goal. It was exciting for them and for us as well. They moved into their separate dormitories, the young boys and men in some and the girls and young women in others. There were a few married couples who were given limited but private quarters. We had sent a supply of food ahead of time so that a welcoming meal awaited them. Everything went smoothly. They promptly elected their own leaders, and the teachers assigned everyone to a training schedule. A few of the Germans working on the farm stayed to help acquaint them with the land, machinery, and care of the livestock. We felt very proud of their spirit and the atmosphere of hope they brought with them. It was something I had not seen for years.

After only a few weeks things had gone so well that they were almost running the entire farm themselves. Not only had they learned the basics of farming but they had initiated classes in Hebrew so that they would be able to speak, read, and write the common language of Palestine. I went to Wilmersreut every chance I got and asked them what they needed most. The girls asked for blue skirts and white blouses and the boys for blue trousers and shorts and white shirts. And I saw to it that they got them. I had the added satisfaction, too, of seeing the reaction of the Denazification Board when they heard of the use to which the farm had been put.

I was particularly concerned for the satisfactory progress of these young people and for the overall success of the kibbutz because, in my mind, this was just a start. If successful, there need be no limit to the number we could help return to a useful life. To celebrate the burning enthusiasm and drive they showed in taking hold, I felt it would be a tremendous occasion to have an opening ceremony, not just to boost everyone's morale but to demonstrate effectively what we could do. Invitations were quickly accepted by all the officers of the American military government, the representatives of the Joint Distribution Committee and the Palestine AMT, officials of UNRRA, members of other nearby Jewish communities, leaders of the German community in Munchberg and in the Landkreis, and, of course, the proudest people of all, our own community.

It was an unforgettable affair, an inspiring day in the lives of all who took part. Speeches of welcome and praise were delivered by American officers and officials. Captain Spiro spoke eloquently and passionately about the tremendous step we had taken in bringing these young people back to life. The boys and girls of the kibbutz, dressed smartly in sparkling white shirts and blouses and blue pants and skirts, glowing with vitality and renewed health, sang and danced for us, whirling in the hora and other traditional Jewish folk dances. It was a deeply moving and highly emotional experience for everyone present. Our guests were obviously impressed by what they saw, and we were proud. For us, it was a hopeful glimpse of the future and a bittersweet remembrance of the past, the youth we had lost in the camps, the years we would never recapture. These young people would live those years for us. We looked for a fleeting moment through their eyes.

We had done a tremendous thing for these young boys and girls and for ourselves. We had started the first kibbutz in our part of Germany, and it was a success. As far as we knew there were only two others, one on the ranch formerly owned by the infamous Nazi Julius Streicher, near Regensberg, and one other in Bayreuth. A whole new avenue of rescue had opened up. Why stop with one? These vigorous young people had ignited my enthusiasm and enlarged my goals. I thought many times in the months that followed of the debt I owed them for the fine, shining example of hope they had shown me.

In the weeks that followed the opening of the Wilmersreut kibbutz we continued to watch over the new members of our community, anxiously at first and then confidently as they maintained their enthusiasm and continued to pour their energies into their work, succeeding in every way beyond our wildest expectations. Lilly and I went there often, frequently taking along a guest or two from the JDC or the AMG or whomever happened to be visiting.

By contrast, time now began to weigh even heavier on the adults, and with the growing realization that our exodus was still along way off they became more anxious to return to their professions and occupations. By order of the AMG, displaced persons, especially those who were former concentration-camp inmates, had to be extended certain privileges and priorities by the German authorities in opening businesses or securing professional positions and jobs, whenever available. We gave them every help we could to get them started, from filing a letter of application for a business permit to locating an automobile or other vehicle still in short supply if their work depended on it. It was particularly difficult to get a permit for a business because of the shortage of materials, especially in the textile industry, which was the principal industry of Munchberg.

An application by a displaced person and/or a former camp inmate usually took a great deal of effort to process as we pursued the various stages through the office of the Landkreis and the German authorities involved, but the results were more than satisfying. Some of our people who had strong backgrounds in trades, such as textile manufacturing, were employed by the AMG on our recommendation as custodians of local factories temporarily seized under the denazification law.

Chapter
28

QUITE SUDDENLY a very disturbing element was introduced into our otherwise progressive calm. While attending one of the frequent meetings at the AMG with the representative of UNRRA, we were presented to Colonel Zimmerman of the military police and informed that Munchberg had been chosen as the site of a displaced persons' jail for all of Bavaria.

At first I had some difficulty in understanding this announcement. The fact that there was a sufficient number of displaced persons in custody to warrant a jail was startling. We had not experienced any convictions in our community. The colonel went on to explain that the prisoners would be serving sentences passed on them by the military government courts, and since they could not be held in any German jail for more than three months, the American military government had decided to establish this permanent detention camp for them. The jail was to be established in a former slave-labor camp whose original inmates, mostly French and Italian slave laborers, had been transported home not long after the liberation, after which it had been temporarily occupied and subsequently vacated by American troops. But the camp had remained, complete with barracks, barbed wire, and guardhouses.

I left the meeting surprised and troubled. Munchberg was a relatively small city to have been chosen for this jail, and I was upset to be suddenly reminded that the days of camps and barbed wire were far from over. I called a meeting of our community officers and related the events of the meeting, advising them that we could expect the camp to be filled very soon with men shipped from all over Bavaria, displaced persons from all walks of life and of many nationalities—Poles, Rumanians, Hungarians, Jews, and non-Jews. "The American officers have requested our cooperation in keeping civilians away from the area, and I have promised them that we will comply. But the officer in charge, Colonel Zimmerman, has invited me to visit the camp when it is functioning, at which time I will try to do what I can to help the men inside," I assured my friends.

Several weeks later, after the prisoners had settled in, I called the colonel and he invited me to tour the camp with his staff. A full regiment of military police had been assigned to Munchberg under his command. During our tour no attempt was made to restrain me from talking to anyone. It was immediately apparent that the men were well treated and that living conditions were adequate in the circumstances. I was unable to converse with many of them because I could not speak their languages, so I talked mostly with Jews and Poles. I asked why they were there, and from the replies, honest and direct, it appeared that the offenses for which they had been sentenced were more technical than serious, at least in most of the cases I heard. Some had been charged with dealing in the black market when they claimed that in fact they had merely exchanged small quantities of their own personal rations for other goods or supplies.

None told me of any criminal act or act of violence that would warrant a jail sentence, and their imprisonment seemed to me grossly unfair in the light of their background and suffering. "Do you need anything?" I asked. "Is there anything we can do for you on the outside?" They had no complaints or grievances, but they did ask for spiritual comfort. They wanted a rabbi and

258

kosher food, or a priest or minister, depending on their religious affiliation, and I promised we would do our best to help.

After my return I discussed the disturbing tour with Lilly. She was the court reporter and interpreter as well as secretary to the Public Safety Officer in Munchberg. Maybe she would have some answers. "On what are they basing these convictions?" I questioned her. "Are these new laws?" I was more than a little dumbfounded that the German Penal Code was being applied to displaced persons with little, if any, special consideration for their presence in this country. I did my best to try to understand. True, there were safeguards. When the German police placed a suspect in temporary custody, day or night, he had to be taken to the AMG for an immediate hearing by the Public Safety Officer before he could be jailed. This applied to all displaced persons and/or former concentration-camp inmates. They were usually held for trial by the American military governor of the district, and the Public Safety Officer acted as prosecutor. In many cases the military governor acted as judge, and the clerk of the court, which function Lilly also performed, read the charges.

Even with these safeguards I was still concerned. I could not bring myself to accept it as justice. There was something very wrong with the whole situation. I had looked closely at those men. Most of them were young, as were most of the surviving DPs, and I knew they shared the common dream of all to emigrate as soon as possible, most of them to Palestine but some to the United States of America. How could they ever hope to enter the United States? Even if they qualified under the newly established DP quota, any conviction and jail sentence, no matter how minor the offense, would permanently bar them.

On subsequent visits I delved more deeply into the details of some of the individual cases, and the facts I learned only seemed to confirm that the punishment was far in excess of the crime. Men told me they had been arrested for trading a package of cigarettes from their rations for a shirt, or a piece of chocolate for something else. If they were found guilty, the

259

judge (the military governor or other American officer) could impose a jail sentence of up to one year or a fine of ten thousand marks, or both! Defendants charged with graver and more serious offenses were transferred to Bayreuth to the Intermediate Court for disposition and trial.

I asked some of the men who had defended them at their trials and was astounded when the answer was invariably "nobody." When they came before the judge to be charged, they had to accept legal representation, such as it was. If there were insufficient American officers to act as defense counsel as well as prosecutors, the only alternative was to accept a German attorney, which was naturally abhorrent to them so that very few did. Rather than endure a trial, where they would have to speak through yet another German interpreter, most of them had thrown themselves upon the mercy of the court and accepted a short jail sentence or the payment of a fine. It was incredible that these men had had to submit to this distortion of justice, unaware of the irreparable harm to their futures that went along with conviction and sentence.

The influx of people into the kibbutz, augmented by the several hundred men in the camp, had increased the demands on the supplies from UNRRA to such an extent they decided to establish a local office to exercise control. They had, in fact, already had representatives inspect the proposed site for the jail and had previously toured the camp after the liberation when the slave laborers were still there. A full UNRRA team moved into Munchberg under the permanent supervision of an Englishman, Mr. Scanes, who lost no time in calling on us. He was amazed to learn of the scope of our operation and the number of people settled in the Landkreis and expressed himself as being genuinely impressed and more than satisfied with our controls and our eligibility for UNRRA aid as borne out by the records and lists he had inspected. We carried on our conversation through his secretary, a Latvian girl who was herself a displaced person who accompanied him, translating into German and English. At the end of our meeting I promised I would take him on a complete tour of all our settlements so he could observe them first hand.

Now that we were to deal directly with each other, it became convenient to establish Mr. Scanes's offices adjacent to the Jewish Community Center, where living quarters for his staff could also be provided. The adjoining villa, which coincidentally had originally belonged to the same German family who owned the villa we occupied, became Scanes's permanent offices in Munchberg.

On Lilly's first free day we gave him a complete tour of Munchberg, Helmbrechts, the kibbutz at Wilmersreut, and the jail camp. And he seemed quite impressed. I told him how grateful we all were for the good UNRRA was doing in helping so many people who had come back from hell to nothing.

In this elderly Englishman we had found a new friend and a dedicated worker. I was deeply honored when after only a few weeks in Munchberg he made me an official UNRRA team worker.

UNITED NATIONS RELIEF & REHABILITATION ADMINISTRATION

Director:
A. W. van Zuylen
Deputy Director:
E. PHILIP SCANES

TEAM 186
DISPLACED PERSONS CENTRE
MUNCHBERG, Germany

18 June 1946

Telephones:
Munchberg 395
Helmbrechts 952
House, Munchberg 278

To Whom It May Concern:
SUBJECT: NATAN SCHAPELSKI

Mr. Natan Schapelski has been designated PRINCIPAL OFFICER and LIAISON of the Jewish Farms and Communities in Landkreis Munchberg and Naila by UNRRA. All orders and directions will be issued to and through him.

E. PHILIP SCANES
Director Munchberg Sub Team
Deputy·Director UNRRA Team 186

I visited the jail camp often, and whenever a representative of the JDC or Phillip Scanes was available I took him with me. I felt the greater number of important visitors I could bring the higher the morale of the prisoners would be. It would help them just to know that a lot of outside people knew about them and were concerned.

Colonel Zimmerman granted permission for our rabbi-cantor to conduct services on Friday evenings and Saturday mornings for the Jewish inmates, and we sent in kosher food, especially for the Sabbath, from our Community Center kitchen. Since none of the non-Jewish former concentration-camp inmates in our community were members of the clergy, I suggested to the Germans that they supply a priest and minister for the other denominations. Colonel Zimmerman gave me a special pass to enter and leave the camp at will, and I frequently attended Jewish services there, with Captain Spiro joining me on the High Holy Days and Passover.

It wasn't long before a continuous pilgrimage of prisoners' families, relatives, and friends began to arrive in Munchberg. On discovering that I had free access to the camp, they came to our house asking for news of their husbands, sons, and fathers and begging me to carry messages to them. I did what I could to ease their anguish. To help spread the word of the humane treatment of the prisoners, I took a group of reporters from the Bamberg Jewish-German newspaper inside so they could observe the living conditions first hand and report what they saw.

In the spring of 1946, the first Passover since the liberation, I had the moving experience of celebrating three *seders* on the first night, the first of them inside the camp, presided over by Captain Spiro. The JDC had sent matzoth and other special holiday food for the entire community, and every family received a sufficient share, with enough left over to take into the jail camp so those men would not feel excluded. Colonel Zimmerman gave us permission to bring in the necessary help to distribute the food and prayerbooks, and a small mess hall was assigned for our services and *seder* night meal. It was a very moving and joyful experience to be performing our religious rituals freely, even though these men were again imprisoned after their years of suffering and deprivation under the Nazis. Some newspapermen from the *Bamberger Press* were present, and they were deeply touched by the conflicting picture they saw—a Jewish-American army chaplain and cantor and a displaced person and former concentration-camp inmate conducting *seder* services for Jewish men convicted of violations of German law and imprisoned by their American liberators in a former German slave-labor camp.

Captain Spiro and I went on from the *seder* to our second *seder* at the Community Center, where Lilly joined us. It was even more joyful because all of the participants were free. From there Lilly and I went on to our third and final *seder* with my family, Sala, Max, and David, in our home.

It was a deeply moving Passover, this spring of 1946, bringing back a flood of memories of so many *seders* in the years before the darkness had descended on our lives. The smells of the kitchen were familiar and comforting, the faces around the table beloved and the ancient rituals easy to recapture. But there were so many faces missing, so many places set in our memories where no one came, nor would ever come. In our hearts we waited not just for the Prophet Elijah but for them.

Chapter
29

WILMERSREUT KIBBUTZ WAS AN UNQUALIFIED SUCCESS. The JDC and Palestine AMT already had more young people ready to settle in kibbutzim. And so I began more meetings with the AMG to find a place for them. I no longer needed to consult the commanding officer directly. His aides, captains and lieutenants, heard my plea and were receptive. A farm in Zell, not too far from Munchberg, that had also been the property of a high-ranking Nazi was turned over to us, and another 100 to 150 enthusiastic young people were brought in. Wilmersreut kibbutz sent over some experienced staff members to help them get settled, and within a few weeks we had another auspicious outdoor opening.

Zell, too, proved to be a success, and without wasting time I pushed for yet another site, which was granted us at Stambach—our third kibbutz. The three farms developed and maintained close ties with one another and helped each other in every way.

Each new success gave me an appetite for more, but there

was nowhere left to turn. Munchberg had already absorbed three kibbutzim, which was the maximum our Landkreis could support. I looked at the adjoining Landkreis, Naila. To my knowledge it had only a few displaced persons and no organized community. At a meeting with the Americans I strongly recommended that Landkreis Munchberg should not be the end of our project, that we should look elsewhere. "Naila was also relatively untouched by the war," I told them, "and they have not, as yet, given any real refuge to DPs. I would like your permission, sir," I said to the commanding officer, "to approach the officers in Naila and to use your name as a reference." He agreed to my request, and, armed with his recommendation, Lilly and I went to Naila to visit the AMG and to call upon the Landrat, Herr Milk. Although our letter of introduction carried the highest praise of the Munchberg AMG, we had to start from the very beginning and recite the history of our community, our aims and accomplishments and the successes we already enjoyed with the three existing, thriving kibbutzim. We explained again who our people were, from where they had come, and stressed that we were here only temporarily. "You can be sure it is neither our intention nor our desire to remain in Germany, gentlemen. We will leave as soon as there is a place for us to go. Until that time, it is our duty to find places for these young people where they can begin to rebuild their shattered lives."

We went back again and again, strongly supported by Mr. Scanes and especially by Captain Spiro, who spoke eloquently on our behalf, and by representatives of the JDC. Meanwhile, the AMG in Naila sent teams to inspect the existing kibbutzim first hand. Their reports must have borne out our claims, for finally the ice was broken and a farm in Landkreis Naila was turned over to us for our fourth kibbutz. Now, our responsibilities covered a much greater area, and to maintain a continuity of supervision and supply my authority as spokesman for the Jewish displaced persons and chairman of the Jewish community was extended into Naila. It became almost a full-time job to administer the four settlements, as well as to make our physical presence felt by visiting them frequently. We could not neglect one or favor another, so we tried to attend Oneg Shabbats on Saturdays at all of them whenever we could. Here, too, we brought along members of our community and newspapermen, and we organized working sessions and meetings whenever the opportunity presented itself. These visits were as uplifting to us as we hoped they were to the young people. It pleased them to have us there, and they went out of their way to welcome us with food grown on the farms and served outdoors, and we joined in their songs and dances.

It was continually interesting to us to watch the life pattern that was evolving. The relationships between the four settlements were close. They competed in inviting each other back and forth for festivities and celebrations. In each one every man and woman, boy and girl had a specific job to do, and any children were cared for in a special nursery. They each set aside a special house for a meeting place and community center where their duly elected leaders and representatives presided. In addition, they attended and took part in general meetings and elections at our center in Munchberg, where they had an equal voice and vote. Except for the staples we distributed from the JDC and UNRRA supplies, they lived off their own labors on the farms, and the Landrats' offices supplied us with ration cards for their uniforms and civilian clothes. The Central Community in Bamberg sent doctors regularly, and in emergencies our own doctor or a local doctor was available to them. There was seldom, if ever, any need to approach the AMG on their behalf. In fact, the AMG was as proud of their accomplishments as we were. The kibbutzim had become a showplace for them as well as for us, and many times our good friends from the Munchberg and Naila headquarters brought visitors from other AMG offices to see what they had helped to accomplish.

All of this was in strange contrast to the continued troubling reports of conflict and poor relationships in other communities, some so bad they indicated a complete lack of cooperation on all sides. It was invariably the same unhappy and frustrating story of a mutual lack of willingness to understand each other, further hampered by the barrier of trying to communicate through German interpreters. The very existence of the DP jail in Munchberg was a tragic example of the results. If there had only been a better relationship in those other cities, some of these men would not now be serving sentences in Munchberg. If someone had represented them, communicated on their behalf, some of these convictions could certainly have been prevented. We had hundreds of people in Munchberg and Helmbrechts and in our four kibbutzim and were very close to the Russian zone on the Czech border. Our exposure to opportunity for breaking the law was as great if not greater than in many of the other communities, and yet nothing similar had happened in Munchberg.

No one from Munchberg or Naila was in the jail. Our reputation for reliability and independence continued to grow with the AMG and among ourselves. We talked out our problems rather than fought them out. We exercised control over ourselves and tried not to inflame or anger the people in whose midst we were forced to rebuild our lives. The proof of our success was everywhere. I had only to look at the faces around me as I raced through days and nights far too short for all I wanted to accomplish.

Chapter
30

THE PEOPLE REGISTERED with the Jewish community and the Office for Former Concentration Camp Inmates had achieved limited legal status by virtue of our records and the records of the AMG. But as they began to move about more freely, it became increasingly apparent that apart from this they had no formal identification they could show to any authorities. Many of them did not speak German and were helpless if faced with questions, or the need to establish their place of residence or background, unless there was a sympathetic interpreter nearby to come to their aid.

I felt these people should be given some official identification that would be acknowledged by all the authorities, American and German. I discussed it at several meetings with the Public Safety Officer and representatives of the Counterintelligence Corps and various other officers and officials. They concurred, and it was decided to issue an official passport.

We put a notice in the papers requesting everyone registered to apply to my office for his *Kennkarte*. On application, they would be carefully screened, and it would be formally established that they had been cleared by the Betreuungsstelle Fur Opfers des Faschismus, the Office for the Care of Victims of Fascism.

When I was assured beyond doubt that they had met the requirements, the card was prepared, photograph attached, the seal of my office stamped on it, and my signature affixed, authenticating it as official. The people streamed into the office and we processed them as carefully and rapidly as we could. As soon as they were cleared, their *Legitimation Ausweis,* official identification, was sent in packages to the Counterintelligence Corps office, where it was double-checked. In almost every case my clearance went unquestioned, and the Counterintelligence Corps countersigned and counterstamped the card and returned it to my office for distribution.

Our people held these cards during the remainder of their stay in Munchberg, and all new arrivals received them the moment they, too, had been cleared. Once issued, the cards were valid without renewal. I had the honor of being issued the first card, No. 1, dated August 28, 1946, and countersigned by Julius Schlesinger of the CIC on September 6, 1946.

Chapter
31

In late 1945 I had been invited with the leaders of other Jewish communities throughout Germany to participate in a meeting at Munich where David Ben-Gurion delivered an impassioned speech about the establishment of a new State of Israel. It had inspired us with hope.

But now the news from Palestine was not at all encouraging. Great Britain had closed Palestine to Jewish immigrants because of the fighting that had erupted between the British troops and the Jews who had armed themselves.

The dream of so many European Jews to settle in a Jewish homeland had suffered an unexpected setback. Shiploads of Jews were being seized by the British and interned on the island of Cyprus while Palestine exploded. Any open emigration from Germany was discouraged.

Each time a new report of conflict reached us I could expect a telephone summons from Scanes, a loyal Englishman and now a troubled man. If he asked me to call at his office, I went alone, communicating through his secretary, but if he asked me to his house, Lilly went along to interpret for us. On each occasion his complaint was the same—how unfair it was for the Jews to rebel against British control of Palestine. "After all, Mr. Schapelski, we have been in Palestine for a very long time," he would charge, "and it's terribly wrong to expect us to withdraw and leave Palestine to your people." I never really understood what he expected from me personally or what he hoped to gain from our discussions. Finally, one day, provoked beyond control, I asked him bluntly, "Why don't you leave Palestine to the Jews and let them carry on alone?" Neither my answers nor my questions satisfied him, but he continued to call me every time a report reached him of further violence. I spent hours listening to him, trying to argue and reason with him, but to no avail. Then in 1948 news of the bombing of the King David Hotel in Jerusalem reached us, and he became not only angry but positively hostile. Unable to restrain myself any longer, I told him, "Mr. Scanes, all this bloodshed and violence can be quickly stopped if your people will only make up their minds to get out and let the Jews and Arabs come to their own understanding."

"What do you mean?" he replied testily. "We British are protecting the Jews. If we leave Palestine it will be only a matter of days before the Arabs slaughter your people."

"Well, Mr. Scanes," I retorted, "why don't you try it and leave their fate in their own hands?"

Our arguments were interminable and inconclusive and placed an enormous strain on our otherwise friendly relationship. The vital work his UNRRA team had done and was doing for our community compelled me to maintain an attitude of courteous tolerance. I could not afford to jeopardize what we had achieved. Throughout his arguments I sensed an unspoken question. Even though he never put it to me point-blank, I realized that his real concern was the possibility that the young people from our kibbutzim were going to be spirited away to join the illegal exodus to Palestine. And in truth they were. The training period of the first group was over, including surreptitious military training, and now with their education complete and their health restored, they were ready to move on to Palestine to take up the task of settling the new land. Their secret orders had come, and, like soldiers entering battle, they obeyed, prepared to face any hardship.

I had been involved in the plan by the Palestine AMT because I knew too many of the young people by name and by sight for it to be carried off without my knowledge. I knew that every detail of the plan had to be kept secret from Scanes. His loyalty would have demanded that he report to his government any movement of our people, even though he technically represented the United Nations. My only concern was the AMG and the effect this would have on their relationships with the British. I talked privately with some of the American officers in whom I had special confidence and trust. "Just supposing that some movement of people in and out of the kibbutzim took place without your knowledge, would a situation like this cause any embarrassment to the AMG or reflect back on our community? Mind you, I'm only asking a theoretical question," I assured them. They understood the true implication of my words and gave me to understand that they had no desire to know of any such movement officially. On the other hand, they were not going to send soldiers out to stand guard over the kibbutzim to prevent any movement.

With this tacit understanding I came to the conclusion that the cause was too important not to proceed. I knew these young people would have to make terrific sacrifices, that not all would reach Palestine, that many would find themselves instead interned once again with so many others on Cyprus. But once the decision was reached, the plan swung into operation smoothly and efficiently. At night, truckloads of new young people from DP camps rolled up to the kibbutzim to replace the exact number of girls and boys, young men and women who were leaving. The familiar faces disappeared in the darkness on the reloaded trucks, rolling away toward friendly ports in France and Italy, where they joined other groups waiting for ships. However, their names remained behind, for we left our lists unchanged, and the new recruits assumed the identities of those who had gone ahead so there was never any apparent change in the population of the kibbutzim. Hundreds of these brave, dedicated young people passed through Wilmersreut, Zell, Stambach, and Naila. Many of them experienced internment on Cyprus, as we had feared, and many died fighting for the Jewish homeland they were dedicated to establish and preserve.

The determination of these young people was now typical of most displaced persons of any age in the communities and camps. No longer were we held captives by fear of reprisal against our families, as we had been during the war. Our families were gone, and we had only ourselves to protect. Our dependence on the outside world was no longer all-inclusive. The general conviction was that we must take independent action if we were to succeed in establishing a Jewish state and that if lives had to be sacrificed they would be sacrificed. Six million dead was the price already paid for a Jewish nation. We were determined that, having paid it, it would not be in vain. The British blockade did nothing to dampen the determination or stifle the courage of those who were ready to go. Many of the people in our own community were eager to join them, and a few who were without pregnant wives or young children succeeded. We were witnessing the greatest miracle in our history. Our people, who had wandered for thousands of years, were finally to have a land of our own. It was hard to wait! However, Lilly and I knew, as we stood so many times saying *"Shalom"* to the truckloads of young pioneers, that we and our family would stay on in Munchberg until the day came when not one person remained behind who needed us.

The last trucks left in 1948, when the State of Israel was officially born in the United Nations, and I returned the kibbutzim to the American military government with our gratitude and a pledge that we would never forget the generosity and understanding that had made our accomplishments possible. Later, those same farms that had sheltered our developing youth passed back into the possession of their original German owners.

Chapter
32

THE WINTER AND SPRING HAD RACED BY, it seemed, almost
without our being aware of the change of seasons, except for the
disappearance of the snow and resurgence of life both in nature
and ourselves.

The war had been over for more than a year, and many of us
who called Munchberg "home" considered ourselves "old-
timers" if we had been there for more than three months. The
stabilizing influence of our community and the increasing return to individual independence by the men in jobs and
businesses made life seem normal, at least on the surface. There
was a place to go in the morning. Men left to do a day's work
and came home in the evening feeling like useful human beings
again. They could provide for their families instead of relying
completely on outside aid. The fact that we lived and functioned in a world within a world, a hostile world at that, we
tried to ignore. So the feeling of relative permanence gave us
more and more incentive to begin living what passed for normal lives under the most abnormal circumstances. In my own

family we had reknit the close ties that had existed in the dear, dead days gone by. Sala and Max shared their home with David, and when our cousin Regina was brought back to us, she also made her home with them. Their home became the center of family life for our other cousins, Sonya and her husband Max Lettich and Eva and Izak Tanc and their infant son, Joshua. Lilly and I lived next door, and the hours away from work we spent together.

Once we had accepted the fact that our stay in Germany was destined to be more than a brief waiting period, David, Max, and I started a textile manufacturing and wholesale business to which I devoted whatever free time I had.

The Community Center was the focal point of our lives. Our people came there for food, clothing, and medical attention, to attend religious services, to celebrate holidays, and to take part in the regular social and business meetings at night. In addition, we were visited by a stream of friends from the organizations dedicated to helping us. They shared our work and our joy, as we seized every opportunity to celebrate happy events to take the place of the tragic memories. Many of the men and women who had come to Munchberg together or who had met there decided to marry, and the center was the scene of their weddings. And as time passed, the sight of a pregnant woman became more and more common, each one especially precious to us who had lost almost all of our dear ones. Every birth was an event and a cause for rejoicing. The new parents brought their infants to our small synagogue in the center to be named, and, in the tradition of our faith, the Hebrew names of our dead were passed on to the babies to honor the grandparents, aunts, uncles, and cousins they would never know, whose memories and dreams they would have to fulfill.

We celebrated not only our own holidays but those of our friends who were strangers like ourselves in a foreign country, far from their own homes and loved ones. On the Fourth of July we gave a party for the Americans, and whenever marriages took place among our Christian friends our center became their center as well.

The business of the community and the management of its widespread affairs needed daily and hourly attention. Banker and I had reached such a solid understanding that a telephone call was usually all that was necessary, and he or his assistant in Helmbrechts would carry on from there in seeking the required housing.

I exchanged visits with the Landrat and Burgermeister frequently. Landrat Szech and I met at least once a week to discuss problems of mutual concern on the overall level of the entire Landkreis. We exchanged views and recommendations on keeping the relationships between displaced persons and German civilians as peaceful and unemotional as possible, and tackled the problems of housing, clothing supplies, and business licenses which concerned him and his office. Our working relationship was eminently satisfactory. He gave his cooperation freely and could be relied upon to support our requests.

Burgermeister Specht's first expression of sincerity and humility never faltered. Our mutual regard grew with each meeting, and I knew that as long as he held office we had a friend among the German authorities. He visited the kibbutz-im with us and showed a genuine pleasure in the accomplishments of our young people. He was a rare man and an even rarer German.

I continued to attend the meetings of the Denazification Board two nights a week despite further deterioration in understanding and unity. More cases were reviewed by the American military government, and additional recommendations for leniency voted by the majority of the board, in cases on which I was the only dissenting voice, were overruled. The Americans became concerned. The conclusion was inescapable that they could no longer rely on the impartiality of the men they had chosen as representative leaders. However, rather than disband the board at this early stage, the AMG decided to expand its own involvement by setting up a special branch where the cases would receive closer attention from their own AMG personnel. Separate offices were established for the enlarged custodianship operations, and Vladimiroff was put in charge. Since hundreds of the businesses of the Landkreis fell under denazification law, a great portion of the economic life of the district was supervised by this office.

My continued presence at the Denazification Board meeting rankled the others who would have liked a free hand in clearing the record of one Nazi or Nazi sympathizer after another. But they could not shake me loose. Their actions were compensated for, however, by the frequent calls I received from Vladimiroff and the AMG asking me to sit in on their reviews of cases which had passed unsatisfactorily through the Denazification Board. So while the board technically still functioned, I had the opportunity of expressing an independent opinion to friendlier and more determined ears.

The office my assistant maintained at the City Hall for the affairs of the German former concentration-camp inmates continued to operate full time also. We talked by telephone for the most part, but whenever an emergency arose or an important decision had to be reached, I went there personally. It was often difficult to establish the true backgrounds of some of the Germans who came to the office for official recognition as former political prisoners. Among the refugees from the Eastern zone were Germans who claimed to have been prisoners liberated from camps by the Russians. But I remembered only too well the German criminals who had ruled over us so viciously in the camps, and the earlier incident with the one man who had caused friction between me and the AMG was also still fresh in my mind. So we moved very cautiously in doubtful cases. If any German who came to my assistant's office felt he had not received fair treatment and deserved a review of his application, he could come to my office and be heard. These displaced Germans, like our own people, wanted to return to active business and professional lives, and if they qualified I traveled with them to Munich to appear on their behalf before the German authorities and vouch for them.

The many-faceted circle of my life had brought new friends from strange walks of life. The Counterintelligence Corps, whose headquarters were in Bayreuth, maintained a branch office in the Munchberg City Hall. I developed a close friendship with the two agents in our district, Schlesinger and Meyer, from our first meeting in late 1945, through our mutual involvement in the Denazification Board and other matters.

Schlesinger and Meyer shared similar backgrounds which uniquely equipped them for their work. They were both from Jewish families who had left Germany before the war to begin new lives in America. They spoke fluent German and could easily pose as young German nationals.

The CIC had the dual function of seeking out and running to ground the high-ranking war criminals who had disappeared at the end of the war and of observing and reporting on political life in American-occupied Germany. The Nazi leader in Landkreis Munchberg, Kreisleiter Deitel, had been interned almost immediately, but there were many others whom the CIC had yet to find. They also had a particular interest in displaced persons, especially those who came across the Czech border and from the Russian-occupied zone. In the intensive screening of all newcomers, some who claimed to be fleeing from new political persecution were actually proven to be Communist infiltrators sent into our zone as agents of another government.

Through my friendship with Meyer and Schlesinger, I had one of my most nerve-wracking postwar experiences. While visiting in Schlesinger's office one day he asked if I would care to ride along with him while he checked out a tip that a very high-ranking Nazi was living in Stambach under an assumed name. I jumped at the chance, and we sped off in an unmarked Czech Tatra. Schlesinger, of course, wore inconspicuous civilian clothes. We found the German's house unoccupied, though it was obvious someone lived there. Schlesinger walked around and talked to the neighbors, inquiring innocently if the man he described was known to them. "Oh, *ja,*" they told him. "He's not too far away. You will find him in the forest cutting trees. Just follow that road," they said. We drove into the woods until the road ended and then set off on foot. The ring of an ax biting into wood soon reached us, and I began to feel less eager about the encounter. "What are you going to say to him?" I asked Schlesinger as we neared the clearing from which the sound came.

"Don't worry," he reassured me. "I know how to handle these men."

We approached cautiously, and my breath stopped when, through the trees, I saw the size and bulk of the man wielding the huge, dangerous-looking ax. "Don't you think you had better get your gun out?" I whispered.

"I don't have my gun with me," Schlesinger whispered back, and then he stepped into the clearing and whipped out his badge. "I am from the CIC. Are you so-and-so?" To my amazement and relief, the German put down the ax and shook his head quietly. "I am taking you into custody," Schlesinger informed him, and we marched him back to the car with my heart still pounding. We rode back to Stambach with the man sitting submissively behind us, and Schlesinger left him under guard at Stambach with orders for his subsequent delivery. I had helped capture a Nazi war criminal!

The jail camp continued to receive DP prisoners, and while my mind and heart bitterly resented the injustice of their punishment, there was little I could do except try to make life as easy as possible for them and provide a link to the outside world. We still had no arrests and no open conflict in the Landkreis, but the general feeling of surface quiet began to splinter and break as the tolerant attitude between the Germans and the Jewish displaced persons crumbled due to a recurrence of the old, ever-familiar anti-Semitic remarks. Landrat Szech and I had many discussions about the deteriorating situation. He attributed the increase in friction to the crowded living conditions and the general feeling among the Germans that they would like to get rid of their unwelcome guests as soon as possible. Little did they know how dearly we would have loved to move on ourselves. Since we could not, I was determined to halt the spread of this infection before it damaged the work we had poured into our community.

I sat with Vladimiroff in his office one day and listened to him relate his anxiety over the same situation. "You know, Natan," he told me angrily, "I just came back on the train and had to listen to Germans near me talking openly about their hatred for the Jews. I even heard a few of them lament the fact that Hitler did not finish the job he set out to do and destroy all of them once and for all." His words sank deeply into my mind, and when I returned to my office I decided the time had come to act, openly and officially. Mere discussion, while necessary, was obviously not effective or direct enough.

I dictated an open letter to my secretary addressed to all the key offices and agencies in the Landkreis—to the American military governor, the CIC, the Landrat, the Burgermeister, and the leaders of all the political parties, as well as every other high official and authority I could think of. Because this move on my part affected everyone in the community, I called in a few key people from our own board and read the letter before dispatching it. Basically what I said was that I knew they were as aware as I was of the incidents that were taking place with greater frequency in the Landkreis, of the remarks and insults being made openly against displaced persons, especially Jews, and the growing amount of resentment among the Germans at our presence in their midst. I went on to comment on the unpleasantness I personally was experiencing at having to receive Germans in my office and listen to their complaints of minor inconveniences because they had to share living quarters with us. I recalled that very little time had passed since blood had ceased to spill and that the very ground around us was still wet with the bloodbath loosed by the Nazis. I appealed to them as leaders of their people to take steps as rapidly as possible to prevent any future outbreaks of such talk because it could only lead to extremely unpleasant consequences on both sides. For our part, I assured them we were doing the very best we could to keep friction at a minimum, and I promised that as long as I was the leader of the community I would see to it that we would do everything in our power to prevent this situation from coming to any drastic or damaging conclusion.

The urgency of the two-page letter brought a flood of calls. The

AMG made known their strong approval and support of the letter to the Landrat and Burgermeister, and their reaction, in turn, was impressively sincere. Landrat Szech asked my permission to duplicate the letter for distribution to the major factories in the Landkreis with his own covering letter. He wanted to take this method of reaching and impressing more of the German people directly, and I had no objections. Two days later while visiting one of the factories in the area, one of the Germans in charge told me they had received and distributed the letters among their employees and at least expressed to me that they shared my feeling and would do everything they could to instill that feeling in their employees.

Landrat Szech decided to carry the matter into a meeting of the Gemeinderat, the body made up of representatives from all the communities in the Landkreis over which he presided. He invited me to attend the meeting because he wanted an open discussion on the letter and its contents. The meeting in the Munchberg Landsamt was packed. Peter Gersh, a good friend, accompanied me as an observer from the community. When the Landrat had read the letter, the matter was thrown open for discussion and I listened, surprised and shocked at the controversy it aroused. Quite a few of the Germans sitting on the Gemeinderat took exception to the seriousness with which had approached the problem. "It's not as bad as they say," I heard from all sides. "And even if remarks are made once in a while, is it necessary to bring it out into the open like this and make such a fuss about it? Why couldn't this be handled more discreetly? We didn't ask to be occupied like this, so how can they blame us?"

Their refusal to acknowledge responsibility only made me angrier. Most of the disparaging remarks came from those who spoke for the smaller, outlying towns and villages where the intensity of the problem was undoubtedly far less, but their blindness was no less infuriating. When my chance came to speak, I turned on them coldly. "Gentlemen," I asked, "do you suggest that because the situation is not bad enough you need not do anything? Do you infer that just because the camps are not still functioning and there is no blood running in the streets the situation is not serious? What will it take to convince you, more bloodshed and murder? Isn't it enough that Landkreis Munchberg had the sad distinction of having had a slave-labor camp here? Let me remind you," I told the stone faces, "that some of you gentlemen right in this room live very close to that camp, and many of you watched the transports going by day after day. You know that this soil is still wet with our blood, and yet you sit here and question whether there is any real need for action or even if the situation is actually serious. I am afraid to ask you what you are waiting for to make it serious enough. But I will ask—what are you waiting for? I suggest you act and act now! Gentlemen, you are the judges; the responsibility is yours!" I got up in disgust, and Peter and I walked out alone.

After we had left the meeting the Landrat carried on the fight and finally got a vote from the Gemeinderat supporting his efforts to improve the objectionable conditions. I went to him and thanked him personally for what he had achieved in the face of such opposition. The result was a gradual improvement, and while our contacts with German civilians were never really cordial, nor would we have expected them to be, the episodes which came to my ears were less bitter and less frequent. Our own people found it as hard as the Germans did to look the other way and turn the other cheek, but we had bigger stakes than an exchange of insults and harsh words. As long as we had to accept this German town as our temporary base, we had to exercise our patience, hold our tongues, and clench our fists.

Chapter
33

AMONG THE MANY PROBLEMS demanding our attention, a very special one still remained unresolved. What could we do for the precious few surviving children orphaned by Hitler and his Nazis and still scattered over the face of Europe.

The Joint Distribution Committee and the Palestine AMT were trying to bring together in West Germany all the children they could find. Some had been collected from the camps where they had been kept as human inventory, guinea pigs, for the experiments of Nazi doctors and scientists. Some had been left alive by some miracle in the desperate flight of the SS in the closing hours of the war; others came from convents and churches where they had been hidden by brave nuns and clergymen, regardless of the danger to themselves; still more from sympathetic Christian families who had sheltered them ever since frantic parents, in final desperation, had thrust them into their care; others from only God knew where. There were hundreds of these children in scattered locations, and Lilly and I participated in many meetings with our friends of the JDC,

UNRRA, and the Palestine AMT, and with Captain Spiro in which we expressed our fear that the shock and injury to which their young minds had already been subjected would become permanent scars if something were not done about them quickly. They needed to be brought together and cared for now. Tomorrow it would be too late.

There was no question in our minds; we wanted as many of them as we could find room for. The more the better. We wanted them very much. They were the young, twisted roots of what was left of the Jewish people in Europe, and from them and from the few thousands of us left would have to come forth the new generations to take the places of the millions who had been destroyed. Our chance had come to open our arms and we welcomed it.

After many meetings and discussions with our friends, Captain Spiro, Lilly, and I began to explore Munchberg and Naila for a place large enough and properly located. Finally, in Naila, we came upon the ideal site. High atop a mountain, perched on a plateau densely covered with forest, sat Schloss Schauenstein. This medieval castle, still intact after hundreds of years, even to its little drawbridge, had been converted by the Germans during the war for use as a manufacturing plant and as a shelter for refugees. Part of the castle was still being used by sisters of an enclosed religious order. Their self-imposed remoteness from the world was suddenly disrupted when Captain Spiro and I called on them. His American uniform threw them into confusion, and they greeted us with a tremulous "Heil Hitler!" We looked at each other in amazement, and the captain answered, "You are behind the times, ladies. The regime has changed." After we had inspected the castle and satisfied ourselves that this was indeed the place we wanted, another series of meetings took place with the commanding officer of the AMG in Naila and with the Landrat, Herr Milk. We assured them that the children would be our sole responsibility, that we would assume all the burdens of their welfare and asked only that the AMG and the German authorities place a part of the castle at our disposal as a home.

We kept up the pressure at every possible opportunity both officially and off the record, stressing the plight of the children and their terrible history. Landrat Milk invited Spiro and me to visit with him and his family at their home, and our discussion about the children led us inevitably into reviewing other tragedies of the war. In speaking of the overall insanity that had gripped Germany under the Nazis, the name of the German General Milk was mentioned, and the Landrat commented quite matter-of-factly, "You know, he was my brother."

Spiro and I exchanged bewildered looks. At our previous meetings Herr Milk had given us to understand that he himself had been persecuted as a Jew. "Landrat, how is this possible?" I asked.

"I knew you would be surprised," he replied. "Let me tell you a true story you will find very hard to believe. My father was a Jew, but my mother was a full German. My brother was a famous aviator in the Luftwaffe. When the persecution began, his career would have ended because of our father's Jewish background, but my mother came forward and swore to the government officials that she had conceived my brother with an Aryan, even though she was married to and lived with my Jewish father. They accepted her claim that my brother was a good clean German Aryan, so he remained in the Luftwaffe to become a general and one of Goering's closest aides, while I was persecuted as a Jew."

This strange paradox of the war made a deep impression on me. I could not imagine a mother willing to swear that one child was illegitimate so that he could take part in a war that destroyed her husband's people and made her other child a victim. But it was only one insanity among so many.

With the Landrat's help, the German authorities acceded to the AMG's instructions, and the *Kinderheim* at Schloss Schauenstein was born. Never was a labor of love performed with such devotion and burning dedication. Everyone came forward to help, from the community, from the kibbutzim in Munchberg and Naila, from the AMG, too. Volunteer social workers, serving without pay, came to care for the children, and a warm, wonderful woman from the Palestine AMT took charge. The castle's huge rooms were carefully surveyed to select those best suited for dormitories, dining rooms, kitchens, and classrooms. We checked the old tile coal- and wood-burning stoves to see that they would heat the high-ceilinged halls, whose thick walls kept the castle comfortably cool in the summer but freezing in the winter. A succession of trucks began climbing the steep, winding road, bringing equipment and supplies from Bamberg, Bayreuth, Naila, and Munchberg. We worked in shifts around the clock. So many came forward to help that we actually had to turn some away. There were more willing hands than work to be done.

It took almost two weeks to ready the portion of the castle we now called our "Children's Home," and as we faced at last the day we had worked so hard to bring about, the realization dawned that, desperately as we wanted them, we shared a common apprehension of the emotional impact this first meeting would have upon us and upon the children. For them it would the first time in years they would be surrounded by grownups of their own kind. Without doubt it would bring back agonizing memories of their parents, no matter how dim these memories might be for some of the younger children. And for us who were so incredibly grateful that they had survived, who wanted eagerly to see Jewish children again, who except for a few new babies lived in a community barren of young faces and small, warm bodies to be loved—for us it would be an agonizing moment too!

Lilly and I stood waiting with Spiro and the others when the first trucks rolled up, and we helped the children down from the convoy. While most of them had been under sufficient care to begin regaining their strength, a few were spiritless, physically and mentally, and in their fright at this new jolting move in their already confused lives they had forgotten how to smile. I stood there watching, my throat tight and dry. I thought again of the *punkt* in Targowa and the children we had smuggled out in the soup pots. I remembered the little girl who had asked me where she should go to find safety. I had no answer for her then. With all my heart and strength, I pledged we would make this home an answer for those who were left.

The boys and girls were all from eight to fifteen years of age. The Nazis had seen to it that the babies had not survived. Our kibbutzim sheltered those who were older and more independent, and the younger ones moved into the home. The helpers from the kibbutzim and the community aided the social workers in settling in the children that first night, feeding them and getting them ready for bed. When it grew dark and we could no longer find an excuse to stay with them, we had to tear ourselves away to go home, not one of us dry-eyed.

I went back the next day and every day after that as more trucks came with their precious cargo, bringing children who had forgotten or who had never learned Yiddish and who had taken on the languages and customs of the people with whom they had been left. Captain Spiro came often and brought along American Army doctors to check the children until such time as the headquarters in Bamberg could send a Jewish doctor for them. We worked constantly, arranging and rearranging the quarters as the home expanded, until we had over four hundred boys and girls.

For weeks I walked around like a man in a daze, unable to let a day pass without driving out there and, once having left, unable to put them out of my mind for a moment. Their sad eyes followed me wherever I went, and when I tried to sleep at night I saw their pale and lost faces. Barring an absolute emergency, I could not bear to stay away from them, and if there was a day Lilly and I were unable to make the trip to Schloss Schauenstein, we saw to it that an officer or other representative of the community went in our place.

As the days passed, the children became more accustomed to their new surroundings and better acquainted with one another. The older boys and girls helped care for the younger ones, and all of them were treated with every kindness and loving attention. A school was started, but because none of the children had been exposed to Hebrew education for years, or any formal schooling for that matter, the classes had to be on the most elementary level, regardless of age. They were taken outdoors to exercise and play games and for walks in the surrounding forest, and we arranged for small groups to go on excursions by motor so that they would feel they were free to move about. As they came to trust us the terrible shyness and fear left them, and we began to see more smiling faces and hear happy, childish chatter again.

They had come to us without a single earthly possession except the clothes they wore, so we tried to gather school supplies and toys they could keep as their own. Some of our men who had been shoemakers volunteered to make shoes for them, and others did what they could. Everyone was drawn to them. The American soldiers came in groups with chocolate and candies from their post exchange and anything else they could think of that might please them. And hardly a day passed without someone calling to ask for a ride to the home. There was no need to encourage anyone to spend time with them, for we all felt the same. We hoped by our visits to reassure the children that someone cared for them and loved them. We wanted them to feel close to us and one another, as if they belonged to one large family, which in a way did; they belonged to all of us now.

When they had settled down a little more, we took them on buses to picnic at the kibbutzim and to Munchberg to show them around the center. It was vital on such occasions that they be spared emotional scenes. The sounds of weeping and screams were still too fresh in their memories, so when we knew they were coming we alerted our people to control their instinctive reactions and try, instead, to show the children warmth and affection while holding their deeper emotions in check. It wasn't easy.

Many came to me and asked with tears in their eyes to be allowed to adopt a child, especially the older couples who had lost their children and could not hope to have any more. It was heart-breaking to have to refuse them, but after giving it serious thought we realized we would have to discourage adoption because it would be better for the children to keep them together rather than split them up again to start yet another new life of uncertainty. How many shocks could they endure?

We tried to think what their dead parents would have wanted for them. One thing we knew: They would not have wanted to die for nothing. These children, their final legacy, belonged to a greater community, and their home would have to be a Jewish homeland, from which they could never again be scattered across the face of the earth. The world one day would recognize the justice of the fight for a country where these children could grow to maturity without the fear that their children, in turn, would also be left orphaned merely because they were Jews. They must be kept together for that day.

Munchberg and Naila had become a very significant area in Germany. We housed a representative selection of the surviving remnants of Hitler's plan to destroy the Jewish people, some very young survivors and some quite old, with the greater part of us somewhere in between. The more I thought about the children, the more memories came flooding back. Had I met their fathers in Birkenau or stood next to their mothers in the freight car on the transport to Auschwitz? Perhaps on the death march their brothers had dropped next to me in the snow. Most of the older children knew their real names, but the little ones answered only to the Aryan names they had been given for their own preservation. No one would dare keep a name like Goldberg or Cohen at a time when such names were death warrants, even for a child. There had been an estimated one million two hundred thousand children among the six million martyred dead. What did a name matter to us? The child was the important thing. It was up to us now to see that the unbearably small number left would not have to spend the rest of their lives in a nightmare of memory and loneliness.

For the children's sake, we tried not to let our conversations with them lead into discussions of the past. We could not erase their scars, but we could try to keep them busy with every type of activity and surround them with love, hoping it would at least ease their pain. Their diets were watched over zealously to see that they ate the healthiest foods, and our own kibbutzim shipped fresh milk and eggs from the farms and ranches. At times the flow of supplies was so heavy we gave up trying to control it. No one wanted to be left out, and as a result generous offerings poured in from all sides. The children wanted for nothing—food, shelter, or clothing. For company, we often brought caravans of cars, two or three or four at a time, loaded with people eager to spend time with them. And the workers, supervisors, and teachers performed miracle after miracle in creating a full and secure atmosphere for their precious wards.

Mr. Scanes accompanied Lilly, Spiro, and me on weekends if he was free, and from his very warm response to the children I could not help but feel that despite his political bluster he must have realized deep inside that the Jewish people had an unchallengeable right to a homeland of their own and that the fighting in Palestine over which we had exchanged so many heated words was justified. Surely these children had removed all doubt. After what they had been through, they were entitled to a homeland where there would be no possibility of further persecution. The representatives of JDC and the Palestine AMT knew, as did Lilly and I in our hearts and minds, that these children would one day, finally, leavé on a journey to such a land.

With the approach of the High Holy Days, the JDC shipped in the special food for our widespread communities in the towns, the jail, the kibbutzim, and the Children's Home. With the traditional foods were included Yahrzeit (memorial) candles so meaningful and significant to all of us.

Each year at the High Holy Days in the past we had traditionally lit a memorial candle for each of our dead. For most of us this would be the first time since 1939, seven years, that we had been able to practice our religious rituals openly in our own place of worship and could mourn all those we had lost.

Kol Nidre services were planned for the synagogue in the community center, but I did not know what to do about the Children's Home. I went to talk to the leaders there. "What do you think we ought to do about the High Holy Days? Should we hold services on Kol Nidre for the children or will it only upset them?" I asked. They had already discussed the situation and arrived at a decision. They felt that since the children already knew about the coming Holy Day and were, in fact, looking forward to it, especially the older children who remembered, there was no choice but to go ahead. We could only hope that despite the harrowing effect it would undoubtedly have on the children, it might also prove to be a valuable emotional release. We had deliberately tried to suppress their thoughts of the past until now. We could not expect to do so forever.

I agreed with them, never dreaming the full effect it would finally have. In the late afternoon before Yom Kippur, I was driven alone to Schloss Schauenstein, promising Lilly and our family that I would meet them later at the synagogue for services. At the castle, the children were gathered in one enormous hall, around a gigantic table. At sundown, services began, and I stood to one side, watching, not fully aware for several minutes of what I and the other adults were about to witness. Each child held a Yahrzeit candle, and when the time came each boy and girl lit his or her candle and placed it on the table as each walked by. In a few brief moments hundreds of flickering lights blazed out at me and the children began to cry, softly at first and then in tearing, uncontrollable sobs. The sight of the candles and their faces blinded my eyes, and the sound of their weeping roared in my ears. I felt as if I had been struck a staggering blow. The sight made by those hundreds of candles and the children who had lit them for their dead parents and families engulfed me. The suffering they had known and everything I had lived through myself lived again in that moment. Each of those lights burned for a mother or father lost forever, to a child doomed to grow up never knowing the love of its parents, to a child who could never completely erase the scars on its body or soul of a childhood too horrible to imagine. My own tears ran scalding down my face, and I could not bear it another moment. I stumbled out of the room and to the door with the sound of the weeping growing louder and louder in the chamber behind me. My German chauffeur jumped to open the front door of the car, where I usually sat, but I brushed past and threw myself on the back seat. I had to lie down. "Is something wrong, Herr Schapelski?" he asked me.

"Drive, just drive, please," I said.

I lay back and gave way to the blackest despair I had ever known. The car crept slowly down the face of the mountain while all the tortures of hell went through me. I looked out the window at the night sky and mutely begged God to send thunder and lightning down to destroy the unfeeling world which had let this holocaust consume us. All the unanswerable questions I had suppressed for months came screaming to the surface again. Will mankind ever be able to atone for its guilt? Will any free man ever be able to say this was not his responsibility? How could this have happened? I could only find more "whys" without answers than I had ever found before. I had never known such pain and anguish as I did that night. The twilight for me would forever be a setting for those weeping children and the lights of the Yahrzeit. I wept for everyone, for my own mother and father, for Yadja and Rochelle, and for all our family and friends. The memories of Sosnowiec, the *punkt* at Targowa and the ghetto at Schrodula came flooding back as fresh and as painful as if they had happened yesterday. And with each personal memory the plight of the children sank deeper into my brain, reminding me of all those I had seen murdered. What had they done other than to be born? They had come into the world hungry for life. Then, why this, why this? I cursed all people who could have stopped it and did not, and I called down God's vengeance on the inhuman monsters who had set forth to commit mass murder with such cold-blooded inventive premeditation, the planned and willful massacre of an entire race, child, youth, and adult, man and woman, by an educated, "civilized" nation. I felt deep hatred and pent-up revulsion against a world capable of such cruelty, apathy, and destruction.

As the car neared Munchberg I began to wonder if I would

ever be able to regain my sanity and control. Would I be able to go on day after day saying *"Guten tag"* to Germans, each one guilty? Would I be able to stand up in front of our community and say, "Be patient. Try to understand the Germans. Be tolerant." And yet, did I have the right to give in to my own pain and anger when there was still so much work to be done? No answers came back to me out of the darkness, so I talked to myself. "All right, Natan, it's too late to change the past, but you can continue your work here and now. Put these questions aside and bury the hatred because there's too much to be done to let them interfere." I told myself I was needed, and I knew my need to be needed was my own salvation.

When the car drew up at the center, the driver's face was drawn with concern, but he said nothing as he helped me out. Inside, the services had just begun; they had waited for me until the last minute. I went to stand with Lilly, Sala and Max, David, Regina, Sonya and Max, Eva and Izak and all my friends, and I prayed.

Chapter
34

ONE BY ONE the American officers who had served for a time in Munchberg were transferred, and replacements came to take their place. Our respected friend Lieutenant Ralph L. Bowers eventually received his orders, and we parted sadly from a fine man to whom the entire community of displaced persons was especially indebted. At his leave-taking I recalled the many times when faced with situations that found us desperately in need he managed to find a solution or offer invaluable advice and help. He and others of our departing friends left with me farewell letters, which I came to treasure along with their memories.

Military Government
LIAISON AND SECURITY OFFICE
Kreis MUNCHBERG

Det. B-256
16 August 46

SUBJECT: Personal Letter
To: Natan Schapelski, Munchberg, Wilhelmstrasse 20

On the eve of my departure from Munchberg I take the opportunity to commend you for the fine work you have done in conjunction with the Jewish Committee in Munchberg. Your tireless efforts have resulted in marked accomplishment. You have done a great service to your people here and to the community. My sincere belief and hope is that you will continue.

Your accomplishments exceed any personal praise that I may render to you.

Ralph L. Bowers
1st Lt.   CAC
Asst. Director

SUBJECT: Open Letter to the Jewish Committee
To: Jewish Committee Munchberg, Gartenstrasse 50

As I am being transferred from Munchberg I wish to take this opportunity to express my appreciation to all members of the Jewish Committee. You have proved yourselves worthy of commendation in many ways. When I compare today's Committee with that of one year ago I find only steady improvement and accomplishments. I am fully confident that you will continue to better yourselves and the community as well. My sincere wishes for the future are with you.

Ralph L. Bowers
1st Lt.   CAC
Asst. Director

Whenever possible the incoming officers were briefed about the Landkreis and the town by the men they succeeded and were given a short history of the year that had passed. In this way the chain of friendship we had forged through these trying months was maintained. A new Public Safety Officer, Captain Mayville, arrived, and shortly after, Major Abbott departed, leaving Munchberg temporarily without a military governor. In the absence of a commanding officer, ranking officers acted until the permanent replacement took office. We were eager to learn who the new military governor would be, and I looked forward to paying the usual courtesy call which was our customary introduction to all new arrivals. But our first meeting with the new military governor was not to take place that formally.

One day while visiting the military government offices I stood talking to Lilly with the other girls working in the secretarial department. I had almost finished my business and was about to leave when the door opened and a tall, imposing officer strode into the room. Lilly turned to him at once and spoke across the room. "Major, may I introduce Mr. Schapelski, the leader of the Jewish community?" As she spoke, I started across the room with my hand outstretched. Without acknowledging the introduction or my hand, the major immediately launched into rapid English, and I turned back to Lilly for interpretation. "He wants to know, Natan, why there are so many Jews and DPs living in this Landkreis." I was so taken aback that I could not answer for a moment, and before I had a chance to recover he had already turned and left the room.

Lilly and I exchanged troubled looks, unable to speak freely. I returned to my office confused and disturbed. If this first meeting was an indication of the new military governor's attitude, it could only mean trouble for our community. But in all fairness to him, I would have to wait and see what happened; after all, the attitude of all the officers we had come to know at the AMG to date had always been most helpful and friendly.

That night when Lilly came home she was also very concerned. "Natan, I really don't know. Unless perhaps someone from the German authorities has already visited him and influenced his attitude," she answered.

"Well," I said, "if they used their courtesy call to try to prejudice him against us, then I am more concerned about them than the major."

Except for the few German officials I knew to be sincere and honest, the majority of the remainder only went along with the wishes of the AMG in cooperating with us as long as it was demanded of them by the military governor. If this feeling of resentment got out of hand, the repercussions could be damaging to the delicate balance of relationships and the good image of the community. Dare we stand by and see all our work destroyed?

Lilly and I talked it out and decided to leave the situation alone for a few days and not to approach the major officially until we had some further indication to guide us. Again the decision was taken out of my hands. I was informed by telephone through his secretary that the major wanted to see me. I went with deep misgivings, reintroduced myself and waited for him to restate his question, but this time he did not query me on how many Jews and DPs lived there. Instead, he advised me through the interpreter that he would like to visit our center and look over the facilities. I asked the interpreter to tell him that we would be honored to receive him at any time.

Several days later he arrived in the morning accompanied by officers of his staff, and we received him with the respect and dignity his position commanded. I conducted them on a tour of the villa from the warehouse to the top floor, pointing out all the operations and functions of the various departments. The officer acting as interpreter suddenly interrupted the tour by advising me, "The major would like you to know he is considering exchanging this villa for our present headquarters." Though I was startled I made no comment, and we completed the tour without further discussion. I was at a loss to understand this sudden change in attitudes. Did it reflect his personal views or was he acting on orders? I simply could not understand it, and my concern increased.

Without giving me a chance to sit down with him and enlighten him about our background and problems, he again requested that I visit him at his office. This time quite simply and directly he informed me that he wanted our center. I had promised myself that whatever happened, I would not permit the villa to be taken from us. A line had to be drawn from the start or there would be no end to the reversal of all we had built. "Major, we have all our facilities in the building, some of which we have built with our own hands, such as the warehouse, the little hospital, and our synagogue. I can see no justification for asking us to move out when it's simply a matter of exchange. Besides, Major, I request you to consider that you would be asking us to move into what was formerly the Nazi headquarters and not only to try to re-establish our vital work here but to worship under this roof. It's unthinkable. Besides, it would be an extreme hardship on so many people, including the UNRRA operations. We would have to start all over again under tremendous handicaps," I argued. Since the exchange would not result in any gain for the AMG, I could not see any valid reason for it, and I made it clear I would not yield. If he persisted he would have to confiscate the villa formally. The meeting ended in tension as he concluded the discussion by affirming that he would take it whether I liked it or not.

The situation was now desperate. It would be a shattering blow to the frail feeling of security that sustained our people in Munchberg and to the vast pride we shared in our accomplishments if word of this threat leaked out. Lilly and I decided to keep it to ourselves, hoping for a miracle. We did not want the German authorities to learn of it either and use it as a basis to begin resisting cooperation. After all, to the Germans we were merely an inconvenience that prevented them from living in the comfort to which they had been accustomed, a permanent witness to the barbarities they had committed that each wished to deny. They could only welcome any excuse or encouragement to close the doors we had opened with such effort and sacrifice. The only person I consulted was Mr. Scanes, because I knew sooner or later we would need his backing and the prestige and support of the UNRRA organization. I did not know where I would turn or what action I would take if confronted with actual seizure of the villa. It occupied my mind day and night. The center was the very foundation upon which our community was built. If that foundation was torn away from us, the entire structure could fall and mortally injure countless people only newly recovered from their deep agony and wounds. The frustrating thing was that there was nothing I could do, nothing within my power I could use to stop it.

As if the situation were not already grave enough, an officer at AMG called me. "We are holding one of your people here. A complaint has been made against him, and we would like you to come over so that we can release him into your custody, Mr. Schapelski."

"What has he done?" I asked.

"It's not serious, but we would like to have you here."

I raced over to the AMG and found one of the young men I knew from the kibbutz at Wilmersreut, a twenty-year-old boy, being held by the military police.

"What happened? What is he charged with?"

"I don't know what I did wrong," the youth told me. "I was driving into town to pick up supplies at the warehouse, and when I went past the prison camp one of the men called me over. I left the horse and wagon and walked to the fence. There weren't any guards around; nobody tried to stop me. The man asked me in Polish to mail a letter for him. I took it, and as I was walking back to the wagon, a military policeman arrested me and brought me here. That's all I know, Mr. Schapelski."

I was relieved to learn it was nothing really serious, and I repeated the facts to the officer. "I know he meant no harm, and I am sure it will never happen again. He had no way of knowing he was doing anything illegal. I would like to apologize for his having caused you any trouble, and I promise if you will release him in my custody I will see to it that it will never happen again."

"I'm sorry, Mr. Schapelski," he answered. "I will have to

make a written report and send it through channels. He may leave with you, but we will hold you responsible for seeing that he stays in the area in case there is any further action to be taken."

I gave him my assurance and left with the boy. When we got outside I told him to return to the kibbutz immediately and to stay there and tell everyone in Wilmersreut that they were not to go anywhere near the prison camp under any circumstances and especially not to talk to anyone there. As far as I was concerned, I felt justified in assuring him that the matter was closed or would be in a day or so, since no crime had been committed. But such was not to be the case.

In a matter of days it was announced that the case would be brought to court and the boy placed on trial. This, added to the strain of waiting for the military governor's next move, was almost more than I could bear. When I learned that Captain Mayville, the new Public Safety Officer, was to act as the judge in the case I went to see him. I said, "Captain, how is it possible that such an innocent act could develop into a court trial? The boy cannot read English, so even if there are warning signs around the camp they meant nothing to him. You must understand that he answered the prisoner's call only because he still remembers how it felt when he, too, was in a concentration camp and how much it would have meant to him then if he could have sent out a note. It is only a matter of months since the end of the war, and already he is being punished for doing an act of kindness he and all the rest of us would have given anything to have experienced when we were behind barbed wire ourselves."

"I'm very sorry, Mr. Schapelski, but the case has been reviewed by my superior officer and I have been instructed to proceed to trial. The decision is not mine to make, I hope you understand."

"Then may I ask you, Captain, if you are going to act as judge, who is going to prosecute?" I asked because normally this would have been his function.

"The military governor," he replied, "will prosecute."

That meant the major himself had ordered the charges pressed and would appear personally as the prosecutor. It was, to say the very least, extremely unusual. Why should he want to involve himself to this degree in so minor a matter? "Captain, tell me what I can do to help clear this up or assist this boy at the trial," I asked.

"You have no official status, but you can be present as a consultant or interpreter if you wish. And I'm sure if the court needs any background information, it would help if you were available."

Over the next few days I pleaded the case with him, off the record, and came away with the feeling that he had no heart for the job he had been commissioned to do. I went to Colonel Zimmerman of the military police and expressed my disappointment at his staff for making so much of a very minor incident. We talked off the record, too, and again I got the impression, unspoken but sensed, that he, too, had no desire to prosecute. He did tell me he was surprised himself to learn it had gone so far; he had expected that the boy would be reprimanded and sent home. Instead, it appeared for some reason that an object lesson was to be made from this one innocent act of human kindness.

The trial was set for a Thursday in the chambers of the German civil court. The courtroom was packed with people from our community and the kibbutzim, as well as curiosity-seekers. Captain Mayville sat on the bench, and the major appeared as the prosecutor. Lilly interpreted for the court, and I sat with the defendant. I had advised him against taking German counsel. "Tell the truth exactly as it happened; don't be afraid and don't be too concerned. Everything will be all right." I reassured him and wished that I could convince myself it would be that simple. The judge called the court to order, and the clerk of the court read the charge sheet. "How do you plead?" the captain asked.

"Not guilty."

The trial proceeded. The prosecutor presented his case, calling the arresting MP as a witness and presenting in evidence the letter the prisoner had passed through the barbed-wire fence. When the evidence was complete, the judge questioned the boy, and he told the same true and simple facts. He had not seen any guards or any signs in any language he could read. Someone called to him. He stopped the wagon, got down and went to the fence. A prisoner asked him in Polish to mail a letter; he accepted it and went back to his wagon. A military policeman came and took him into custody. The prosecutor asked that the court find the defendant guilty as charged.

With the few, simple truths before the court, I asked for permission to speak, and when it was granted I asked questions of my own. "First of all, may I inquire why this boy is here?" The court advised me he had committed a violation of the Penal Code and recited the code number. "These numbers mean nothing to me, your honor, since I am not familiar with these laws. But you have heard this boy tell you the truth about what happened. He innocently violated a regulation of which he knew nothing, and he has been put on trial for it. Let's bring back the SS beasts who deprived him of the right to be educated to a point where he might have understood the laws under which he is charged or been able to read the signs he disobeyed, and let's put them on trial instead! But first, let's give this boy a chance." I said, "Gentlemen, if he is found guilty, then the entire Jewish community, all the displaced persons here and, in particular, I myself are the guilty ones, guilty of failing him. It would seem to me that we and justice itself are on trial, not him. Perhaps you did not allow us enough time to educate him. We are still busy trying to settle the few survivors who are left. We have not been able to explain to such a boy or to the many other boys and girls just like him that there are situations they will face that an education and normal everyday life would have trained them to handle. If this boy is found guilty, I suggest to the court that I serve his sentence for him."

There was no more I could say. I could only hope that he be spared a jail sentence for the sake of his future immigration status and for the sake of the overall reputation of the community. The fate of any one of us inevitably affected all.

The trial had begun in the middle of the morning and continued after the noon recess. It was almost three o'clock in the afternoon before Captain Mayville retired to consider his verdict, and we sat tensely to await his return. The prosecutor had vigorously insisted on a conviction, and I did not envy the captain the decision he had to make. His superior officer had pressed the case and had acted personally as prosecutor, and he now had to hand down an impartial and just verdict. The people in the courtroom seemed to be aware that a great deal was at stake, and the suspense was tremendous. When Captain Mayville returned and announced that he had reached a decision, we all fell silent. "I find the defendant guilty as charged!" My heart stopped. "However," he continued, "although ignorance of the law does not excuse the defendant from punishment, the court finds that the extenuating circumstances placed before it are such that we are imposing a token punishment of fifty marks' fine as being appropriate."

A vast sigh of relief came from our friends, and I was jubilant. The young boy slumped with relief and then broke into a big smile. I paid the minimal fine on behalf of the community, and we left the courtroom. It had been an exhausting experience dragging through several weeks, involving not only our pride and his future but the emotions of all the young people in the kibbutzim. But justice had prevailed through the responsible action of a decent, humane man. I went to see Captain Mayville as soon as it was proper and thanked him profoundly for myself, for the boy, in the name of the community, and for all the free people to whom the word "justice" meant life itself.

After my momentary exhilaration at the outcome of the trial, my nervous state quickly returned and grew with each day, waiting for the final blow to fall. Would the order to vacate the villa come tomorrow? And what would I do if it did? How could I answer to all these people who depended on me? I could not sleep, and I could think of nothing else. The rumors we had hoped to avoid spread gradually, and people began to ask if it was true that we would have to move. I could not face the hopeless look with which they inquired, so I avoided a direct answer. It was all I could do to force myself to go to the office and keep up the pretense of normalcy when all I thought of was "Is this terrible thing really going to happen?"

Lilly begged me to eat and try to rest, but I could not. I paced like a wild man around the apartment and again at the center when I was able to move myself to go there. It reached a pitch where I could endure it no longer. I stood to lose nothing by taking the initiative, and so one day while having a general discussion at the AMG with Captain Stanchos, who spoke fairly good German, I saw the major walking toward us and decided to make my move. I rose to my feet, said "hello" and for the second time offered my hand. To my complete surprise and overwhelming relief, he grasped it, shook it and through the captain started to question me quite calmly and with obvious interest about the community's activities and the settlements we had established in Landkreis Munchberg. "I've had a chance to discuss the Jewish community and the displaced persons' activities with the other officers and my staff, and I would like to know a little more about them. I may say I have heard nothing but good reports."

"Thank you very much, Major," I said gratefully, hardly believing my ears.

"I'd like to hear more about the condition of the people and find out if there is anything I can do to help," he continued.

I was so taken by surprise that I could not believe I was talking to the same man, he had changed so radically in such a short period of time. I started to feel guilty. Had we jumped to conclusions and prejudged him because our concern was so great? Had we unintentionally fallen into the same trap that had plagued the other communities, compounding a misunderstanding by closing our minds and relying on assumptions and surface reactions?

I went home that night almost lighthearted and told Lilly the whole meeting word for word. She shared my surprise, for there had been no indication at her office that any change had taken place.

Thereafter I took advantage of every opportunity I could to

spend time with the major, and he demonstrated continued interest in our operations. While I did not develop an immediate rapport with him because of the uncertainty over the villa, he began to gain our confidence and trust, as the weeks passed, both as a person and as an American officer.

Winter came again to Munchberg. The first snows fell early as they usually do in the Bavarian Alps. In keeping with the long-standing European tradition, especially in Western Europe, the birthdays of officials were honored by other officials and authorities with courtesy calls and the presentation of tokens of esteem and recognition. I found out that the major's birthday was near, and the Jewish community and the displaced persons authorized me to represent them in following the custom.

With my friend Bill Gersh I drove through the snow-banked roads to the major's house, where he had recently been joined by his wife from America. As we approached we met the minister from Munchberg, the head of the local Chamber of Commerce, and the Assistant Burgermeister on their way back down the hill, and we exchanged greetings. "The major and his wife are not home," they told us. "The housekeeper says they are at Captain Stanchos' house, so we're going there."

We turned around and followed them, and when we arrived I let them go in ahead. When they had paid their call and left, I went inside, asking Gersh to join me because the weather outside was so bad. As a token from the whole community we had purchased the latest-model Swiss stopwatch and had it nicely wrapped. Since Captain Stanchos spoke German very well, I asked him to interpret and tell the major that in the name of the Jewish community and all the displaced persons of Munchberg I wanted to present a small gift to him as a token of our esteem and appreciation with our best wishes for his birthday. He translated the words to the major and his wife. The major accepted the package and began to unwrap it. The picture is still vivid in my mind. As he opened the package and lifted the lid of the small black leather case, exposing its contents, the most remarkable thing happened: He began to cry!

What had I done? I was stunned by his reaction. The more he examined the stopwatch the harder he wept. Finally, still holding the case, he turned away from us and walked quickly into the bedroom and closed the door.

"Captain, what have I done wrong?" I asked, bewildered. Captain Stanchos stared at the closed door and shrugged his shoulders. "I don't know, Mr. Schapelski." "Please, Captain, ask the major's wife if she knows what happened," I begged him. Her reply was obviously confused. "Mr. Schapelski, she doesn't know either," the captain told me. "She cannot account for his behavior. She has never seen him react this way before." I looked at Gersh; he looked back at me, dumbfounded. And then I asked the captain if he would kindly allow us to remain until I found out what I had done. He agreed, and we all stood there on edge for what seemed like an eternity. Still the major did not come out. Finally, his wife excused herself, and she, too, went into the bedroom. We waited again; neither one came out for at least five more minutes. At last they both came back. The tall, impressive Army officer stood before me with tear-reddened eyes. I was nervous and apprehensive. "Captain," I entreated, "please ask the major what I have done." And I started to repeat that our gift was intended as a gesture of good will and respect. But the major did not permit me to finish. He came over to where I stood and swept me into an embrace, folding his arms around me and talking to the captain all the while rapidly in English, which I could not, of course, understand.

The captain tried to keep up with him, repeating his words: "As a child he had lived in a neighborhood where there was a jewelry store, and in the window of that store had been a stopwatch—something he had wished for with all his heart as only a young boy can wish. His father had promised to give him such a watch when he reached his thirteenth birthday, but when that day came the depression in America was in full swing and he could not afford it. His father had renewed the promise for his sixteenth birthday, but again the dream had not materialized. Once again, when he joined the Army, his parents had still been unable to give him what he had wanted for so long. In later years he had, of course, almost forgotten his boyhood dream, but now, thousands of miles from home, after years of war, a mature man with tremendous authority and great responsibilities in a foreign land, his childhood dream had been fulfilled through an unexpected gift from a man who could not possibly have known what it would mean to him."

I could feel the tension leave the room as we were all caught up in the depth of his feeling. He couldn't stop talking about it. It was like being recognized in a strange country, where you would least expect anyone to know your name and call out to you. Gersh and I left with full hearts, and I went home smiling and very much moved, thinking how often human beings can be so close to one another while thinking they are so far apart. It was truly remarkable how such a simple gesture could break down, once and for all, any barrier that still remained between us and show each of us to the other as being equally human and sensitive. I told Lilly the whole amazing experience, and she was as touched as I had been.

That same evening while I was at the office meeting with delegates from organizations out of the city, the guard came in to announce that the major was there. He was indeed there, right on the heels of the guard, sweeping into my office, excited and happy. He threw his arms around me again. "I hope I'm not interrupting anything, Mr. Schapelski," he said.

"Not at all, Major. This is a great honor. May I introduce you to my friends?"

He greeted everyone around the table and expressed interest in our discussions. Lilly was kept busy interpreting for us. "Can I drive you home, Mr. Schapelski? I have my car outside." I declined gratefully. My own car was waiting. "You know you have promised several times to take me on a tour of your settlements and projects. When are we going to do it? Tomorrow?"

I had to promise we would take him the following day to see everything in the Landkreis, Munchberg, Helmsbrechts, the kibbutzim, the seminary, and, in addition, he wanted to see the

Children's Home at Schloss Schauenstein, even though it was in Landkreis Naila outside his jurisdiction.

The next morning he called for Lilly and me with his chauffeur, the captain and two other officers, and we left in his huge American car. He was tremendously impressed with every project, particularly with the kibbutzim and the caliber of the young people he met there and the superlative condition of the farms and ranches they were operating. Their progress, their behavior, their attitude, and what they had learned from scratch impressed him and his officers greatly. The last place we took him was to Schloss Schauenstein to see the children. He was so moved by the home and so taken with the children that it was obvious he spoke with difficulty, his voice filled with emotion. He looked at the children and listened to some of their histories and the circumstances which had brought them to us. "I want to do something for them if you will let me," he asked. "Where do they keep their toys, their school supplies, their clothes?" We showed him that each dormitory had closets for the thirty or forty children occupying it. He turned to me and said, "That's not good enough. I am going to send each child a little footlocker of his own." I tried to explain to him that the children were getting along fine without such possessions, but he would not listen. When we returned to Munchberg he immediately phoned the officer in charge of the munitions dump and ordered him to deliver a shipment of empty cartridge cases to Schloss Schauenstein. It was a gesture from the heart of a truly fine man. He made it very clear to me there was nothing within his power he would not do to help these children. And he never forgot his words.

And so we two, who had met under such unfavorable conditions, both strangers in an unfriendly land, with no common language, each wanting only to do the best for his own people, each burdened with great responsibilities, had broken through the wall that separated us and found we were, after all, very much of a mind and heart. I know that I (and I am sure that he felt likewise) deplored every day we had wasted in misunderstanding and conflict because of our inability to communicate with each other. I cherished his friendship all the more because it had been so dearly won.

Peace and harmony returned to our relationship with the AMG, even better than before.

Chapter
35

INCREDIBLE AS IT SEEMED, a year had rolled by since our first election of officers for the Jewish Community. I was reminded of this by a directive from the Central Committee in Bamberg. They required each recognized Jewish community to hold annual elections of officers and stipulated in detail how many offices had to be filled per hundred members of the community, right down the line from president, vice-presidents, secretary, treasurer, and so forth. Outgoing officers had to requalify for the ballot by obtaining the requisite number of signatures from registered members of the community.

This year the restrictions seemed unjust. No one could run as an individual. An entire slate of officers had to qualify and be voted for as a group on the final ballot. I felt it was undemocratic and so expressed myself in letters to the president of the Central Committee in Bamberg, stating my belief that every voter should have the privilege of choosing whoever he wished on an individual basis rather than having to cast his vote for a slate of candidates regardless of whether or not all the nominees met with his approval. But they had their orders from Munich and could do nothing about it.

Friends drew up a petition to place my name on the ballot as part of a slate with Ignatz Rotter, Joe Komet, Mr. Reif, Lilly, Drexler, and several others. After obtaining our individual consent, they circulated the petition and collected the required number of signatures. Mr. Kluger ran on the only opposing slate. Any member of the community in Landkreis Munchberg over the age of sixteen could vote, but the young people on the kibbutz in Landkreis Naila could not. There were over three hundred voters in the immediate community, and on the Munchberg kibbutzim there were several hundred more.

The day of the election arrived, and everything ran smoothly. It was a Sunday—a custom we followed in subsequent years. We had poll watchers, and some of our leading citizens who were non-partisan did the counting. The kibbutzim brought in their sealed ballot boxes from the farms and ranches to be counted in the center. Sealed ballot boxes also came in from the adults at Schloss Schauenstein. I was working late in our home when a telephone call informed me that the ballots had all been tallied and I had received over 90 percent of the total vote. It was an overwhelming victory. I was very proud of the solid vote of confidence the people had given me. I had another year to serve and looked forward to it eagerly.

Here and there one or two of our friends left the community, some fortunate enough to have a relative in America or some other country, but there were always the new arrivals to take their place. Those who had gone into business prospered, and more were encouraged to follow their example. Even the shortage of supplies eased a little late in 1946. Our family business was also prospering. Max and David began to travel to Munich, Frankfurt, Dusseldorf, and other major cities on the lookout for new customers and sources of raw materials. And when the occasion demanded it and I could spare the time, I went, too. Everywhere I looked I felt a swell of pride. Each kibbutz was functioning beyond my wildest dreams. Lilly and I continued to visit the young people regularly by day, and by night the trucks whisked them away, leaving their replacements behind. And scarcely a weekend passed that we did not spend with the children. Their returning confidence and health made everyone's life more joyful as they responded steadily to our care. I used every excuse I could to bring our people together as often as possible for meetings, holiday celebrations, dances, anything that would seal the bond between them and keep their sense of unity strong. There was a wonderful feeling of loyalty throughout the entire community. It only needed to be fostered and maintained.

The one great disappointment I experienced was the final total disintegration of the Denazification Board. I had stuck to it through all the months of frustration until finally the American military government, disturbed by its shortcomings, disbanded it and established a special office in its stead where custodianships were to be directly reviewed and assigned. By this time the Allies had found the central files of the Nazi party intact in Berlin, so there was no more guesswork involved. I had the gratification of seeing quite a few court trials involving Nazis who had lied about their political affiliations on their questionnaires, only to be caught when their dossiers were pulled in Berlin. Those who had previously stood trial and yet continued to hold property, practice professions and operate businesses found the Custodianship Department stepping in to remedy the prior errors in judgment.

The Palestine AMT came to us again with a problem and a request. There would be a great need for teachers in Palestine. Somehow, somewhere, a pioneer force had to be built to meet that demand. The AMT representative asked if I could find a place in Munchberg to establish a teachers' seminary. "But why always Munchberg?" I asked. "This once couldn't you find another place? You know how crowded we are already." I was genuinely curious as to why other communities had not spoken up and asked for the opportunity to settle people as we had. "You know as well as we, Natan, that Munchberg is one of the very few places where we have had such outstanding success. It's only logical we would want to continue where we have already found a healthy climate of cooperation from all sides and where the community itself commands such respect and prestige."

"I know that and, believe me, I am very proud. But why push everything into this one area? Have you tried anyplace else?"

"Yes," they said, "we tried to find a place around Munich because we thought it would be best to have it close to the displaced persons' camps, but we failed. We wanted it to be separate from a camp. We realize it's a big order to fill because it means not only classrooms but dormitories and living quarters for single people and couples, students, teachers, and staff. And that in turn means kitchen facilities and sanitation. And it can't be done on a farm like the kibbutz. It should be in the town."

The meeting was lengthy. The need was beyond question, but I wanted to think it over carefully and then look around to see if suitable locations even existed before I approached the AMG and German authorities. "How many people do you anticipate?" I asked.

"Well, Natan, we hope to have from fifty to sixty students, so you might as well count close to one hundred with the staff."

I talked to Lilly, and we concluded that if there was a chance we could bring this about, far be it from us to say no. We talked to Captain Spiro, and his enthusiasm encouraged us even more.

"Listen, my friends, if you here in Munchberg don't do it, who will?"

Our minds were made up. I began to look over the facilities Munchberg offered. Directly across the street from our center was a huge factory that had been owned by the Kalbskopf family, the former occupants of our villa. The industrial complex covered acres of land with mills, warehouses and buildings. It was in excellent condition and only in partial operation under the custodianship of a German, Carl-Heinz Muller, whom I had met at the AMG. He had a very good relationship with the American officers and had been complete-ly cleared of any Nazi party membership. He seemed to be an exceptionally decent man. I went to visit him, and he listened cordially to the reasons for my interest in the complex. "I only want to go through the vacant buildings to see if there is a place we could use before I approach the AMG," I told him.

He reminded me that he had no authority to make any commitments but very graciously took me on a tour. We came to one part of the factory which had just been vacated by American troops who had been billeted there. There was one vast room capable of accommodating hundreds of people which must have been used as an assembly hall for workers when the factory was in full operation. It could serve ideally for classrooms and lecture rooms. There were excellent kitchen facilities adjoining it, also unused since the American soldiers had left. The rest of the rooms, which had been used in the past for warehousing materials, were empty and no longer required. I could see that our taking over these facilities would interfere in no way with existing production, reduced as it now was. If there was a place in Munchberg for a seminary, this was it. Besides, it was close enough to the center so we could oversee it easily.

I thanked Herr Muller for his courtesy, and later with his approval I approached the officers in authority. Lilly interpreted for me. I pleaded that this was a vital project for our young people who would one day emigrate. Proper exposure to good teachers and qualified professors from America and from Palestine to complete their education would be invaluable to their futures. The sincerity and reasonableness of our request gained ready sympathy. I promised to be personally responsible for the young people's welfare and guaranteed that they would not become a liability to the community. Similar promises in the past had never been broken. When I had finished the major asked only that I give him time to check with Muller for his opinion, which I already knew. The next day the answer came: "Yes." With an unbelievable minimum of discussion and a complete absence of problems, they had granted our request. Now it was up to Muller and me to work out the details. He not only offered no obstacles but overextended himself to give us every consideration and help.

When I notified the Palestine AMT and JDC of our success, they were elated. They counted this as an accomplishment second only to Schloss Schauenstein, because they had been searching for such a place since late 1945. Soon shipments of beds, blankets, dishes, and food supplies from UNRRA and the JDC began to pour in. Mr. Scanes was very pleased and cooperated fully, although, for obvious reasons, we refrained from telling him the ultimate purpose of the school and that its student teachers would one day be going to Palestine. Throughout the organization of the seminary there was an amazing absence of problems. The American officers, UNRRA, the JDC, and the AMT actively assisted us, and the Landrat and Burgermeister offered no resistance, only encouragement. It renewed my puzzlement about the lack of similar accomplishment in other communities, some far larger than ours.

The executive director for the seminary was the first to arrive. He moved into a small house on the grounds of the factory and helped set up the overall operation. He greeted the young people as they arrived and settled them into their quarters. They were quickly followed by the advance guard of teachers, professors, and traveling lecturers, who were given private housing close by. The students had been selected from various DP camps where they still lived in vast numbers more than a year after the liberation. They were young Jews from many different countries. For the first time they would be unified into one people and learn a common language, Hebrew, while being taught the tools of the teaching profession. The JDC and AMT had deliberately selected those who had gained some education before the war and who had expressed a desire to teach.

Dignitaries and representatives of every organization came eagerly to the opening ceremony. It was a landmark occasion. A very proud elderly woman from the AMT arrived bearing a gift that was to become a symbol of courage and faith for all of us. It had been smuggled somehow out of Palestine for us, just to say, "We are with you, we need you." It was a gift beyond price. Our people fighting there had sent us a flag. For the first

315

time we raised a Jewish flag—the blue Star of David against a white field—over a continent where no Jewish flag had ever flown before.

The assembly hall was packed as I welcomed the new members of our Munchberg community. "We are joyful and proud that Munchberg was chosen as the place for your training and education," I told them. "And I promise you we will do everything in our power to make your stay here a happy one until you leave us to do your chosen work. You are part of our community family now, for this is how we regard ourselves. Consider yourselves among your own brothers and sisters."

Many others representing the various agencies and authorities made welcoming speeches also, and we felt, when the ceremony concluded, that we had successfully assimilated them into our community, so close was the feeling of unity and purpose.

The seminary was busy from morning to night. Classes were held in shifts when necessary to compensate for lack of teachers or space. Soon it, too, became a showcase for the American and the Jewish agencies. They pointed again with pride to what we in Munchberg had been able to accomplish once more, in contrast to their unsatisfactory experiences elsewhere.

Our community in only a year of existence had amassed a shining record of achievement and progress. The hardships had lessened. We no longer had to fight for sufficient food and shelter. Helping hands reached out from all sides; the Americans, now more than ever, furthered our work with their compassion, understanding, and support. The JDC, the Palestine AMT, and the UNRRA were behind us constantly, offering encouragement, guidance, and warmth. Instead of destruction and death, hopelessness and futility, we felt the surge of creativity flow around us. The children in Schloss Schauenstein were thriving and becoming, in truth, children once more. In the kibbutzim, the farms bloomed under the hands of the young men and women who came secretly at night and left, just as secretly, months later, strong and fresh, ready to face the new and different hardships awaiting them in

316

Palestine. And just across the road we could observe the thriving activity in the seminary as it bustled with young people hungry for an education and others just as hungry to fill their need. I awoke each morning eager to begin a new day, fed and nourished in my heart and spirit by the visible and tangible evidence that life was renewing itself. Problems still faced us, but we had learned to meet them with a passionate conviction that they existed only to be solved.

One morning Lilly left on AMG business to deliver some important papers to the military government offices in the town of Tischenereuth, about twenty miles southeast of Munchberg. She was accompanied by an American soldier in a jeep driven by a German man. She had never been in the town before and was surprised to see some barracks obviously occupied by civilians. Reaching forward, she tapped the driver on the shoulder and asked, "What are those buildings over there?"

"Oh, Frau Schapelski," he answered, "that is a DP camp." Unaware that such a camp existed so near to us, even though in a different Landkreis, she completed her business in the military government office and on the way out of the town asked the driver to stop at the camp barracks. Almost immediately upon entering and identifying herself Lilly found herself face to face with a group of girls who stared back at her in unbelieving recognition. They stood frozen for a few seconds, and then clung together, embracing one another in tears and a torrent of words. For the first time since her friends had left to return to their own homes over a year ago, she was face to face with some of the girls who had left the last camp at Neustadt near Coburg and walked in the tragic transport from which she had escaped.

"What happened to you?" she asked through tears. "How did you get here?" They told her that after she and the other girls had fled through the woods, the SS had searched the area for a while and then moved on, afraid to stay too long in one place and risk capture themselves. "They kept us marching. You know how it was. But after you ran away we felt we should

317

try to escape, too. We knew it was no use to keep going on like we were, so about twelve of us made the break near here, near Tischenreuth, and we stayed in the woods until the Americans came through."

"What happened to all the others who were still left," Lilly asked, "or do you know?" The girls looked at one another and then at her. "You know how many were already dead when you left, Lilly," they answered.

"Yes, but there were still so many, not just on our transport but the others were met. All those men and girls, what happened to them?" The memory came flooding back to her—a column of emaciated, ragged men crossing an open field past their transport, dragging a cart piled high with bodies. As the two columns neared each other, the men had called out in Hungarian, "Bread, bread," and the girls, at the point of starvation themselves, had thrown them whatever crusts they could, while the SS beat them and drove them on. It was while watching that column disappear into the woods that Lilly had decided she had nothing to lose by trying to escape; it was too obvious that only death lay ahead, whether by starvation or by execution.

"Well, what happened to the others?" she asked again. Quietly at first and then overcome by their memories, the girls began to tell her what they had seen and what they had found out after the liberation. "They kept the transport going, not stopping for a minute. While we were still with it we met up with another transport of men, and one of the older women in our line saw her son for the first time in years. She screamed at him and he recognized her, but the SS wouldn't let them touch each other or speak. Not too long after we ran away the SS realized they would never make it to the Czech border. The Russians were closing in on that side and the Americans were advancing from the rear. So they shot the rest of the girls in our transport. The other transports must have ended in the same way."

Lilly was shaken and dazed. "Then that means that from the original four hundred girls, there can't be more than thirty or

thirty-five of us still alive. And all the other transports, too."
She couldn't finish; it was too agonizing to contemplate.

The women, some of them newly married and settled in the camp, exchanged quickly the more pleasant events of the past year, and Lilly left them, promising to return soon. She came home that evening white-faced and exhausted, knowing she would have to tell me about her experience and relive once more the tragic conclusion of the story I had learned from her so many months before. I was as shaken as she at the unexpected revelation that so many murders had taken place so near to where we lived and worked. "Let's go back to Tischenreuth tomorrow," I said, "if you feel well enough."

"Oh, yes, Natan," she said. "I want to go back there with you right away."

Since I did not speak Hungarian, the native tongue of most of the women, Lilly translated for us. They recounted the travels of their transport in more detail from the time it left Neustadt until they ran away—not long after Lilly and her friends had escaped. The SS had tried whenever possible to keep the march off the roads and away from the cities and towns so they could not be seen. They drove them through woods and across fields and had marched through Helmbrechts only because the guards had hoped to leave them in the camp there, but it was too full to take them in. "Do you know the route you took or the names of the towns you passed near?" I asked them. "We never knew exactly where we were, but there were thick forests and rolling farmland most of the way." From their descriptions and the name of an occasional town, I tried to note down some bearings by which their approximate route could be traced. "What happened to the bodies of those who died?"

"They left them where they dropped; they were in too much of a hurry to bury them or let us bury them. Most of the time they just pushed them into the ditches along the roads."

"Then they are still out there somewhere?" I asked, knowing the answer already.

On our way back from Tischenreuth my head began to

pound as I tried to comfort Lilly. "How could something like this have been kept quiet for so long? There must be a lot of Germans who knew about it. Someone had to have buried the bodies." That meant that more than just a few were in on it and had kept silent. We sat up that night, talking on and on. "My God," I said, "there are men and women, our people, lying somewhere out there in ditches and fields, hidden in unmarked graves. We cannot just sit here knowing this. Something has to be done about locating them and giving them a decent burial. I'm going to see Major Anderson in the morning."

Lilly and I sat in his office the next Monday and she spoke for both of us in recounting the events which had brought us there. His face grew paler and more drawn as he realized the enormity of the crimes we had uncovered. When we finished, he was silent for a few minutes and then asked, "Was this office aware of any of this before I came here?"

I said, "No, Major, I don't think it could have been, because we knew nothing of it ourselves in our own community."

"Do you know if the German authorities were aware of it?"

"To my knowledge, Major," I replied, "they were not, but of course I cannot be certain."

He drew himself up sharply. "All right, Mr. Schapelski, what do you want to do about this?"

"With your permission, Major Anderson, I would like to go to the Landrat and the Burgermeisters in Landkreis Munchberg and discuss it with them. First, I want to find out if they knew anything about it, and then I want to see what we can do about finding out where those bodies are. Beyond that, I haven't been able to plan."

"Very well," the Major said. "I want to see steps taken immediately to help you do whatever you feel is necessary to bring these innocent victims to a final resting place." He became stern. "You go to the Landrat and the Burgermeisters with my full authority and tell them that this office is very concerned that this situation should reach our attention at such a late date and then only by chance. Then you come back to see me and we will proceed from there."

I carried his message to the Landrat's office and to the Burgermeister's in Munchberg and the other towns. They admitted, of course, knowledge of the camp in Helmbrechts; it was common knowledge, after all. They remembered the transports, too. "What did you think happened to those people?" I asked them.

"Well, we assumed that there must be bodies somewhere, but we didn't know how many or where they were," was the vague reply.

"You have no idea at all of how many there must be lying out there?" I pressed them.

"There must be hundreds," they assumed.

"Well, gentlemen, we will have to do more than just assume now. I do not intend to rest until we find every single one of them, wherever they are lying, in ditches, in fields, anywhere, and we will bring them into the light of day and show them to the same people who told us yesterday and are telling us today and probably will tell us tomorrow that they did not know about these terrible things, that they were shocked to find out what had been happening in their Germany, without their knowledge or participation." I spat out the words through clenched teeth. "Now that you are aware of the situation, I will keep you informed of what I intend to do about it." They promised me their full cooperation.

When I had visited all the German authorities I returned to my office briefly and found a message from Major Anderson asking Lilly and me to report to him on my return. She joined me at her office, and we found Major Anderson with our good friend Captain Stanchos. I made my report, and together the four of us went over my plan. I told them I intended to spend every hour scouring the countryside and tracing the routes of the transports. I wanted to question the farmers and people who lived in the woods and forested areas. "I know it will be very difficult to break the ice with the Germans. They are not going to help us, but if I can get two or even one to tell me something, it will be a start and we will know we're on the right track. If we can recover one body, it will lead us to the rest." I stopped. Each time the realization of what lay out there in the rain and cold swept over me, my fury grew. For so many months I had buried myself in the pressing work of each day that I had managed to stave off the confrontation I would some day have to face with the horrors of the past. I had urged our people and pleaded with them to treat the Germans with tolerance and patience for so long. I had not dared give in to bitterness for fear it would show in my words and acts and thereby destroy everything I was fighting to build. But this was too much.

The major's voice called me back out of my reverie. "Who will go with you, Mr. Schapelski?" he asked.

"I intend to handle this personally and alone," I replied.

"I don't want you to do it alone," he said. "I would like you to be accompanied by an officer from the military government and have him stay with you day and night until you make a breakthrough." He turned to Captain Stanchos. "Since you speak German, I would like to ask you to join Mr. Schapelski and make it your duty to stay with him and help him in every way you can." The captain expressed his eagerness and willingness to help, and I was very grateful, although I felt it was more than I should expect of them. "No, no, sir," the major contradicted me. "This is an obligation and duty of my office and of every office of the Allied armies. And since you are going to be occupied for weeks, perhaps longer, I would like you to advise the representatives of your Jewish community and displaced persons that this office will stand behind them while you are gone, and if they have any problems, all they need do is report them to Mrs. Schapelski and she will work them out here with me. You have our full support. Our hearts are with you, and we respect you for the task you have undertaken. Captain Stanchos will go with you every step of the way to give you all the power and prestige of our government, and whether voluntarily or with force, if necessary, he will help you get the information you need. I only wish I could go with you myself, my friends."

It was impossible for me to express in words how deeply

moved I was by his generosity and support. I think we both realized that an event far beyond our time was taking place and that we two from the opposite ends of the earth would long remember these days. I told him as much and told him also, "Major, as far as I am concerned the words you have spoken here today deserve to become a part of history so that they are never forgotten. And if the world does begin to forget, I promise you, we will refresh its memory."

Early the next morning I left my office and rode out with Captain Stanchos and a driver. We took the road from Munchberg to Helmbrechts and there began to leave the main, paved highway to examine the terrain. We left the car frequently and peered into gullies and ditches along the dirt roads. They were filled with brush and debris, and even when we used long sticks to probe it was impossible to determine anything. We stopped at a farmhouse and questioned the owner and his wife. "Do you remember transports of men and women coming through here last spring? Did you see any bodies left behind?"

"Nein, nein," they protested. At the next farmhouse and the next it was the same story. They knew nothing; they had seen nothing and knew of no one who had. After the first two days the captain and I began to look at each other dejectedly. It was as if they had rehearsed the same story and the same speech, and yet we knew that some of them had to be lying.

On the fourth day, just before dark, we made our last stop. It must have been the twentieth that day. The farmer, an elderly man, walked across the field in answer to our hail. Captain Stanchos launched into his statement. "I am the representative of the American military government. We know that transports went by here in this general vicinity, and we also know that men and women were shot, beaten to death, or died of starvation. Their bodies are somewhere near here, either buried or hidden. Now, we know you lived here then, so you must have seen what happened or know someone who did, and we want you to tell us."

There was no possibility of misunderstanding. Captain

323

Stanchos spoke fluent German. I joined him in interrogating the man and in trying to reassure him that it was not a question of punishment, that we merely wanted to recover the bodies. But he kept denying any knowledge of anything over and over again. We left discouraged, convinced that he was lying. At the farmhouse we questioned his wife equally without success and then approached the laborers in the fields. Again, no luck. We drove away, slowly as usual, keeping an eye out for a mound of earth or any other indication of a grave site, but there was nothing.

At the next farm we again stopped and began the same ritual. The old man looked at us oddly and stopped us part of the way through our explanation. "You have just come from the farm next to mine, haven't you?" he asked.

"Yes, that is so," we answered.

He hesitated and then said slowly, "Last spring we saw them marching the Jews across that farm, and after they were gone we found some bodies. We dug a hole in the field and buried them, myself and the other farmers."

It was the answer I had been praying for. Despite the horrible reality of the moment, Stanchos and I muttered "Thank God" under our breath. The silence was finally broken.

We sped back to the previous farm and confronted the farmer. It took me all my strength not to strike his lying face. "Why did you send us away with your lies?" I asked him.

"We have proof that you lied," Captain Stanchos told him, "and now you will be put on trial for lying to an American officer about acts of barbarism which you witnessed and denied. Is that what you want?" he asked.

The German began pleading with us, saying that he would cooperate, that he was sorry. "Prove it!" we told him. He began to spew out information, other names and other places in the area, which he knew about and which most of the other farmers knew about. We were right: There had been a conspiracy of silence. It had become even tighter when the news of our investigation circulated. "We know there is a grave right here on your land. Where is it?" He took us out into the field almost halfway between his house and his neighbor's.

"It's been so long that I can't be sure, but I think it must be here," he said, pointing. We would never have been able to locate it. There was no marker or other clue that anything lay beneath the dark and muddy ground. We broke pieces of wood and drove them into the earth to mark the spot.

We returned to Munchberg, where we informed Lilly and the major of our first discovery. We called a meeting of the elected lay leaders of the Jewish community, the Former Concentration Camp Inmates and Displaced Persons to inform them that the conspiracy of silence had finally been broken and that we would continue on the next day and every day thereafter until we had found and marked each and every grave.

Still later that same night I met with Major Anderson and some of his officers. He was so deeply stirred and already so emotionally committed that he decided to join us the next day, and so we four went out together, the American major, the American captain, Lilly, and I, to continue a sorrowful journey we knew we had only just begun.

Now that the one farmer had cracked, we went back to others who had lied, and when they realized it was hopeless to continue their denials and protestations of innocence, they talked and implicated still more of their friends and neighbors. Each time they took us to a place and pointed down, I shuddered. There was never any sign of the murdered victim lying below. Most of the places were ditches, some fairly shallow, others deep, all of them piled high with brush and nature's steady accumulation of leaves and soil. It was the Germans' passion for sanitation and fear of infection that had driven them to perform the burials, not any sense of decency or regret. At each place we left stakes in the ground to guide us when we returned.

The time had now come to plan exactly how we would lift away the earth and reclaim our dead. There would have to be a mass funeral as soon as a decision could be made as to where their final, sanctified resting place would be. Whatever we did, it had to be conceived and executed so it would live forever in the memories of everyone involved—the survivors who needed

325

no incentive but who had the need and, God knew, the right to mourn; the witnesses to the crimes who by their silence and stealthy acts of concealment were as guilty as the beasts who committed them; and the staunch friends who stood by us with conscience and conviction.

The officers of the military government requested that the work of uncovering the bodies be performed by former high-ranking Nazis. They felt it would only be an act of justice that the men who had built the Third Reich into the greatest instrument of death our world had known, the men who had instigated these crimes against humanity and who had caused the deaths of hundreds of thousands of their own American soldiers, should bear this labor. Major Anderson made this his irrevocable decision. "It's very late to remind them that we know who they are and what they have done, but it is something we must do. Will you please see to it that you receive a list of their names from our Security officer and get the lists also from the Landrat's office so that we don't overlook anyone?"

His orders were obeyed without question, and we compiled a list from which we picked some fifty of the highest-ranked Nazis living in the Landkreis, those who had never been interned as war criminals and those who had already been released. Orders from the American military governor were sent to each of them to report to various grave sites prepared to receive instructions to dig. The orders explicitly stated that the AMG would accept no excuse for non-appearance, not even that of physical disability, and that if anyone failed to show up at the place and time stated, they would face immediate trial for failing to obey orders.

I volunteered to appoint representatives from among the displaced persons, Jewish men, so that one or two of them would be present at each site to supervise the exhumation and continue the search for other possible sites in the immediate area. So many of our men came forward begging to take part that there were more than we could use. On a cold, wet morning two days later, we began. Not to our complete surprise, we

326

found in several places that the stakes had already been torn up and thrown away, making it necessary to relocate the graves. After the first of these, the AMG circulated an order through the Landratsamt and Burgermeistersamt that any repetition of this crime would be drastically punished, and they posted military police to enforce the order.

The first morning of the digging, key officers went out to witness the sad culmination of our search. At each site each former Nazi, regardless of age or station in life, was handed a shovel and told to start digging. Our men stood over them, watching with mixed emotions as the earth came away. First the soil, black with rain, and then not too far below the surface the first bodies. It was a sight unbearably horrifying even to us who knew what to expect and almost too stark for the officers who accompanied us. The bodies lay so close together and so badly decomposed that it was virtually impossible to determine age or sex. We forced ourselves to watch in ever-mounting horror as each shovelful of earth lay bare still more of our people, some of the bodies no longer intact and others still wrapped in the pitiful remnants of the rags that had clothed them and strips of leather as makeshift shoes clinging to what remained of their feet. We knew they had probably been young because the transports had been made up mostly of young Jewish men and women. The Germans were silent and white-faced as they bent over their shovels. One by one they approached our men and complained of the odor from the graves. "Could we wear masks?" they asked. "No." They returned to the digging.

At the end of the first day I returned to my office filled with anguish and anger. Almost immediately the telephone began to ring. As the Germans returned home, they called me, one by one. "Listen, Mr. Schapelski," they swore, "I was never really a Nazi in my heart. I was forced to join the party for the sake of my family. Don't make me go on with this. I am not able to do hard work in this rain, and the bodies make me ill." Another call and still another, all protesting their innocence and asking on one pretext or another to be excused. And in most cases they inferred quite plainly and often quite openly that they would pay me anything I asked. Two of the calls came from the brothers whose case had come before me in the early days when the Denazification Board was really functioning. They offered payment of any amount if only I could get them relieved. Neither they nor any treasury on this earth had enough money to buy back their souls from the devil for what they had done. I told each one calmly and coldly that if anyone resisted the instructions of the American military government and the Allied Armies of Occupation, he would be faced with trial and imprisonment. "My personal recommendation is that you report as ordered and do your work diligently," I repeated as the calls continued, controlling my urge to give vent to my feelings and scourge them in words that would readily have sprung to my lips.

Each day I visited each site accompanied by officers of the AMG, representatives from all the organizations, people from our community, and with Captain Spiro. And sometimes Lilly and I went out alone to stand side by side and watch silently. The graves lay along a definite route that had become clearly marked, but we would never be able to determine which of them held the bodies of her friends. She came out bravely with us time after time, pointing out the areas she remembered, explaining over and over where the transports had gone and how the continued shooting and beatings had left more and more bodies behind, abandoned where they now lay.

When eventually days passed and we located no new sites, it was time to prepare for the funeral. The Landrat asked me to select at the Landkreis's expense whatever kind and quantity of wood I wanted for caskets, and he placed the facilities of the Landkreis at my disposal. Munchberg had only one place where they manufactured coffins. I went there and arranged for the first delivery in the morning. Their inventory was not sufficient for such an enormous job, so I asked that they work day and night to provide enough for all the graves. I gave them a list of the sites and asked them to deliver as they completed work each day. Each evening we notified them of the locations for delivery the following day.

And so as the days passed we brought out of the German soil the remains of what had once been the youth of our people. Only a minute fraction, it is true, for the rest were ashes in the fields around Auschwitz and other death camps. My mind and eyes tried to flesh out their pitiful but cherished bodies. What did he look like, that one with the rags still clinging to his bones? And who was she? That must have been a young woman with the shreds of the camp garment disintegrating in the air. Had Lilly known her? I did not know their names, but it didn't matter. I knew them, each of them. They were myself and each of us still alive. And we were their future, for they would live on through us.

Many of those who had come out to lend their presence and sustain our spirits when they heard of the work we were doing, had finally to turn away, unable to bear the sight when the bodies were being lifted from the shallow graves and placed in individual coffins. Sometimes one body could not be separated from another, and the two had to be left joined in death in one casket. Even the Americans who had become inured to violent death on the battlefield were visibly shaken, and my heart ached at their staunchness in standing by. Not one person who stood at one grave left there quite the same for the rest of his life.

We stored the caskets in barns and outbuildings on the farms nearby, under German police guard, and as the digging drew to a close we rotated the crews so that each of the "former" Nazis put in equal time. When it was apparent after two weeks that our task was almost complete, I began to look for the proper place for a cemetery.

Whenever I had a moment to spare, day or night, I drove through the countryside looking at one place after another. Gradually, I became more and more disturbed. I saw beautiful places, especially past Helmbrechts, rolling meadowland, lush with grass and flowers and trees. There were so many possibilities that it was difficult to make a choice. I had no sooner decided on one place than I changed my mind and found some reason to select another, which in turn I could not accept. Until one night, unable to sleep, I went over in my mind, as rationally as I could, my inability to reach a final decision. Suddenly I realized why I could not do it. It was unthinkable that we should raise our dead from their unmarked graves only to recommit them to the same soil, even if the surroundings were more acceptable. Some day we would have to leave them behind, unprotected and most assuredly unvisited. It would be only a matter of time before their graves would fall into disrepair and perhaps even be desecrated when we were no longer there to protect them. No, if they were to rest in German soil, it would have to be a place among their own people, where we could be fairly certain their memories would be revered and cherished. The next day I drove to Hof, where a Jewish community had existed for many, many years and an ancient Jewish cemetery was still intact. I met with the German authorities and the Jewish community and asked them to set aside several plots in the old cemetery for a mass grave. They willingly agreed, especially the members of the Jewish community, who were eager to do their part.

The deadline we had set for the funeral finally came. We had constructed a dais for the caskets and a platform for the services. It was a dark, wet Tuesday morning, but our many good and dear friends came out in the pouring rain to join with us in honoring our dead. The American officers were there, hunched up in their heavy jackets, their faces swollen with emotion. Our dear friend Schlesinger from the CIC joined us, too. Mr. Scanes came to represent UNRRA; the Joint Distribution Committee and Palestine AMT sent their people to witness and take part. Every public official and dignitary from the city of Munchberg and the entire area was present, including the Burgermeister, Herr Specht, and the Landrat. It seemed that every civil servant of the German authorities was also there from the German police on down. The kibbutzim sent delegations, and some of the older children from Schloss Schauenstein came to see and remember. Photographers stood by to record for mankind's memory this most awesome moment, a moment no one who was physically present would ever forget.

The services were scheduled to begin at ten o'clock, but the rain continued to pour down, and I had to decide whether to go on with the ceremony or move everyone into the hall of the sports arena nearby. No, I thought, no storm and no rain shall stop us. This we will not hide from the eyes of God. A famous European cantor from Hof had asked to conduct the chanting of the ancient prayers, but the rain had delayed him, so our own cantor stood ready in his place. At ten o'clock we began. First there were speeches, then prayers. Captain Spiro, the rabbi, in his American uniform, recited the Hebrew prayers Molev Rachamim, and our cantor sang. We said Kaddish for our dead, weeping in the rain, unable to tell which of the drops on our faces were tears and which were rain. Major Anderson and other dignitaries delivered eulogies, unforgettably simple and sincere, the more moving because they had witnessed everything with us every step of the way. At one side of the field lay a row of covered caskets holding almost a hundred bodies; no one would ever know for sure. I took my place on the platform and spoke. "This is a tremendous experience for us here today, but it is only a tiny part of history, only a morsel of the entire truth—the horrifying truth that six million of us were murdered like this or under even more brutal circumstances. What did six million Jews do to the German people? What did one million two hundred and fifty thousand Jewish children do to the German people or, for that matter, to anyone? What crime did these who lie here today commit against any man? None! Yet they were brutally murdered, as we would also have been had the war not ended. These, our flesh and blood, our dead, are nameless. We know only that they were Jews. But we know that they were murdered and by whom. There was no one to witness Auschwitz and Birkenau for us because ashes cannot speak. But now, these, our visible dead, speak for them and for us. They are our witnesses. None among us knows whose brother or sister lies here today. They are the brothers and sisters of all of us, even those of us who have had none. Because we are all their fellow men. Did we perhaps know some of them in the camps or pass them in a death march? Who knows? But someone knew them, loved them, and wanted

331

them to live, as we want to live and as we *shall* live for them. We shall see to it that the world will never forget the stain of guilt that lies across it. This we vow before God as the heavens weep with us this day."

Captain Spiro also spoke and flung an indictment in the faces of the German people, challenging them to tell him now in the presence of these dead that they did not know what was happening in their country. "Yes, I know there were no gas chambers or crematoriums in this community. But it didn't take gas chambers or crematoriums to bring death to these people." Throughout his speech he never once minced words.

The candles we had lit burned and sputtered in the rain on a flag-covered table. When the final eulogy was delivered and the final Kaddish prayers said, we loaded the caskets onto the waiting trucks, some draped with Jewish flags and others, supplied by the American Army, draped with the American flag. Over the headquarters of the AMG the American flag flew at half mast. The caravan of cars and loaded trucks moved out and wound its way slowly and solemnly through the rain to Hof, as if we were reluctant to recommit the bodies to the ground.

In Hof, we were joined at the side of the two large graves by the Jewish community there, and we repeated the services, still not drained of the emotion that gripped each of us. Spiro spoke again at the open grave with the rain soaking his uniform. He raised his arm and pointed at me. "History will not forget nor will humanity ever let fade the memory of the burden that man chose to carry. Let them mark this day and mark it well, for we are all witnesses to the shame and guilt the world must carry forever."

With his final words still ringing in our ears, we laid them to rest at last there in the ancient cemetery in Hof and cast the dirt over them, whispering our prayers for the eternal rest of their souls, pledging we would never forget them, these nameless few we had finally claimed as our own.

Chapter
36

THE YEAR 1946 drew to a close with the icy winter of Bavaria a harsh reality around us. The beginning of the new year saw the influx of new arrivals slowing down, with the additions coming mostly now from people moving into Munchberg to join their family, friends, and former neighbors as we found room for them. To all intents and purposes, on the surface at least, the problem of the displaced persons was finally under control. While some had found refuge in communities like ours, many had of sheer necessity wound up living in the DP camps, with their physical welfare in the hands of the UNRRA agencies, Palestine AMT, and AMG. For them, as well as for us, there was still no place to go, but we in Munchberg had taken hold of our own destinies.

The men who had been successful in securing licenses to transact business had gradually regained their dignity and self-respect as their hard work began to show results. A few experienced merchants had started small retail stores, and the limited number of professional people in our midst—doctors, dentists, etc.—had opened small offices and taken up the tools of their profession again.

Even though the desperate anxiety of the first year had almost completely been dispelled by our tremendous progress, the hourly and daily routine of watching over all the various settlements still kept us very busy. There were always problems and decisions to be made involving the kibbutzim, the Kinderheim at Schloss Schauenstein, the new seminary, and the regular communities in Munchberg and Helmbrechts, as well as the regular meetings to be held with representatives from the various organizations and the careful maintenance of the close relationship we had built so solidly with the AMG.

There was very little harassment from the German civilian population. The level of cooperation from the German authorities, particularly from the Burgermeister and Landrat in Munchberg, was high, and this attitude reflected downward to the ordinary citizens, who followed their example. The AMG experienced very few problems and heard few, if any, complaints from us or from the German civilians, for we saw to it that any differences or frictions were smoothed over and solved before the AMG even became aware that a problem had existed. Since this was still not the usual situation in other communities, Munchberg became even more the prime "example" of a peacefully administered community.

It was inevitable, however, with so many hundreds of people, that even in Munchberg we would witness occasional arrests and trials of DPs, especially since we were so close to the Czech border, where many illegal crossings were being made. The possession of an excess quantity of cigarettes or other supplies not justified by the normal ration card was illegal and pointed to possible black-market operations. The AMG called on me from time to time to appear as an observer and as an interpreter from Polish to German, if one was needed at a DP's trial, and the far-reaching effects of these arrests began to concern me.

Many of our own people in the community had built their hopes on emigrating to the United States and other countries where they had relatives or friends, and some had already become involved in the complicated machinery of applying for quota numbers. I was acutely aware of the laws that existed in many countries that any criminal conduct, whatever the charge, that resulted in a conviction and jail sentence absolutely precluded entry into the country for the family member so sentenced; and if one member of a family suffered this fate, it meant the end of hope for all the others, for no emigrating family would leave a family member behind. This tragic but necessary restriction to keep out "undesirables" also applied to those who suffered from communicable diseases, such as tuberculosis, which brought back vivid memories of the outbreak we had brought under control that previous year.

I felt that the only way we could try to prevent such tragedy among our own people was by constant education. We held weekly meetings at which I stressed over and over again that our status was only temporary in that whatever the provocation or temptation, we had to think of the future and maintain self-control. I went to great lengths to explain the laws which had sprung up to suppress the black market, and I warned them, with great emphasis on the consequences, that even if they came into possession of a few packages of cigarettes legally and used them to trade for another commodity, they had broken the letter of the law, that however innocent their action was, it was a black-market transaction.

On my own initiative I went to AMG headquarters and tried to prepare the groundwork to offset what I foresaw as almost inevitable—the eventual arrest of one of our own people. "You see, Major," I told him, "these people find it hard to understand why they shouldn't be allowed to trade a few cigarettes they don't smoke for something else they really need. It's very difficult to explain the existence of a law to people who have absolutely nothing criminal in mind. We are living here on a razor's edge, knowing one day sooner or later we will move on and yet trying to build a life here at the same time. You must take the past into consideration to protect that future should any of these things happen." He was receptive and understanding as always, and with the constant indoctrination and

335

explanation on both sides I had every reason to hope that should a case come up involving one of us, we could expect some leniency at least.

However, as it turned out, there was not one conviction of any of our people from Munchberg that resulted in more than a fine. No jail sentences were passed, closing the doors to other lands.

There were occasional trials of DPs who had crossed the border illegally, and these were in some cases convicted and sentenced to jail for various terms, depending on the individual circumstances of their cases.

It was a never-ending source of pleasure to include the Americans in our social events, weddings and other celebrations, and they in turn invited us to their parties and holiday festivities. We had come to count on each other as friends, and with the confidence born of familiarity it seemed natural to expect it to continue without change. But we had forgotten the policy of the American occupation forces. It was a sad day for us when we learned that Major Anderson had received orders transferring him to another command. We took leave of each other regretfully and with genuine emotion. It was a blow to lose the close collaboration and support of a man we had come to value so much. And it was a personal loss for Lilly and me to have to say goodbye to a dear and respected friend.

We said many words to each other in private, and then, in public, at a farewell dinner attended by his officers and our leaders, I had the opportunity to express my feeling for him publicly—feelings that all the years between have never dimmed. "If you will forgive me for saying this, Major," I addressed him and the guests, "I think that when you came to Munchberg you had not had the chance to study or understand the problems you would face. And yet all of us here know so well how fast you grasped the situation and proved your compassion for those who had suffered so much. More was accomplished in the past months under your leadership than in all the months before you came, and you can claim to your everlasting credit much of the success of so many projects devoted to rebuilding lives. You are, sir, a fine representative of your great country and a fine human being." I paused, reflecting on all the memories we shared. "Major, I know you are as proud as I am looking back, remembering how rough it was when we started and how differently and with what accomplishment we are parting now, even though we are sad to see you go. Look around, my dear friend. Look at the farms, at the seminary, at the people here, and at the children. Look what we have achieved together. We could not have accomplished it alone. You have created for yourself a permanent place in the history of our time, and I am very glad to have a chance to repeat before these people what I have already said to you in private—that it has been an honor and a privilege to know you and Mrs. Anderson and to have had the opportunity to work with you. We shall never forget you here in Munchberg, nor shall we forget you wherever we go. We pray that God will bless you both wherever you may be."

The interpreter finished translating my words, and then the major rose. "Mr. Schapelski, it is the wish of my headquarters that I be transferred, so I am leaving Munchberg, but I leave knowing that whatever little part I played in your tremendous achievements will be among my proudest memories. I witnessed something here that I thought would be impossible, but Landkreis Munchberg is the living proof that with inspired and dedicated leadership there can be understanding and cooperation among all peoples, and I am proud and grateful to have shared that experience with you. My wife and I wish you all the very best of luck and good fortune. Goodbye, my friends," he said and took leave of us. The following day a messenger brought me a letter he had left behind. Its formal wording couldn't conceal the message of enduring friendship it contained.

MILITARY GOVERNMENT LIAISON &SECURITY OFFICE
Det. B-256, LK Munchberg
APO 407, U. S. Army

15 February 1947

SUBJECT: Letter of Recommendation
TO: Whom It May Concern

This is to introduce Mr. Natan Schapelski, chairman of the Jewish communities Munchberg, Helmbrechts and Naila. I have met Mr. Schapelski during my term as Military Government Officer of this Landkreis. Mr. Schapelski has always fully cooperated with Military Government and all other authorities. His communities are organized in an exemplary manner. His personal qualities and his work performed as UNRRA and IRO Liaison Officer have gained my highest esteem. Any consideration and help given to him by Allied and German Authorities would be highly appreciated by this officer.

Robert C. Anderson
Major, FA
Director

Chapter
37

As the business life of our community expanded, the contrast grew between the people capable of earning a living for themselves and those still totally dependent on aid, either because of lack of education, insufficient experience or, in many cases, because of health still impaired by their suffering in the camps. Their basic needs were still met by the agencies operating through our community, and all they could do was wait patiently until their quota number was called, or they could emigrate to Palestine. It was heart-breaking, however, to watch some families become hardship cases when they could not afford the special medical care and drugs they needed. I felt the time had come for the community as a whole to stand by those less fortunate.

I called a meeting one evening and recommended that a committee of five men be elected to form and administer a Free Loan Society. I suggested that three of the members be from the business community, one from outside the business community, and that one of our officers serve as an observer with a full vote. "Those of us who can afford it will contribute to an interest-free revolving fund for those who are in need," I explained. "There are many among us," I continued, "who are too proud to take charity even when they desperately need money. I feel we have an obligation, those of us who can afford it, to offer them a chance to borrow with dignity. I would like to hear some discussion on this."

The majority of those present felt it was a very good idea, but there was some unexpected opposition from some of the businessmen, two especially, who voiced an objection to having an officer of the community serve on the board with voting rights.

"But we cannot afford to let such a fund come under the control of a few men without a balancing vote," I explained. "This is why I recommended we elect two who are not engaged in business themselves. Anyone who comes to apply for a loan must be judged on the individual merits of his case; this must be the only consideration."

They still objected. These same two men knew they would be called upon to make substantial contributions to the fund. It seemed to me they had forgotten that they owed their start in business only a few months before to the help of the Jewish community, and my temper began to rise. The meeting room was packed and the discussion grew quite heated; but suddenly I could take it no longer, and without waiting to hear any more arguments, I got up and walked out with Lilly at my side, and the meeting broke up.

But the problem could not be solved by walking away from it. And I would not let the opposition of a few men stand in the way of a much needed service for many. Three days later I called a general meeting where a formal vote could be taken. With very little discussion the recommendation to establish a Free Loan Society, Gemilath Chasedim, for our Munchberg community was passed almost unanimously. At the same meeting the committee was elected, and I appointed Mr. Reif, a vice-president of the community, to sit on the board. Two of the other four members were the same two who had opposed me from the beginning.

And so in Munchberg, in 1947, we saw reborn an ancient tradition among our people, a tradition of helping those less fortunate by making it possible for them to borrow money discreetly and with dignity, interest-free. Immediately after the committee was formed we met with the key sucessful businessmen to raise the first funds. Ganger, Kluger, Reif, Komet, Gersh, Max, and David were among them. Each contributed a certain amount of money to a general fund, and we set up an office in the center to accept applications. While we did not need permission from the AMG to take such a step, I informed them as a courtesy and received their approval.

The plan worked. The people came, hesitantly at first, embarrassed and ashamed. But they were received with such respect that their dignity was restored. Their applications for loans to help with medical expenses, to start a small business or profession, or to aid in the expense of immigration procedures were processed rapidly and confidentially. In this way we loaned out hundreds of thousands of marks, all interest-free, and in some extreme cases no repayment was even expected. Perhaps one or two managed to take advantage of it, but in the main we gave much needed help to those for whom it was intended. Later, many people who had repaid their loans promptly and proudly came foreward and volunteered to lend money to the fund themselves so that others could be helped. And this was the real, long-range result I had hoped for. Their immediate need for money had been filled and their anxiety lessened; then, with their self-confidence restored and their badly warped outlook on life repaired, they were ready to face the future with new appetite and eventually even to help others now less fortunate than themselves. This was a giant step on the road back to a full and normal life. To the long list of accomplishments of the Munchberg community we could add, as far as we knew, the first Free Loan Society formed after the war.

With the gradual return to normalcy, if such it could be called, also came the return of personal differences—sometimes between business partners, sometimes between a man and wife. Unlike the old days when the rabbi passed his decision on their quarrels, a decision as binding as law, there was no elder to whom anyone could turn. Where could they go? Not to a German civil court; it was unthinkable. Nor even to the American military court; in fact, to no court. How could they understand our problems and render decisions with the wisdom we had been raised to expect from our leaders and elders and to honor without argument? There was a need and no one to fill it, so I inherited that responsibility, too.

Many evenings brought telephone calls asking me to hear a dispute, large or small, but none the less urgent, and I would call the parties to my office for a talk. At times, if word reached me that trouble was brewing, I took the iniative and made the first telephone call myself. "Come on in and let's see what we can do," I would say. Many cases were solved merely by open and frank discussion with very little arbitration on my part; others no amount of persuasion and reason could settle, so I would render a decision, and the parties involved would abide by it.

I tried to bring into the open the true causes of dissension, and when there was no clear-cut case of right and wrong, I urged the people to compromise their quarrel and recognize the foolishness of breaking up a business or a marriage without real cause. I was humbled to be accorded such respect by people of all ages and walks of life and to have my judgment taken solemnly and finally. It was at times like these that I sorely missed the guidance and strength of the learned elders and rabbis who had not survived the holocaust.

Chapter
38

FOR A FEW MONTHS AFTER Major Anderson was transferred, Captain Mayville acted as military governor, carrying on in the same spirit as before. Then one evening Lilly came home and told me that a new military governor, a Major Cleary, had arrived, transferred from Landkreis Wunseidel.

I called at his office shortly after, and Lilly introduced us, explaining who I was and then interpreting for me as I expressed my pleasure at meeting him. I used the occasion of our first meeting to fill him in briefly on the background of the community. He seemed quite interested and courteous. "We have a great many displaced persons here, Major Cleary, and we also have a number of settlements outside the city—in Helmbrechts and on farms both here and in Naila. There is also quite a large teachers' seminary here, and we have over four hundred orphaned children in a home in Naila. I believe you will find that both the Jewish Community of Displaced Persons and the Former Concentration Camp Inmates have an excellent record of cooperation with your office as well as with the

Burgermeister's and Landrat's offices," I explained, "and I hope that in the future we will both be able to continue to work together for the benefit of these people." His attitude was very pleasant and cordial, and he expressed through Lilly his similar hope. "Please inform Mr. Schapelski that if there is anything I can do, I hope he will call on me," he answered.

Our first impression of him was very favorable, and Lilly and I were pleased with the meeting. Unconsciously, we breathed a sigh of relief. With each new change we had no way of knowing what to expect.

A week or two later my telephone rang. It was the president of the Jewish community in Markdredvitz. We exchanged greetings. "What can I do for you?" I asked.

"Well, I just found out that our military governor from Wunseidel, Major Cleary, was transferred to Landkreis Munchberg. Is that right?"

"Yes, that's correct. We like him."

He paused a moment and said, "Well, Mr. Schapelski, I think you should know we lit candles of thanksgiving after he left."

"But why?" I exclaimed.

"He just wasn't interested in the DP problems, period."

We chatted, I thanked him, and hung up, perplexed. I had found the major most kind and polite. Now, as a result of this telephone call, I felt apprehensive. Were we facing another possible conflict? I hoped not!

I watched Major Cleary closely in all our subsequent meetings and exchanges of information and opinion, but I could detect no opposition or disinterest. He listened courteously and was always ready and willing to help. I asked Lilly, "Do you see something in him I don't see?" We had discussed the call from Markdredvitz at some length.

She said, "No, he is very reserved but very polite and kind. I just don't understand it."

We offered to take him on a tour of our settlements, and he accepted readily. At each stop he expressed great admiration for what he saw and seemed genuinely impressed and

344

complimentary. We told him of the tragic circumstances which led to the recovery and subsequent burial of the bodies, and he was quite obviously moved. With each passing day we became more convinced of his sincerity. At no point did he demonstrate any quality that would have borne out the remarks of the leader of the Markdredvitz community. The inescapable conclusion was that they had contributed to their own problem. They obviously had failed each other there.

Curiosity finally led me to ask the major about his experiences in Markdredvitz. He said simply that it had been very unrewarding. The DP community there was not unified; his office had seen them only as individuals asking for personal help. There was no overall plan, no interest in the whole. He had anticipated the same in Munchberg and had been agreeably surprised.

It was the same old story of a lack of mutual understanding and tolerance, of demands on both sides made without proper explanation, resulting in resentment and conflict, the insurmountable barriers to progress and constructive cooperation, whereas here in Munchberg we had developed the other extreme.

Major Cleary administered the responsible and powerful position of military governor in the best tradition of those who had gone before, forging another strong link in the chain of friendship we had fought so hard to maintain. We spent considerable time together and exchanged views on how best to help avoid problems. I went over our training program to educate the people not to engage in any violations of the law, however minor, and urged him as I had urged Major Anderson before that if someone from our community came before him, especially a first offender, to bear in mind the circumstances which brought us to this place and time.

In the early summer of 1947 our community reached its highest peak of population and activity. Every few months the nighttime exodus from the kibbutz took place, and a growing restlessness began to be felt in the community as the desire to emigrate increased.

Lilly was under tremendous pressure from her work as court cases continued to pile up—some of them top secret, some minor, all of them adding to the exhaustion she already felt. One tragic case involving the alleged rape of a German girl by an American soldier dragged on for weeks, and she had to sit through the trial, interpreting endlessly until the very day before our daughter Vera was born. And even in the hospital, shortly after Vera's birth, they came to see her on business, giving her little chance to rest. Two weeks after Vera's birth, Lilly returned to work at the urgent request of the AMG, and we had to content ourselves with seeing our beautiful baby daughter only in the free moments between the other demands on our time.

One day in July, at the AMG offices, Major Cleary and I discussed the fact that over the months some of our people had unquestionably built up an accumulation of reserves of food-stuffs, cigarettes, and materials they had not used, and it was logical to assume that sooner or later they would be tempted to trade for something they needed more. "What are we going to do when this happens, Major? It's almost a certainty there will be some arrests and trials. Who will defend these people in court? Some of them don't even speak German well enough to use an interpreter."

"I share your concern, Mr. Schapelski, but what can I do? I have my orders and must act upon them."

"But, Major," I said, "these people are entitled to counsel. They don't trust a German to speak for them. And legal counsel of other nationalities is not available. What can we do to help them protect themselves and get justice?"

The major stood up, walked over to the window of his office and looked down at the busy street below. After a few minutes he turned back and through Vladimiroff, who was interpreting, said to me, "If this is the case, then why not you? You understand them. If there is a problem, you can speak honestly for them. As of today I am appointing you to act as an official Friend of the Court for all displaced persons in this Landkreis."

I protested. "Major Cleary, I have no background in law.

346

How can I stand up in a court and take it upon myself to defend anyone?"

The major replied, "Mr. Schapelski, you are a practical man trusted in this community. You have just explained to me what can happen when justice is not done. This is your chance to see that it is. I feel that you are the right man, and, besides, Mr. Schapelski, there is no one else."

I had visions of the prosecutors in court reeling off legal precedents, citing case numbers and code numbers of the various statutes involved. I had no legal training or background of any kind. "Major, this is too important to me to give you an immediate answer. May I have twenty-four hours to consider it?"

He said, "I cannot force you to take this job, but in the best interests of everyone involved I urge you to."

I had no choice. I had raised the issue, and now, faced with his challenging appeal, I accepted. I prayed I would be able to live up to my commitment, frightened more than a little by the responsibility I had undertaken. Up to now the only defending I had done had been behind the scenes, informally and in generalities. Now it would have to be done publicly and formally, within the strict confines of professional legal practice, in which I was totally untrained. The community was very proud and pleased, but I was apprehensive. The keen awareness of the consequences of failure weighed very heavily on me, and I continued to pray that I would not be tested too severely.

Less than forty-eight hours later my trial by fire began, and it had nothing to do with the possible black-market cases I had foreseen. I received a desperate telephone call from a friend, Mrs. Schwartz. "Mr. Schapelski, my husband, Morris, he's been in an accident. Please come quickly."

"Yes, right away," I promised and dashed out the door. On the way to their home I saw a crowd of people standing in the street and, beyond them, a car smashed through the plate-glass window of the Poch Department Store. "What happened here?" I asked the nearest policeman. "Did anyone get hurt?"

"No, Herr Schapelski. By some miracle no one was hurt

except the driver of the car, Herr Schwartz, and he's not bad," he answered, holding back the crowd.

I could see for myself how dangerous it could have been. I walked on rapidly to the Schwartz house, and Mrs. Schwartz, Max Webb's sister Laya, told me the following story. Her husband, Morris, had gone into business and with the help of the community had been able to get the use of a car. Since he was unable to drive, he had hired a chauffeur, but today he had decided to try for himself and had lost control of the car. It had run away from him, down the hill and into the store window, narrowly missing a number of pedestrians and shoppers. He had been treated for minor cuts and then taken to the police station. He was formally charged with driving without a license and endangering lives and property.

So the first case I had to defend was a serious one and one for which there could actually be no defense. All I could advise him to do was tell the truth, plead guilty, and throw himself on the mercy of the court. Normally, such cases were heard in the courthouse in Munchberg, but this case was heard in the offices of the military government, with Major Cleary presiding as judge. Captain Mayville acted as prosecutor, and Lilly was present as interpreter and court reporter. Morris Schwartz and I were the only others in the room. A policeman waited outside to be called as a witness, if necessary. Morris was asked to state his name, age, and address, which he did. Lilly as clerk of the court read the charges and asked how he pleaded. "Guilty," he said, "and I throw myself on the mercy of the court—but with an explanation."

I rose and asked the major for permission to speak on behalf of the defendant. "Proceed, Mr. Schapelski."

"Major, this man committed a very careless act. He operated a car without a license and without experience. The evidence against him speaks for itself. His negligence destroyed property and could have injured other people. But permit me, Major, to go into this man's background and some mitigating circumstances. This is his first offense. His record is clean except for the number he has tattooed on his arm. His only prior conviction was that of 'political prisoner' of the Nazis. He survived the concentration camps and the horrors of the war and found himself here in Munchberg. He is a married man now with children. He has applied for emigration to America and is waiting for his papers. I am not trying to explain away the seriousness of what he has done, but I am asking that he not be deprived of his chance for a new life. He is prepared to make full restitution for the damage he has caused and pay whatever fine you impose. But if you should find him guilty and impose a jail sentence, then I do not think that justice will be served. It's not a matter of his spending time in jail—it's more important than that. It is a sentence to spend the rest of his life here instead of America. And we impose it on his wife and children, too, who would not leave without him. Because he used such bad judgment, should we repay him in kind and say to him that because of this one lapse, because he was so foolishly anxious to learn to drive a car, we are going to send him to jail and by so doing stop him and his family from going to America forever? Major, I know that these are considerations that in normal times would not have to be taken into account. But the times are not normal, and I suggest that justice be tempered with fact. I give you my personal guarantee and the guarantee of the community that if this man is released, he will never operate an automobile here again until he is qualified and that we will take the car away if he does not take adequate lessons and use his chauffeur until he is licensed to drive himself. I will also take responsibility for seeing that full reparations are made to the store. I leave it in your hands, sir, and hope that this court will show mercy and not let his family suffer for this one foolish act, that you will give him another chance." I finished and dropped into my chair next to Schwartz.

The major looked down at his papers, rereading the charges and thinking. Finally, he looked up and asked Schwartz to rise. I stood with him. "Mr. Schwartz, you acted in a careless and negligent manner. What you did was very dangerous. You could have injured and perhaps killed innocent bystanders and yourself. But it is difficult to assess punishment in your case.

349

Under the circumstances and in the face of the evidence, I have no choice but to find you guilty." My heart sank and I could feel the blood leaving my face. I had failed. "But," the major continued, "I have taken into account your counsel's explanation, and in view of this I am going to fine you one hundred marks and hope that by your future acts you will never give us cause to regret our decision."

"Oh, dear God," I breathed. I could see Schwartz's face brighten, and Lilly looked over at me happily.

When I had recovered I asked permission to address the court again. "Major, we want to thank this court for its compassion and generosity, and I promise you in the presence of these witnesses that this court will never have reason to regret its decision." And it did not. Morris Schwartz and his family continued to lead exemplary lives and two years later emigrated to the United States.

Chapter
39

THE LIFE OF THE GERMAN POPULATION gradually returned to normal as the postwar restrictions eased. But the more freedom they were granted, the more they demanded. Every improvement in their conditions only encouraged them to make renewed complaints about having to share living space with the DPs.

On the other hand, we were pressed for even more housing as people married and had children. To ease the problem somewhat we came up with the idea of building four-family apartments, primarily to fill the needs of German former political prisoners, since after all this was their country and ultimately their permanent home. Sooner or later we would be leaving.

It took months of complicated negotiations with Landrat Szech and Burgermeister Specht, but we finally reached an agreement. Plans were drawn, and we broke ground for the first project. The costs of the land and building were paid out of West German government funds. A list of the eligible Germans registered with the office of the FCCI was submitted to the registration office, and those with families were given priority as the buildings were completed.

In my negotiations with the German authorities I alerted them that if emigration did not open up for us by the summer of 1948, we would be forced to find more permanent housing for the Jewish members of the community, too.

In the process of restoring more freedom to the German people Mr. Scanes and his staff gave up the villa where their offices had been and moved to smaller quarters. The AMG permitted its German owner to reoccupy it. The reoccupied villa and ours shared a common garden of two acres with a swimming pool between. The pool was closer to the center and in good weather was in constant use by our people for much needed recreation and therapy. It was suggested by Major Cleary that now that the German family had moved back, we should relinquish the use of the pool to them, since it was part of their property. I said, "Major Cleary, I don't think the pool originally belonged to the reoccupied villa. It is obviously closer to ours." Inwardly I was surprised by the request and determined not to give in. "May I suggest that I have the records in the City Hall searched," I volunteered, "and we will rely on what they show."

He agreed, and I had a title search made immediately. The records clearly showed that the pool was on the same parcel of land on which our villa stood. I was relieved and very pleased. I returned to the major's office with the official record, and the matter was dropped.

There was increasing restlessness on both sides. The Germans wanted to get rid of us but not half as much as we wanted to leave. The DPs were tired of being "displaced" among the very people who had displaced them. They were anxious to know where they would eventually find a home and when.

The fighting in Palestine had increased. Ships of refugees were being seized. Very few got through the blockades. More of the youngsters from the kibbutzim were being joined by families from the community on the illegal transports and ending up interned on Cyprus. The desire to start a new life and to belong somewhere could not be contained. One entire family from Munchberg gave up and out of desperation crossed back into East Germany and returned to Poland just to settle its future, bleak as it would be back there. Only the business and professional people did not fall victims to the restlessness because they were occupied.

Our own family was growing. Shortly after Vera's birth in May, a daughter, Helen, was born to Sala and Max. The family textile business was prospering and kept David and Max occupied full time.

My work continued to be taxing during this restless period. I had to keep everything we had gained these past two years at the same high level of service to the community, keep the relationships with the Germans peaceful, and continue to justify and earn the cooperation and respect of the Americans, who were themselves under pressure, finding their positions now more difficult to maintain. It seemed that I spent most of my time trying to exert a calming influence every place I could, even though I, too, shared the urge to move on.

The problem was no longer bringing in more people or trying to establish new settlements outside the cities but trying to maintain or, if possible, improve what we had. Girls and boys from the kibbutzim intermarried with members of other settlements and with people from the seminary. Suddenly, an expectant mother on a kibbutz desperately needed private living quarters in which to bear and shelter her child. Or a young newly married couple in the seminary wanted a place of their own. Where were we to put them? Out of further desperation I converted the top floor of the community center into a number of private apartments, and four or five families joyfully moved in. It was only a partial answer to an enormous need. Everything was crowded beyond capacity.

The brighter side of the picture was the continued smoothness with which the kibbutzim, the Children's Home, and the seminary were operating. At the seminary there was a constant influx of teachers and students. Some of the teachers came for short visits, and others stayed on for months, instructing the students in Jewish culture, Jewish history, the contemporary and ancient history of Palestine, and opening the way to a knowledge of Hebrew and other languages. It was an enriching experience for all of us. Lilly and I attended the lectures whenever we could and watched the young people being prepared for their roles as educators and leaders in the exciting future that lay ahead.

Chapter
40

WHEREAS IN THE PAST, since taking the position of Friend of the Court (or public defender for the DPs), it had been an infrequent occurrence to hear of arrests involving members of the community, now quite suddenly there was scarcely a week in which we did not have one or more. Fortunately, the majority were minor cases settled in private meetings with the AMG and German police. The charges were either unsubstantiated or the evidence so weak that they were dropped. When this happened, the AMG would send me formal notification to inform the defendants that no further action would be taken. But if the charges were serious enough, a pretrial hearing was held, followed by a trial if the evidence warranted it.

The German police and American military police had their hands full trying to catch and prosecute genuine black marketeers. But in their diligence they often prosecuted well-meaning people for simply giving away cigarettes or chocolate received through the JDC or UNRRA. There were other cases unquestionably more serious. At the border crossing into

Czechoslovakia the American military police arrested two Polish men leaving the Western zone. This in itself was quite unusual. Most people wanted to get into our area, not out. They questioned them thoroughly, and the Poles told them a story of having smuggled a quantity of whiskey into our zone and selling it to a family in Munchberg. The MPs lost no time in bringing them back to the house they described. It was the home of the Gersh family, the largest intact family group in our entire community—two sisters, two brothers and their mother, and the husbands of the two sisters. I got an immediate call for help and rushed over with an interpreter.

The MPs were requesting permission to search the house. Since they were from Rehau, in another Landkreis, they could not search the home of a displaced person registered in Munchberg without a search warrant signed by the Munchberg AMG. Hoping to forestall the situation and wishing they would simply go away, I insisted on a warrant. But they went to the AMG, secured their warrant, and returned. They went through the house room by room, looking everywhere, and for their trouble they found one bottle of whiskey, which they confiscated. We had had ample time to conceal this one bottle from them, but we had not tried. They, of course, had hoped to find a houseful of black-market merchandise, but on the basis of the discovery of that one bottle they still wrote a report on which charges were brought against the two Gersh brothers.

The trial was set, and the military police from Rehau brought the two Poles to testify against the defendants, William and Peter Gersh. When I had a chance to present my defense I asked the court to consider the contradiction between the claim of the two Poles that they had sold a large supply of whiskey and left it in that house and the actual physical evidence of one bottle found by the MPs. "I ask the court to remember that no attempt was made to conceal this bottle of whiskey, which the defendants could so easily have done. And I submit that one bottle of whiskey does not constitute a warehouse of black-market goods." I concluded by making a motion that the case be dismissed for lack of evidence. We waited anxiously for the verdict. A jail sentence, if imposed,

356

would mean that the entire family would be cut off from emigration to the United States. When the judge announced a verdict of not guilty for lack of evidence, as moved, we were jubilant.

There was another case with a more tragic outcome. Two young women and two young men, each from different families, decided to pool their resources and take to Munich whatever cigarettes, canned goods, and merchandise they had accumulated, in the hope of converting them into the necessary tools of their trade, sewing machines, etc., that they could take with them to the new land. The Reichsmark was so inflated that it had virtually no value; one could buy nothing with currency, so their reasoning was simple and understandable.

On the Autobahn between Bayreuth and Nuremberg their automobile crashed into the railing on a bridge overpass, spilling four badly injured people onto the road. They were surrounded by the cigarettes and other goods scattered from the wrecked car. When the ambulance arrived, so did the German police.

One man and one woman were critically injured and taken to a nearby hospital; the other two were treated for minor injuries and jailed. I immediately informed the AMG in Munchberg of the circumstances, and as soon as their conditions warranted I applied for a change of venue so they could be tried in their own community. At first the AMG offered little encouragement, but after days of argument over legal technicalities my petition was finally granted because the merchandise found in the road had been loaded into the auto in Munchberg—my main argument for change of venue. The two less injured young people were placed in the custody of military police from Munchberg. But the other young man and woman still lay hospitalized. She suffered the most from her injuries and eventually lost the sight of one eye. What a tragic price to pay for breaking the law of a land that had already taken so much from her!

I could not deny the evidence; it spoke for itself. I could only base my defense on the issue of what had happened to these people as victims of the greater crimes committed against

357

them. "Yes, it is true they had goods in their possession which they had accumulated. But, by the same token, they did not use them for profit. They had a dream for the future, and this dream needed tools to make it come true. Once their people had these tools, but they were taken away from them. A million times they were taken away. You will ask that if they wanted these tools, a sewing machine or the like, why didn't they buy them? Why did they have to break the law? You and you and you and I know we live in a country where money is meaningless, where you can buy nothing for money, only for goods. I submit that in the extraordinary circumstances of our time, these people have to be judged on the basis of common sense, because for the time being there is no real law under which they can expect justice."

I felt I had convinced the court and waited almost confidently for the verdict. It was "Guilty"! I couldn't believe my ears. Then the sentence was announced. "The defendants are found guilty as charged, and the court is imposing a fine of fifty marks and the confiscation of the merchandise. Court is adjourned!" Thank God, I thought, no jail term. Young lives would have been destroyed. I thanked God for the American sense of justice. The more problems that arose and the more I sensed the restlessness around me the more I concentrated on interpreting and explaining the different factions to each other, and the more the communities around us disintegrated, the more I was determined Munchberg would continue to be an example in spite of everything.

As time progressed it got no better; it got worse. Instead of the prospect of peace in Palestine, the fighting increased. The Arab countries declared that if the British pulled out, they would push the Jews into the sea. Cyprus was one big DP camp, and few actually landed on the soil of Palestine. This did not discourage those from Munchberg or from the kibbutzim from still trying to go there. But as the hope of an early departure drifted further and further away, the bitterness and tension mounted.

Chapter

41

THE SUMMER PASSED UNEASILY into fall, and we celebrated the High Holy Days for the third time in our temporary little world. And then in November the excitement of the annual election of officers once again held our attention for a while. With almost the same slate running we were overwhelming re-elected. There were more weddings in the family—Cousin Regina to Joachim Komet, Cousin Sonya to Max Lettich, and Cousin Eva to Izak Tanc. Eventually snow blanketed the steep, winding streets of the town once more, muffling the noises of the cars, motorcycles and jeeps, and the year 1947 drew to a close.

The European custom of exchanging greetings and expressions of friendship and respect among the officials and authorities again took place at the New Year. I sent my letters off and received many warm greetings in return. One of these I have treasured all my life. Max Specht, Der Burgermeister der Stadt Munchberg, put his heart and conscience openly on paper in words of deepest sincerity.

Munchberg, December 31, 1947

To the Head of the Jewish Community
Munchberg
Gartenstrasse 40

I would like to express my sincerest thanks for your congra-
tulations which you conveyed to me. I also would like to express
my satisfaction concerning the excellent relationship between
the city administration and the Jewish Community in
Munchberg in the past. It is my warmest wish this should also
continue in the future. In case any differences of opinion should
occur at any time, they have to be settled with the same understanding and dispassionate approach as in the past.

My personal approach to the Jewish people is unshakable and
it is my conviction that six million dead *cannot* be forgotten. And
I shall keep this opinion whether I will be Mayor or once again
just a simple laborer. I hope that no circumstances will ever
occur to force me to change my conviction.

I wish the Jewish people for all time to come, a happy future. To
you, dear Mr. Schapelski, I would like to convey my special
thanks for your understanding cooperation and express to you
and your wife my sincerest best wishes for the New Year.

Respectfully,

Max Specht, Mayor

Slowly the tide turned. The kibbutzim began to dwindle
noticeably. Now that they could leave openly, no new arrivals
came to take their place. The people still trapped in DP camps
were leaving also as fast as they could. The United Nations took
up the question of a Jewish homeland, and our spirits rose with
the possibile recognition of our new country, the State of Israel.
Encouraged by the news, still more of the people from our
community began to leave. The fever was contagious. Everyone

saw the handwriting on the wall. The day was finally coming!

The biggest wrench for us was letting the children go. A few of the older boys and girls had already joined the transports of trucks to Marseilles and made the sea voyage like the young pioneers they were.

The whole world now felt the urgency of the displaced-person problem to which heretofore it had virtually closed its eyes. The British government began putting pressure on other countries to open their doors to the DPs so that it would ease the strain in Palestine, and the results were quite successful. The governments of various countries established special quotas, and some, like the United States of America and Canada, opened resettlement centers in Germany to receive and clear applications for emigration. One was set up in Schweinfurt to serve Bavaria, and the Joint Distribution Committee and UNRRA sent in representatives to help out.

Hundreds jammed the center as soon as it was opened. Palestine was the first choice of most, but many had relatives or friends willing to sponsor them in other lands. Some wanted to go to Canada, Australia, or South America, but next after Palestine, the largest number chose the United States, the golden land.

At the resettlement center the people were put through a rigid investigation process involving every phase of their lives. They were given medical check-ups to prevent the emigration of someone who had a communicable disease. Their records in the community in which they had lived were rigidly examined to see if they had broken the law or served jail sentences. And they were asked for guarantors or sponsors in their chosen land who would guarantee employment there. I heard heartbreaking cases of hopeful families who believed their applications would be automatically accepted only to discover someone in the family had an unsuspected ailment which was discovered only during the medical check-up, disqualifying the entire family. When the medical examination and other records were approved and the CIC confirmed that the applicant was not and had never been a member of a Fascist or other subversive conspiracy, he qualified to go before the consulate of the country he wished to enter as a stateless person.

When people in our community encountered problems with their papers, they came to us for help. If their record showed a court conviction and fine, I wrote letters clarifying the background of the case and vouching for their character. If their record showed a past or current illness, we arranged for our local doctor to re-examine them and issue a certificate as to their present state of health and if they were ill to get an extension of their papers until they recovered.

It was a very exciting time after the long wait, first years, then months, and now weeks. A new day was dawning for everyone around us, but for Lilly and me it was still work and more work. While others struggled to get out, we had to hold on and try to administer the dissolution of the settlements in an orderly fashion.

In the kibbutzim the young people still left were tense and impatient; they could not bear to sit back and wait, knowing that they could be so much help to their friends.

The slow emigration to other countries through the resettlement center eased the pressure in the cities and towns, but it was little help in the camps and settlements. These people were interested only in the new Jewish state and were impatient for the day they could call it their own.

In February 1948 another good friend left Munchberg. Captain Raymond W. Mayville, a fine officer and worthy representative of his government, said goodbye and took with him our heartfelt appreciation and blessings. He left us with wonderful memories of his friendship and a generous letter:

362

MILITARY GOVERNMENT LIAISON & SECURITY
OFFICE
Det. B-266, LK Munchberg
APO 696, U. S. Army

10 February 1948

SUBJECT: Letter of Character

To: Whom It May Concern

1. It has been my privilege as a Military Government officer to
work closely with Mr. Natan Schapelski, Chairman of the
Jewish Committee for Kreise Munchberg in Ober and Mittel
Franken.

2. It can be said in all honesty that if it were not for Mr.
Schapelski's unceasing and most praiseworthy attention to his
work and cooperation with Military Government, many of the
problems confronting this office concerning Jewish displaced
persons would have been considerably more difficult in ef-
fecting over-all settlement.

3. I heartily endorse Mr. Schapelski as an energetic, efficient,
trustworthy, and most capable man.

Raymond W. Mayville
Captain   OMP

Chapter
42

THE NEWS WE HAD LONG AWAITED finally came through on May 14, 1948. The British mandate on Palestine was officially terminated, and the new Jewish state, to be called Israel, was proclaimed to the world by the Jewish National Council in Palestine.

For weeks before the suspense in the community had steadily mounted. We all talked of nothing else. Everyone wanted to hear the news as it happened, so we hooked up special loudspeakers inside and outside the center, tied into our shortwave radio; and the kibbutzim even wired loudspeakers out into the open fields so the young people working there could hear. First, the anxious weeks passed. Then the days. Then the announcement itself. A new country had been born out of the battle-torn desert of Palestine—Israel, a Jewish homeland. Thank God, thank God!

The joy and emotion spilled over into tears and smiles. We danced in the streets, we danced in the center. All over Munchberg we could hear the horns blowing in the cars of our people. Women ran home to get white handkerchiefs and white scarves, and with a Star of David hastily painted on them in blue, they waved from every corner, from every hand. A few of the women took to their sewing machines and in an instant, it seemed, stitched together a few big white flags with the pale blue star to fly proudly over our center.

It was a day unlike any other day. As fast as we could we arranged a formal, solemn observance to which we invited all those good friends with whom we had shared so much, the American officers, the representatives of the Joint Distribution Committee and Palestine AMT, and from the German officials the few fine young men who had believed in us and helped us find a way to survive to experience this great day.

We chose the seminary for the occasion because it was the largest gathering place and for another, more meaningful reason: It was symbolic. There in that school carved out of a German textile factory were so many young men and women who had trained long and hard for this very day. What better place could we choose?

We filled the main room and overflowed into the aisles, then the halls and then outside, where loudspeakers carried our words to the hundreds who could not get in. With our heads held high, smiles and tears on our faces, we rejoiced. The people of the AMT were jubilant; no longer were they a group of volunteers. Now they represented a national government in the eyes of the world. Just before the ceremony began, more wonderful news came through: The gates of the camps on Cyprus were open and all the people held there were free—finally able to join their brothers and sisters in Israel and fight side by side, shoulder to shoulder, man and woman alike, armed or unarmed, with whatever they held in their hands. They were going forth to join in a battle which the whole world had written off as lost. How could untrained, unarmed people, by their very tradition a non-militaristic people, prevail against thousands of trained soldiers from the Arab countries? The world was learning to look at the Jews in a new light.

Brilliant and moving words were spoken. Everyone had

something to say of lasting beauty and importance. When my turn came I fought to control my emotions as I looked out over the sea of faces and beyond them to the memories of the past. There was much that I needed and wanted to say to contrast this triumphant moment with the worst years of the war. I wanted to refute the accusation that the Jews went willingly and passively to their deaths. I wanted the world to know how the sadistically clever plan of the Nazi monsters was enforced by using our concern for our own families as weapons against us. I wanted to contrast the willingness with which our same people under different circumstances went out to fight an incredible war in an unfamiliar land against battle-seasoned soldiers with modern arms—and won that war and that land for their own.

"At this very moment, as we meet here together with our friends, friends who in the darkest hours of our life after the war stood with us, helped us and sustained us, whenever and wherever they could, trucks are rolling into towns all over West Germany. They are coming to pick up the men, women and children from the kibbutzim, from the DP camps, from the children's homes, from every place where there are Jews ready to go home and fight for their homeland. Beyond doubt, we will win there as we have won our way back to life here. This is no longer a time like 1939, 1940, or 1941 when our young people were helpless to fight because the lives of our loved ones were held over our heads. There is no one here who does not remember the threat of murder of a mother, father, husband, wife or child if he did not obey a Nazi order. In those dark and bloody years, who among us dared gamble with the lives of our families or even possessed a weapon? They used our love for each other against us. But those days are past now. In this new battle there are no hostages to hold over our heads; we are free to fight back. The battle for Israel has been destined for a very long time, and our people there are not just fighting for themselves or for their children. They are fighting for all of us and for our children and our children's children, too, and for the memory of those who did not live."

366

I turned to address the seminary group seated together. "We are privileged here in Munchberg to witness your hard work and devotion to get an education so that when this day came you would be ready to play your part in building your new country, a country that has such great need for you as teachers and leaders. And I know that you will not hesitate for one minute to join in the battle and see it through even if it should be to the last one of you, because there is no other way. We pray that God will watch over you and bring you through your journey safely and the struggle that lies ahead. Our hearts and our thoughts are with you. *Shalom!*"

At the close the same elderly woman I had remembered from before stepped forward in the uniform of the Palestine AMT and, speaking in Yiddish, asked me as spokesman of the Jewish community to accept a tattered Israeli flag which she had just received from the battlefield in Israel. I took it from her and held it close to me; nothing could have meant so much.

From that day on the exodus really got under way. There was farewell party after farewell party filled with presentations and speeches. Day and night the stream grew into a torrent as trucks rolled from the countryside filled with young people from the kibbutzim and from the towns. The pressure was at a peak. Everybody wanted to go today, not tomorrow, but there simply was not enough transportation. The DP camps burst open and they joined the rush. "Let's go, let's get out, let's go *home!*" Our hands were full not only with the papers of those going to various parts of the world through the resettlement center in Schweinfurt but with the overwhelming number now impatient for Israel.

For weeks I raced daily from kibbutzim to kibbutzim to help load the trucks and attend triumphant farewell parties for the boys and girls who had come to us broken and defeated. Now these same young men and women, healthy and filled with enthusiasm and conviction, danced wild horas for the last time on German soil and clambered up on the trucks with their bundles and packages and memories. Then as the last trucks rolled away from each kibbutz we lowered the flag and returned the farm to AMG control. It was the end of an era.

We spent a great part of the time at the Children's Home. They were as aware as everyone else of the meaning of the new State of Israel; they had already begun to call it "home." Now the wonderful future we had promised them was at last coming true. The Youth Aliyah, the Jewish Agency for Palestine, and the Hadassah made the plans for their trip. Then one unforgettable day we let them go, all together, as they had come. We laughed and cried as we lifted them up on the trucks. They had filled such a place in my heart for years that it was particularly hard for me to see them leave, even though it was everything I had hoped and dreamed for them. I watched the trucks roll out of the courtyard of the old castle and waved back to the children until my tear-filled eyes could no longer see the last truck moving down the winding road.

Now that the need for the seminary had ended, all members of the staff and students in training readied themselves to move on to the new Jewish homeland. We held a closing ceremony even more poignant and meaningful than the opening. So many young men and women had already passed through the classrooms and gone on to Palestine to take up their vital task, their memories haunted us as we gathered to say goodbye to those who would follow. The seminary had gained such renown throughout Germany that dignitaries from distant cities came to pay their respects and add their praise. Every seat in the auditorium was taken, and many stood outside listening over loudspeakers as the parting words were said. Many famous Jewish leaders as well as non-Jews addressed us that day and recounted their appreciation of the work the seminary had done and the unforgettable role it would always play in the history of Israel through the far-reaching influence of its graduates on the youth of the new state. In a tremendously moving ceremony, the flag of the State of Israel was lowered and presented to me as a token of appreciation. It was a great moment in my life and yet another memory I will treasure as long as I live.

We needed no Schweinfurt and no red tape for Israel. Israel

didn't care whether you had an illness or a prison record or even the money to pay for your fare. Anyone among us who wanted to go found the door wide open and people waiting with outstretched arms to welcome us. Those leaving knew that the fighting was as violent as it had ever been, but it cast no fear into their hearts; the urge to set their feet on the soil of their own land was too great.

It wasn't long before we started to receive letters from those who had arrived, and we were heart-broken to learn that some of the fine boys and girls who had been among the first to leave had already fallen on the battlefield, many of them wounded and many killed. What I had said to them that day the State of Israel was born had proven true. They had been called to duty and had not been found wanting.

Even after hearing this sad news—and in the beginning it was tragically bad—not one person changed his mind about going. The JDC and AMT supplied what money they could to rent, lease, and buy old and new ships, and the exodus reached its highest peak in the summer and fall of 1948. Our community in Munchberg grew smaller and smaller.

From the determination of the pioneers in Palestine and the determination of the displaced persons in Europe, each knowing there was no way back, would come the final victory in Israel. The kibbutzim and the DP camps had exploded and sent out reinforcements, each one a soldier in his heart, to join their people and bring about a miracle in the desert. No sacrifice was too great and no age limit too young. Some of the heroes were still children.

Chapter

43

YET ANOTHER CASE that was to have unforeseen consequences grew out of the fever to get moving. A young German boy employed in one of the local textile factories as a wrapper decided to steal an occasional piece of yardage because at this time, before the currency reform, the money he received as salary was worthless. He would cut off a few yards when he was unobserved and wrap it around his body under his shirt. One day he was caught, and the police were called in. He confessed he had been doing this for some time, and when they questioned him as to the disposition of the goods he implicated a member of our community, Mr. Silbergold.

Again, an urgent telephone call from Mrs. Silbergold reached me at the office. The police were in her house with a search warrant, looking for stolen merchandise. "I would like to see you both here in my office right away," I said. "Please come over now." They hurried in a few minutes later, flushed and upset. I urged them to tell me the whole story.

"We did buy some material from the boy, but just once and only a few yards to make a dress for my wife and for our daughter. I swear that's all," he told me.

"How could you do business with such a young boy? Didn't you know it must have been something illegal?" I asked.

The boy had told him he was receiving the goods in lieu of wages. Well, this put a new light on the story. It wasn't customary, but it was plausible in the economy with currency only worthless paper.

"What did you tell the police when they searched the house?" I asked.

"We told them we didn't have any material. We were so frightened," they answered.

"Did you admit that you had bought some?"

"No, no," they said.

"Where do you have the material now?"

They told me they had left it with a dressmaker to be sewn into dresses. I questioned them and requestioned them to assure myself there was no more to the story than what they had told me. When I was reasonably sure I had the whole truth, I told them to go to the dressmaker's shop, pick up the material, and take it immediately to the police department. "Tell them this is what you bought from the boy, tell them how you bought it and what he told you. And tell them you have talked to me and I sent you to them. After that, it is up to the police if they want to make a case out of it." It was the only way to handle it, by making a clean breast of the facts.

As soon as they left I called Captain Schmidt at the police department and told him they were on their way to see him. "I don't think these people knowingly committed any crime. It's logical to believe what the boy told them. They are willing to return the goods now that they know it was stolen. And I feel that under the circumstances this should be punishment enough for them."

He listened and then indicated his agreement, stating that he did not feel the case called for them to be charged with any crime. I was relieved, but my relief was only temporary. He did not live up to the feeling he had expressed to me and immediately filed a report with the American military government charging them with receiving stolen property. He did include our telephone discussion and apparently quoted me accurately, because when Major Cleary called me in to review the facts before the case was brought to trial, he alluded to that conversation.

I went over the details with the major point by point, stressing how the police had found nothing when they searched the house. "But when the Silbergolds told me the whole story, I sent them to the police with the merchandise, and they went voluntarily. If they had decided to keep quiet, there would have been no evidence to charge them with. I think you will agree, Major, that this shows their good faith."

He gave it much thought, and after we had discussed it at great length he indicated his agreement. "I don't think there is a case against them, Mr. Schapelski, in the light of what you have said. So I will not have any charges brought against them and we will let the matter drop," he told me.

"Do you think we ought to have a formal trial to clear them?" I asked.

"No, there's no need to go through all that. There isn't enough evidence to warrant it, so we'll merely file it away with no further action, and you can inform Mr. and Mrs. Silbergold accordingly." I thanked him profoundly for his understanding and carried the good news to the worried couple.

In May 1948 we said goodbye to the last military governor of Landkreis Munchberg. Major Timothy Cleary left us, and our last bond with the AMG was gone. His parting letter amply demonstrated the understanding and compassion with which he had administered the difficult duties of his office. I blessed the day he had come to us from a community which had never taken the time to get to know him and his real worth and character.

372

MILITARY GOVERNMENT LIAISON & SECURITY
OFFICE
Det. B-256, LK Munchberg
APO 696, U. S. Army

TC/1s

15 May 1948.

TO: Mr. Natan SCHAPELSKI, Chairman Jewish Community, Munchberg, Helmbrechts and Naila.

My dear Mr. SCHAPELSKI:

Before leaving Germany I must express to you
my thanks for your helpful cooperation with this office during
the 15 months I have been here. Relations between surviving
Jews here and native Germans are strained in many localities.
Here, under your wise leadership, these relations have been
exceptionally fine. Your tact, patience, and deep understanding
of all human problems has brought about the fine situation that
exists, and has earned for you and your people the respect of
the German population as well as the gratitude of the U.S.
occupation forces.

I wish you all future personal success, and I will
be always eager to report on your fine qualities and high
character to immigration authorities of any country which asks
me.   TIMOTHY CLEARY
                       Major,
                       Director

With Major Cleary's departure as the last military governor,
the void was filled by the United States High Commissioner for
Germany, who brought in civilian staff employed and trained
by the State Department of the United States of America. They
wore civilian clothes instead of uniforms and were professional
attorneys and judges. Judge Elmer Groth arrived in Hof to
become the circuit judge for our area, and he traveled to hear
cases in Ansbach, Bayreuth, and the other major cities in

Bavaria. Munchberg was assigned to the headquarters in Hof together with the other surrounding Landkreise, including Naila, Wunseidel, and Rehau.

Now, in place of the close, personal relationship I had enjoyed with the AMG and military governor, I had no status whatever with the new judicial system, which bore the imposing title of the United States Courts of the Allied High Commission for Germany. Judge Groth was Magistrate of the District Court for the Tenth Judicial District, headquartered in Hof. I was no longer able to appear as a Friend of the Court or act as defense counsel, since all cases were now to be handled in the formal, legal manner by professional lawyers.

When the Munchberg court was closed, Lilly was relieved, thinking at long last she could stay home with Vera and become a full-time wife and mother. But it was not to be. Judge Groth approached her and asked if she would continue to work for him in the headquarters in Hof. It was a difficult decision to make, and we talked it over very carefully. The travel back and forth would, of course, be eased by a car and chauffeur they would provide for her, but she had so looked forward to retiring from this trying work. Ultimately, we decided for the welfare of the remaining community; she should continue to serve. They appointed her Clerk of the Court because of her specialized knowledge and experience in the backgrounds of the people and problems that would face the new court. As a part of her duties she was to supervise the secretaries, interpreters, and court reporters.

The Magistrate Court in Hof was limited to imposing sentences of confinement up to one year and fines up to ten thousand marks. The Intermediate Court, which sat in Bayreuth, had power to impose sentences up to ten years in prison and fines to a maximum of one hundred thousand marks. Beyond that, the Supreme Court in Ansbach handled the more difficult cases, including war crimes, murders, and other capital offenses. They could pass sentences of life imprisonment or death and could impose unlimited fines. Each

374

of the two lower courts could refer to a higher court cases which called for punishment beyond its jurisdiction.

I was pleased that we had no cases on file involving any of our people when the changeover took place, but my pleasure was short-lived. Captain Schmidt had not been content to let the Silbergold matter end with Major Cleary. Only a week after the new court began to function, Lilly told me the Silbergold case was on the calendar. I was astonished and stunned. How could this have happened? "Major Cleary closed it, you know that, Lilly."

"Yes, but remember there was no trial. We should have insisted that he let it go into court. Now, Schmidt has reopened it, and since it was never brought to trial, they are going to charge him again and make him appear before the judge."

"Oh, no," I groaned. We had no one on our side any longer, and now a young German lawyer, von Richthofen, was the prosecutor. I advised Silbergold to retain a German lawyer, that we had no choice. The man who had served on the Denazification Board with me agreed to take the case on short notice. I gave him all the background I could on the facts and what had happened with Schmidt and Cleary, but he went into court relatively unprepared.

After hours of argument, pro and con, the judge announced the verdict. "I find the defendant guilty as charged." Mrs. Silbergold cried out, and her husband turned white. Lilly could not speak, and we looked at each other across the room, dazed. We heard the judge sentence Silbergold to ten months in jail. He based his decision on the fact that Silbergold had been involved in a minor case once before which cast a shadow on his credibility. He was held without bail and remanded to custody after the trial.

I was badly shaken. Aside from the unnecessarily cruel judgment on Silbergold and his family, his jail sentence broke the record of Munchberg for the first and only time. The Silbergolds were to be the first and only family unable to emigrate to any place but Israel because of this conviction and sentence. I blamed myself for not insisting Major Cleary hold a trial. I felt betrayed and that I had misled the Silbergolds into a false sense of security. But it was too late to do anything about it. It didn't help to learn from the German prosecutor, von Richthofen, on leaving the courtroom, that it might have gone more favorably had the defense not been handled so poorly. I was curious. "Explain what you mean," I urged him.

He said, "If I had been the defense lawyer, I would have asked the young boy if he had given any of the material he stole to his own family for clothing. He testified he had a mother and sisters living here. If he had answered 'No,' which I would bet on, then I would have built my case around his character. If he didn't even take care of his own family with the material he admitted to stealing, then he was doing it as a criminal, purely and simply. And if this was his true character, then nothing he said should be believed. In this way, I would have attacked his testimony against Mr. Silbergold, and I think the court would have seen it that way."

He was probably right, but it was too late. Lilly had been right, too. She had predicted that the case would go badly against us. We were faced with a real court which relied solely on factual evidence. An emotional appeal was no longer possible.

In June 1948 the long-overdue monetary reform took place. The Allies replaced the hopelessly devalued Reichsmark, which had figured so prominently in the Silbergold case, with the new Deutsche Mark, and an era of new economic stability began. The remaining members of our business community were now in a better position than before. Their inventories were now valued in good money rather than the almost worthless Reichsmarks with which they had been purchased. The Free Loan Society became even more important for those looking to us in the business world to finance their emigration to countries other than Israel.

The first members of our own family left: Eva and Izak Tanc left with their children for Israel to join members of their family already there.

Chapter

44

LIFE WENT ON, and I tried to hold the community together even as it diminished. David met and fell in love with Fela Bader, a young girl who lived with her family in Munich. After the war she had been among a few hundred young Jewish girl survivors taken by the Swedish Government to Sweden to recover. When she returned to Germany she joined her sister and brother-in-law, Regina and Leo Hoenigstein, and her brother, Mark Bader, in Munich, and through relatives in Munchberg, the Weisstuch family, she and David came to know each other and decided to marry. We celebrated David and Fela's marriage with special joy. It was a beautiful wedding and a significant day. Now all three surviving members of our family were married. Our family would go on!

Several weeks before the wedding I had jumped up on one of the trucks that still brought food to the warehouse. It was raining, and I wanted to check for spoilage before accepting the shipment. When I jumped off my body twisted and I felt a sudden severe pain. Examination revealed a double hernia.

Since the wedding was so close, I postponed doing anything about it until after the ceremony, but the very next day I checked into the hospital in Munchberg, and David and Fela postponed their honeymoon until I recovered. Oddly enough the surgery was performed by the same German doctor whose case had come before me on the Denazification Board. After surgery a serious infection developed, and, fearful of the reaction, the doctor brought in a specialist from Heidelberg to assist him. Penicillin was impossible to find through ordinary channels, but Lilly managed to get some with the help of the AMG. It took some time before I was ambulatory again, and it was trying for me to be physically helpless and unable to get around as I was accustomed to doing.

In September 1948 representatives of the Jewish Agency for Palestine issued a Certificate of Registration to Lilly and to me. While in Munchberg they sat down with us privately and asked us to join in the exodus to Israel. They explained that with our backgrounds we would be assured of positions in the new government. It was a marvelous opportunity, and I was just as eager to join the fight as I had been from the beginning. But we still had obligations in Munchberg. We were not yet free to go. "No, gentlemen, I am afraid we will have to say 'thank you, but no.' We have resolved that we are not going anywhere until the last person in our community who wants to leave has had his chance. When the last one is on his way to his chosen home, we, too, will decide when and where we will go."

The emigration to Israel slowed and became more orderly after the first big rush, and emigration to other countries continued through the resettlement center in Schweinfurt, especially to the United States. Even though we had given up most of our settlements outside the community, our center and the Office for Former Concentration Camp Inmates was still in operation.

Lilly was busier than ever in her new work because the district encompassed all of Oberfranken south to Bayreuth and was a particularly sensitive area because it bordered the Russian zone, the Czech border, and the East German border. Hof was only ten minutes from the border, and the Allied forces found it necessary to set up gigantic camps for the German and Czech refugees who crossed the border illegally every day. Each morning when Lilly came into her office virtually a hundred or more refugees would be standing around waiting for sentence. The German police were swamped with them, and the Court had to try them in groups of thirty or forty at a time. The sentencing became automatic—"Thirty days in jail, twenty days suspended." They were sent to transient camps after serving the ten days, and a separate agency set up by the Counterintelligence Corps screened them to weed out any spies or agents sent over deliberately to cause trouble and unrest. These hundreds of people stayed in camps until they could be absorbed into the population. They represented quite a problem to the authorities, especially in Hof. When the camps in Hof could not longer take them in, they were sent on to other camps.

Judge Groth served for quite a while, and when his tour was over a new civilian judge, Judge Mason LeBaron, arrived to take his place. He had been an attorney in America and was quite experienced. In addition to the refugees, more and more smuggling cases appeared on the court calendar, and Lilly was tied down so much that for days at a time she came home so late and left so early that she got to see Vera and me only briefly. Judge LeBaron made his personal residence in Munchberg, so we came to know each other quite well.

The young German prosecutor von Richthofen also left when Judge Groth departed, and the new prosecutor was a German woman, Frau Stoyer. The judge and the prosecutor traveled as a team and sometimes came to Munchberg to try a local case. Most other times cases involving people from Munchberg were heard in Hof.

Before Frau Stoyer was engaged as a prosecutor the judicial district had paid Lilly a signal honor by offering her the post. She was the logical choice because of her background and skill and because she was a non-German. We discussed it at great length, but we both felt it would pose a difficult problem in

379

view of the potential conflict with her relationship to me and to the community. She had too much internal knowledge of the community and my affairs. If she were to be placed in a position where she had to prosecute a member of our community, it would be impossible. She had to decline the honor which she had well earned and justly deserved.

About this time a few very close friends of ours were ready to leave for America; they had their papers and were due to appear in Schweinfurt for final processing in a few weeks. They got together and pooled all their surplus goods to take to some friends in Munich, which consisted mainly of cigarettes since they were non-smokers. While they waited at the Munchberg railroad station for their train, the police picked them up and seized their luggage with the incriminating evidence. Someone had tipped them off, and we had a pretty good idea who it was.

Captain Schmidt, not daring to bypass me because of my relationship with the German authorities, notified me by telephone of the arrest, though he did not legally have to do so. The three women and one man were released on bail and came to see me. I asked them what they had intended to do with the cigarettes. They told me that since they were leaving they wanted to give them to their friends and family in Munich for their personal use. I saw nothing wrong with this and told the police I felt that this was not grounds for black-marketeering charges. But their suspicions were not so easily set aside.

Trial was set to take place in Hof, and my friends were released in my custody. I decided that I would appear as a witness on their behalf. They were desperate because the date for their appearance in Schweinfurt was drawing close, so I asked for a speedy trial. Lilly and I tried to reassure them that since they spoke the truth, they had nothing to fear. But secretly we wished we were as sure of the outcome as we tried to make them believe.

The Munchberg police who had arrested them appeared as witnesses and brought along the confiscated cigarettes as evidence. I had advised my friends not to engage legal counsel, just to throw themselves on the mercy of the court after pleading not guilty. They followed my advice and told the judge, LeBaron, that they would defend themselves with my help. I felt that by testifying for them as a witness I could establish a basic defense that as members of the DP community they were entitled to possession of the cigarettes and that there was no evidence against them except the assumption by the police that they intended to transact black-market dealings with the goods.

When I saw the high-pressure tactics of Frau Stoyer and her aggressive attack on the defendants, I realized she was out to get a conviction at any cost. This was one of her first cases, and she undoubtedly wanted to score a victory. The court adjourned for a noon recess, and I felt very uneasy. She was shooting at them too hard and too fast, getting them confused and terrified in their answers. I asked Lilly to approach Judge LeBaron during the recess and ask for permission for me to appear as a witness as soon as possible since the two girls were having difficulty expressing themselves through the interpreter. She hurried away to see what she could do and came back with good news. He had consented.

When court resumed session, I was called as a witness and sworn in. First, I made a statement as to the background of the accused—that they had lived in Munchberg since 1945. Then I explained the frequency and quantity of supplies that had been disbursed to each member of the community since that time. "It is quite possible and probable that if they did not smoke, they could indeed have accumulated such a supply of cigarettes."

When I had finished my direct evidence, the prosecutor rose to the attack with her cross-examination. "Mr. Schapelski, will you tell this court whether these cigarettes admitted as evidence"—she pointed to the pile on the table—"are the cigarettes which these people received from your center?" I saw her line of thought. "Well, we never did stamp the community name on the packages; it would have consumed too much time. I can only tell you that we distributed many brands of American cigarettes, and they are among the brands we gave out. But if

381

you are asking me to swear that those cigarettes are precisely the same as what we distributed, I cannot do this, Madam Prosecutor," I concluded.

She pressed on with her questioning for a few more minutes, trying very hard to pin me down to a statement which she could tear apart and thereby destroy my credibility, but I refused to be led into her trap. Finally, she gave up and said, "No further questions."

Judge LeBaron rapped three times on the table in front of the full courtroom and stated, "After listening to the witness, Mr. Schapelski, whom I know personally, and in view of his testimony, his personal reputation and my knowledge of his background and integrity, I will accept his word that these defendants are innocent of committing the crime with which they are charged. Case dismissed." He ordered the cigarettes returned to our friends, and they were free. I breathed a sigh of relief. They would be able to leave as they had planned.

Chapter

45

THE MONTHS OF 1949 AND 1950 spun by. We saw our friends dissolve their businesses and give up their professions and leave. All the settlements were now closed except for the community center. I had more time to devote to our family business, and with the community reduced to fewer than a hundred people I felt it was time for Lilly to retire and take up a normal life. She submitted her resignation, but it was quite some time before they could let her go. She was an integral part of the judicial system, and they needed her desperately.

In 1950 David and Fela left Munchberg to enter the United States, and we knew the time was drawing near when we would have to make our decision, too. The Meyers, with whom Lilly had lived when we met, had long since emigrated to America also and were living in New York. They wrote constantly, urging us to come, but they were unable to sponsor us because they were not yet citizens. Then one day they remembered that there was a Jewish man in New York whom we had befriended as an American soldier in Munchberg. They contacted him,

DISTRICT COURT

MAGISTRATE OF THE DISTRICT COURT FOR THE
XTH JUDICIAL
DISTRICT OFFICE HOF

4 Jahnstrasse
Hof/Saale
18 January 1951

TO WHOM IT MAY CONCERN:

I have known Mr. Natan SCHAPELSKI since November 8, 1948 when I assumed the office of Magistrate in the United States Courts for Germany, Xth Judicial District, at Hof, Bavaria, Germany. Mr. Schapelski is chairman of the Jewish Communities at Munchberg, Helmbrechts and Naila.

I know Mr. Schapelski to be a gentleman of the highest character and integrity, not only because of my personal acquaintance with him but also because of the general reputation which he enjoys as a member of the community of Munchberg.

I vouch for Mr. Schapelski in every respect and consider him a worthy candidate for immigration to any country.

Respectfully,

MASON S. LE BARON
Magistrate
US Courts for Germany
Xth Judicial District

Tel.: Hof 3228

X DISTRICT COURT
UNITED STATES COURTS FOR GERMANY

384

and he gladly offered to sponsor us and sent the necessary papers to Schweinfurt.

We decided to file an application even though we had not yet convinced ourselves this was the right decision. We completed all the formalities and met with the American consul. He looked over our papers, including a letter from Judge LeBaron. "Why do you want to go to the United States? You have an established, successful business here, and I can see that you are well known and highly regarded by everyone. I'm really curious. Why do you want to leave all this behind and start over again in a strange country?"

Lilly and I glanced at each other, and I answered him, "Well, sir, it's true we are well established here, but we do not wish to live or bring up our child in a country whose people murdered our parents and our sisters and brothers."

He lowered his head for a moment and then stamped our papers without further comment.

Our decision had not been easily made. We were torn in so many different directions. I would have gone to Israel in the beginning had my obligation to the people in Munchberg not held me here. Israel still called me. But David and Fela were now in America, and we did not want to separate the family again. Max and Sala had already said that they would go wherever we went. And so it was a nightmare of decisions to be made by me alone. Whatever I decided would affect so many people's lives!

We had had so many wonderful associations with Americans and had come to admire their freedom and their way of life. America held out the hope of everything we had dreamed of for ourselves and for our children. And yet each month that passed we applied for postponement after postponement, stating that the magistrate would not yet release Lilly from her post.

Finally, there was a new crisis. The Korean War broke out, and its repercussions could be felt in Bavaria, where we lived only minutes from the Russian zone. We made our decision—it was to be America. Max and I made plans to liquidate the business as best we could, and the women prepared the two little girls and themselves for the journey. In the days of anticipation that followed, we booked passage on the *Queen Elizabeth* and arranged for travel to the French port where we would finally leave Europe behind.

I experienced an unfamiliar sensation of fear and anxiety. Was I doing the right thing in pulling up roots again?

It meant learning a new language, new business methods, a new way of life. And it meant starting all over again in a new identity. Here I was known, but here I could not live.

In the spring of 1951, almost six years after the liberation, Lilly and I walked through the now empty rooms of the community center, rooms still echoing with the voices of the thousands who had come through their doors. Down in the basement the shelves of the warehouse were empty, no sign of the tons of food that had poured in there to feed the starved victims of the holocaust. Upstairs, we stared into the rooms where the little hospital had been and the storeroom for clothing and shoes. The apartments above us were empty, too. We walked across the main meeting room, remembering the voices of so many who had sat here with us through festivity and troubled times. At the doorway to what had been my office we stood for several minutes, reminding each other of the days and nights of concentrated work and endless meetings and of the hundreds who had come there for our help and to help us. Everything was done and everything was gone, the records packed away, the flags taken down.

Our last stop was in the little synagogue of our community. I reached up and took down the old charred Torah and cradled it gently in my arms. It was the only thing we took away from Munchberg with us, except for our memories. I followed Lilly out the front door of the villa and down the drive. I locked the gates behind us, and we turned our faces west.

386